How to Survive in an Organization

James J. Heaphey

TODAY'S BOOKS IMPRINT

History Publishing Company, LLC
Palisades, New York

Published in the United States by
History Publishing Company
Palisades, New York

Library of Congress Cataloging-in-Publication Data
Heaphey, James J.
    How to Survive in an Organization/James J. Heaphey.
    –1st ed.
    p.cm.
    Includes bibliographical references and index.
    Library of Congress Control Number: 2008923402
    ISBN: 9781933909196
    SAN: 850-5942

Printed in the United States on acid-free paper
9 8 7 6 5 4 3 2 1

First Edition

Contents

Acknowledgments -vi

Author's Note - vii

Introduction - viii

One:
What Is an Organization. . . Really? - - - - - - - - - - - - - - - - 1

Two:
The Myth of Management Wisdom and
Productivity - 17

Three:
The Myth of Performance Evaluation - - - - - - - - - - - - - 35

Four:
Not in This Organization - 45

Five:
What Are People . . . Really? - - - - - - - - - - - - - - - - - - - 63

Six:
The Human Condition - 82

Seven:
Groups and Jobs Shape Our Attitudes - - - - - - - - - - - - 101

Eight:
Power - 115

Nine:
Sources of Unofficial Power - - - - - - - - - - - - - - - - - - - 133

Ten:
Strategy: Presentation of Self - - - - - - - - - - - - - - - - - - 153

Eleven:
Strategy: Ethics, Decorum, Rhetoric, and
Getting Along - 170

Twelve:
Strategy: Avoidance of Entrapments - - - - - - - - - - - - - 191

Thirteen:
Strategy: Legal Matters Dealing with
Management and Meaning - 209

Fourteen:
Tactics: Dealing with Coworkers and
Managers - 225

Fifteen
Tactics: Managers Come in Different Shapes
and Sizes - 244

Sixteen:
Tactics: Manipulating Numbers, Office Space,
Whistle-Blowing - 264

A Working Application - 284

Bibliography - 285

Index - 290

For My Children and Theirs

Acknowledgments

For almost a half a century, I have been learning from my students and clients under the guise of professor and consultant. My best student addresses me as "sensei." I blush and take great pride in that.

But now the truth is out: I learned far more from them than they did from me. The papers they wrote, the case studies they reported on in classes and seminars, conversations they had with me, are the heart of this book, the evidence for my generalizations, the examples of my lines of reasoning, and finally, the reason why it was written.

Many of them will never know the debt I owe or the pride I take in recording their thoughts. I hope a few do, and they feel good about what I have done.

Pam Heaphey, my wife, infused me with the spirit to write this book, then stayed with me grinding out the details. I would dedicate it to her, but we've been there, done that. We both dedicate this to our children and theirs.

Don Bracken, Publisher, and Tom Cameron, Senior Editor at History Publishing Company, were extraordinarily encouraging companions and skillful constructive critics throughout. They believed in this book. What can be more important to an author?

Lin Gall, Glenn Gall, Amber Holland, and Kate Whorf, one of the dedicatees, proofread and critiqued the manuscript for me. Jennifer Johnson proofread for the publisher. Marcia Carlson was the indexer. These are the people who polished the words and clarified the confusions.

James Heaphey
Williamsburg, Virginia
April 2008

Author's Note

There are two major sources for the case examples in this book: articles and books, and personal sources, i.e., what people have told me or written for me in seminar assignments during my forty-six years of experience as a professor and consultant in the field of organizational behavior.

My clients and students were from the private and public sectors, including the military. Because my other specialty is political institution-building in developing countries, I have had many clients and students from a wide spectrum of countries spanning the globe.

I quote from books, articles, and my personal sources. Usually I present the quotes in italics rather than quotation marks. I provide sources of the quotes from books and articles in the bibliography. I chose to use this style to spare the reader from the irritating distraction of footnote or endnote numbers in the text. My examples are from years ago as well as current (2008) times. My purpose in doing this is to emphasize that organizations have been as I describe them for many years.

Introduction

Think of this book as being like a jungle survival guide. There are things you must learn about being in a jungle; such as never run from a jaguar, walk toward it shouting and clapping your hands, always run from dangerous snakes, and stay away from most insects. There is no shortage of jaguars, snakes, and insects in organizations; however, unfortunately for you, they disguise themselves better.

Most people learn about these things as they try to maintain their composure forty or more hours a week. The longer they've been at it, the more, I believe, they will nod in agreement as they turn the pages of this book.

Organizations are probably more like jungles these days because of the white-water economy; however, all organizations—public, private, not-for-profit, religious and military—have always been a survival game.

This book helps guide you through your jungle safely. How much it helps depends on you—on how much you can embrace the strategic principles and adopt the tactics recommended.

And, though it is tempting, don't turn to the chapters on strategy and tactics without reading what comes before those chapters. You can't use the recommended strategy and tactics successfully if you don't understand the illusions on which organizations depend. Don't assume you know what they are. You probably know some of them; for example, you might know that the claim by organizations that they can evaluate an individual's performance is an illusion. You probably don't know all of them, and odds are that you're still being fooled by some of them.

As Buddha advised: For one not to be fooled by illusion, he must first be disillusioned.

Disillusioning you is the mission of chapters one through nine. There are also many suggestions for strategy and tactics in those chapters.

When you read the chapers on strategy and tactics, you will disagree with me on some points, which is good. This book is not a catechism; it is a guide.

—One—

What is an Organization . . . Really?

> The irrationality of a thing is no argument against its existence, rather a condition of it.
>
> —Nietzsche

> One of the most salient features of our culture is that there is so much bullshit.
>
> —Harry G. Frankfurt

> No matter how cynical you get, you can never keep up.
>
> —Lily Tomlin

We have worked in organizations for so long now that we accept them as natural aspects of our existence—like work itself, love, and family. It is therefore unsurprising that we idealize them. As is, therefore, with all things essential to our being, we have contrived a romantically benign image of organizations.

In this dreamland we have created, organizations are fair and decent institutions run by hard-working managers who have risen to the top on the basis of their talent to do so. These managers are educated and trained to follow principles of rationality and efficiency in the allocation of resources under their command.

At times we rant and rave about organizations using words like "stupid" and "grossly unfair." Now and then we realize that someone high up in the hierarchy is stupid or corrupt, or both, but never do we forsake the ideal. When things get so obviously bad that we must be critical, we usually blame the problems on "bureaucracy" or certain individuals. "Bureaucracy" is what an organization is when it falls short of the ideal. Or at least that's how we put it all together for ourselves.

While we fancy ourselves as hard-headed and realistic about organizations, we cling to a benign ideal of organization and its offspring myths as though it were a lifeline—which it is. Ideals help us cope with reality. Unfortunately, ideals can also keep us impotent and disadvantaged in organizations. To paraphrase Machiavelli:

> Many have dreamed up organizations that have never in truth been known to exist; the gulf between how one should live and how one does live is so wide that a man who neglects what is actually done for what should be done learns the way to self-destruction rather than self-preservation.

This book is intended to disillusion you and then enable you to use the illusions of organizations for your own purposes. The critique of organizations is not stated to tell you how to improve them. There are a thousand books designed to do that, every one of them shaken with at least a little snake oil. Nor am I on a moral crusade to lead a revolt against organizations. That would be as realistic as leading a revolt against people whose natures we will explore after looking at organizations. Organizations and people are what they are. No one is going to change them. However, you can learn to cope with them more effectively, and that is what this book is all about.

It is also not my purpose to declare that everything done by every organization is always stupid and is always covered up by hypocrisy. Some managers know what they are doing some of the time. Some organizational policies are good for you some of the time. This book is about your life in the "most of the time."

Everyone, of course, likes the part of this book in which you learn how to use illusions for your own purposes. It's not only tactically smart to hoist the organization on its own illusions, it's also fun; but you can't get there without going through the first part; and the first part involves disenchantment, which everyone dislikes. The frustration of this contradiction was expressed well by a high-level executive, I'll call him "Ted," in a company I was advising on computer-based information systems in the 1990s.

Ted was bothered by my approach. I believe that an organization cannot develop a useful policy on computer-based information systems before the managers in that organization undergo brain-dewashing. The computer industry and some universities have brainwashed managers into thinking that computers do a lot of things that they don't really do. In some cases, the illusions are simply lies; in other cases, the managers are hoodwinked into believing that what computers can do is done without much effort.

Midway through my disillusioning session with Ted and his peers, he interrupted me. "If we listen to you," he said, in a manner indicating that listening to me would be the height of folly, "all the wonderful hopes we have for our organization are shot down. We should be listening to someone who appreciates the powerful potential of computers. You're a naysayer."

I wasn't the last. In the September/October 2007 issue of Public Administration Review, Shaun Goldfinch states that "the majority of information systems' developments are unsuccessful. The larger the development, the more likely it will be unsuccessful."

There's a lot of Ted in everyone. People do not like being disenchanted. So brace yourself.

You Are Absolutely, Positively on Your Own

Nowadays jobs are hot potatoes—difficult to hold on to, and when you do hold on, you feel the pain. In the 1980s and early

1990s workers at the lower levels suffered recessions and competition from cheap labor in countries only geography teachers can find. Middle- and higher-level managers joined the suffering in the mid-1990s, victims of "re-engineering" and other euphemisms for cutbacks. Positioning chunks of managers in the middle of organizations was once taken for granted; today it's considered hazardous fat.

Prior to the mid-1990s only the "liberal" and "soft" media complained about cutbacks. The elite business media praised or explained downsizing in terms of "cycles" and "rightsizing," and "survival in global competition," never considering the need for sympathy for, or advice to, workers who found themselves either out of work or in low-paying work. However, when in the mid-1990s the management class was caught in the flush of downsizing, the elite business media changed its tune. In December 1996, for example, Fortune ran an article titled "You Are Absolutely, Positively on Your Own," in which the author provided the following warning and advice to managers and high-level executives:

> You do understand that the old social contract between U.S. companies and their employees has expired, don't you? Surely you no longer believe that unconditional loyalty, or even doing a good job, guarantees employment. You've probably even memorized that new mantra 'My career is my responsibility.' Yet, if you're like millions of other Americans, you're probably still putting all your career eggs in your employer's basket, hoping that they will be treated gently. And you will probably still react with shock, anger, and dismay when the eggs splatter.
>
> In the current corporate atmosphere, change has become an accepted fact of life and re-engineering is no longer an emergency exercise. The stark fact is that you are ever more likely to be blasted out into the ranks of the unemployed with no safety net, and it could happen over

and over again. According to current Department of Labor statistics, today's new college graduates will, on average, have eight to ten jobs and as many as three careers in their lifetimes.

Another vital truth you should understand is that candor about your career issues is in short supply at many companies these days.

Not even skills with the latest technology or being a highly-skilled professional assures work in what William Wolman and Anne Colamosca label The Judas Economy. They argue that this highly-touted "knowledge economy," run by bankers and investors, is "the triumph of capital and the betrayal of workers." Everyone who works, they say, no matter at what level in the organization, is being marginalized by cheaper labor and less regulation in China, India, and Mexico. The problem with knowledge, they point out, is that it can be taught to anyone. If medical transcribers and computer programmers in Beijing and Bombay will do the job for one-third the cost of U.S. workers, then businesses will invest their capital in China and India.

Another facet of information is that it can run around in modern communications systems at amazing speeds. The diagnosis of your medical test last week may have been done by an analyst sitting at a computer screen in southern India.

Things in the public sector are just as bad, maybe worse. According to former President Bill Clinton and Vice-President Al Gore, one of the greatest accomplishments of their first term (1992-1996) was the decrease in government jobs. They took pride in emulating the private sector by getting "lean 'n mean." One wonders how government workers and managers felt when they heard the President say over and over again to audiences from San Diego to Boston, that although thousands upon thousands of government jobs had been cut from the budget, levels and quality of service had increased. This conclusion was a self-serving, unsubstantiated, evaluation, but it was the kind of simplistic stuff that the public eats up.

The reality of the situation is that large chunks of government work traditionally done in-house are being done on contract. State Department payroll, for example, is done by a management information systems private company.

Such "outsourcing" gives false impressions of savings for the President and Vice President to wave on the White House lawn and also distracts government agencies away from fundamental employee concerns that were long honored—like pensions.

Barry Schrum, an Energy Department employee, found out in 1995 that a mistake had been made regarding his pension plan. He thought he had one. He was supposed to have had one, beginning thirty days after he sat down at a desk in the Energy Department eleven years ago. But he didn't because, as his personnel office told him, a mistake had been made. He was told that he could bring his pension up by contributing $35,000 to it and that this amount would be matched by the government. He sold his home and took a check for $35,000 to the personnel office.

A few weeks later he was told that the personnel office had given him bad advice. Actually, he was told, he would have to pay the $35,000 over an eight-year period. He told all of this to a Congressional committee in 1997. The committee was investigating a foul-up that had left thousands of employees in the same plight as Barry Schrum. None of these employees had been able to get anyone in the federal government to deal with the problem. Personnel offices passed the buck to the Office of Personnel Management, who passed it on to Treasury Department retirement counselors. Management all showed up for the hearings to say, "Administratively, our hands are tied, because current law gives us virtually no options to correct the mistakes."

Committee Chairman John L. Mica made note of the incongruity between this and the Clinton-Gore "reinventing government" mantra. He then ordered the government officials responsible to come up with a solution.

The mistakes are in the management information systems, and the problem is that no one knows how to work through the mistakes. Three things caused this incorrigible misery:

- The new pension plan was far too complex for the average employee to understand, maybe for anyone to understand.
- Information systems management was between private sector bidders, with reshuffling between them and public agencies. The result was confusion.
- The Clinton-Gore downsizing found a rich lode in the personnel, budget procurement, and accounting ranks. Thousands of these employees got buyouts to take early retirements, including, naturally, the best of them. These were the people who had the experience and the wits to deal with the confusions caused by the new pension plan and the gypsied management information systems.

There's an intriguing footnote to this that will warm your entrepreneurial heart. Some of the talented civil service personnel and accounting people who took early retirement started a private company, Government Retirement Benefits, Inc. in Alexandria, Virginia, to train federal personnel officers. They soon found themselves almost overwhelmed by requests from confused federal employees for counseling because the employees didn't trust the answers they got from their own agencies.

For this and many other reasons provided for us by the wonderful world of "efficiency through downsizing," what had remained of pride in government service prior to the reinventing-government charades was diminished beyond recognition. American civil servants used to encourage their children to find government careers. Today, in survey after survey, civil servants tell us they advise their children to stay away from those careers.

No matter where you go to work, you must be prepared to cope and succeed. Unfortunately, some of the principles your parents, teachers, ministers, and conventional morality have preached to you are sometimes very bad for you because they are based on a world that doesn't exist. In other words, when the real world is fleetingly acknowledged, you are commissioned to right its wrongs, suggesting heroic acclaim if you do. They don't tell you John Jay Chapman's warning: Reform consists of taking a bone from a dog.

Organizations are Organized Hypocrisies

Benjamin Disraeli once dismissed his political opponents as having formed "an organized hypocrisy" because the ideas of its "head" differed so remarkably from the sensations of its "tail." He was calling attention to an annoying characteristic of any organization, including his own political party. What the people at the head of the organization say about it has little to do with what is being done throughout the organization.

Some examples of typical organizational hypocrisies, or illusions, are:

- Productivity is essential.
- Organizations care about workers as individuals.
- Organizations have techniques that enable them to place the most qualified individuals in positions.
- The value of programs and individuals in terms of the organization's goals can be evaluated.
- The most valuable programs and individuals are rewarded.
- Organizational training plus continuing direction lead to rational worker behavior.
- Top management is in control.
- Organizations pursue efficient ways of doing things.

Organizations are aptly defined as "organized hypocrisies" because the hypocrisies intertwine symbiotically; each one gains from its interaction with the others. For example, the hypocrisy that management knows how to, and does, evaluate work objectively supports the hypocrisy that organizations pursue efficient ways of doing things, and vice-versa.

In addition, the illusions work well together in artful logical argument. Suppose that you challenge the notion that organizations promote the most efficient workers. You might well get back this reply: It must be so because organizations pursue efficient ways of doing things.

Incidentally, you have undoubtedly heard that organizations in the private sector have to be efficient because if they are not, the competition will wipe them out. Reality is a cold place for that old proverb. Every day we read about companies that have been very successful because they had a better technology, or were lucky, or corrupt, or some combination of those three.

If your antagonist is passionate enough about Adam Smith to use the "in the long run" argument (that's the last refuge, to argue that these truths will inevitably appear in the long run), remind him of someone else's words: ". . . in the long run we are all dead."

Many people withdraw—some cringe—when confronted with the statement that organizations are filled with hypocrisies. Bill Fremson tells us about his own education regarding hypocricies.

A year ago I would have protested loudly at the suggestion that all organizations are filled with hypocrisy. But today I just nod at that, and think 'amen.' Let me give you one example of what's been happening to me.

My first day on the job as a credit manager was a wonderful experience. The company has an orientation program. I was told that family is a number one priority for my organization. But during the past year I have encountered resistance every time I've requested rearrangement of my work schedule to accommodate a family need, like watching my seven-year-old daughter perform in a school play or taking her to the doctor. What they should have told me in that orientation is that the company values my work more than anything else. There's nothing wrong with that. I'm aggravated by the hypocrisies we're all expected to live with. Even worse, we have to pretend as though the company's value statements—mine even puts out a glossy brochure on its values—are carried out in the day-to-day of our work. It's disgusting!

A clinical psychologist teamed up with a syndicated journalist to study the sincerity of company mission-and-vision brochures. They questioned a large number of workers. According to these two researchers, the following comments are typical:

Individual effort is encouraged, but mavericks are terminated.

We talk about cooperation, but build firewalls.

We promote strong performers into do-nothing positions.

We promote quality, but reward quantity.

We manage the many to correct the problems of the few.

They mail us soft cheese and a depressing letter at Christmastime.

Organizational hypocrisies promenade on a grand stage, which partly accounts for their durability. In the early Twentieth Century, Americans established a new religion based on large-scale industrial organizations. These organizations were presented as fulfillment of the American destiny, the final realization of progress in a true democracy. The man who builds a factory, said Henry Ford, builds a temple. The man who works there, worships there.

The "temples" built by Ford and his fellow tycoons were treated as such by the American political and court systems. Workers were provided no legal protection whatsoever as workers. A job was a privilege, not a right; a worker was blessed and should count his blessings even if his paycheck was meager.

Workers are somewhat better off today, but the sacredness of large-scale organizations lives on and provides support for the hypocrisies. What actually goes on in organizations is masked by illusions anchored in the myths of a materialistic religion.

Now and then we gain a glimpse of the truth when managers of organizations expose a more honest version. These moments of truth are usually preambles to an announcement that a reorganization is about to take place. What had been previously presented as a smoothly-functioning company is now declared to be in trouble.

For example, in 1996 Digital Equipment announced that it would cut 7,000 of its 60,900 jobs and spend $475 million on restructuring; this surprised much of Wall Street.

In this case the explanation given by the Digital Board Chairman was that we did not properly execute the strategy we agreed upon. This is one type of explanation—our strategy was sound, but our execution failed. Some other versions are: Our strategy failed. The market shifted. And, of course, We had bad luck.

In the next chapter, I will argue that managers do not have a body of knowledge, let alone a scientific body of knowledge, like, say, your doctor or your auto mechanic has. Imagine your mechanic, even in his more arrogant and uncommunicative moments, telling you that your car failed the day after he gave it back to you because the strategy that you and he agreed upon was not properly executed. Although mechanics, like managers, do not always stay glued to the truth, they are able to name specific things that went wrong.

If the Digital Board Chairman were to read this book (doubtful) and get this far (inconceivable), he might patronizingly say something like, Ah, if only men such as I could enjoy the simple tasks of the mechanic. Notice that he still hasn't told us why his company is in trouble, at least not in language anyone can understand.

Something a person like that chairman can say honestly is that the mechanic and the doctor carry out their own plans, whereas people such as he must depend on others doing the work. Managers don't like to provide explanations like that because it gets uncomfortably close to the observation, not infrequently made, that managers don't do anything.

Prior to those moments of truth when we see admissions of failure, the hypocrisies of an organization are not publicly disclosed, nor are they usually discussed within the organization. Hypocrisy creates its own defense mechanisms. Within every organization there are powerful forces at work to safeguard the hypocrisies. Even the revered "bottom line" can be manipulated by these forces. A Honeywell CEO once observed that long before the bottom line indicates that the organization is in trouble, everything inside has gone to hell in a handbasket. This is what Lee Iacocca came upon at Chrysler in 1979. One of Chrysler's biggest problems, he said, was that even its top managers didn't have a very good idea of what was going on. They knew Chrysler was bleeding. What they didn't realize was that it was hemorrhaging.

Some organizations will insist they are perfect even while indications are quite to the contrary. During the years 1989 to 1997, major scandals at the U.S. Naval Academy made headlines. There was widespread cheating, drug scandals, sexual assault, car theft operations, and Congressional investigations. The Naval Academy's leadership admitted that these things were going on, but blamed them on changing values and pressures in the world outside the Academy. A senior official there said that the academy is trying to do all it can possibly do, but today's society is different. We can't assume that all of the kids coming to the academy have honor, courage, and commitment.

Stonewalling is not confined to the military. At the same time that the Naval Academy was shouting, We're ok, but we don't know about American society, the mutual fund behemoth Fidelity Investments was also pretending to be all right while all signs pointed in the other direction.

Fidelity had grown stunningly in the 1980s on the returns of its brand-name mutual funds. In the 1990s, those same funds lagged in the market. At a company where fund managers rarely left, there was suddenly an unusual number of departures, and the portfolio shop was considered to be in disarray. However, Fidelity would not acknowledge it had a problem and, as recently as 2007, was being penalized for various irregularities that have taken place at least partly because Fidelity has tried to hide its problems.

Another illustration of how organizations deal less than adequately with failure took place in the summer of 1997 when the Chicago School Board kept school children who had not passed basic tests in math and reading in school beyond its scheduled closing. Discarding the traditional practice of social promotion, the schools told the children they must stay in school that summer until they either passed the subjects or were reassigned to their present grade level.

There seemed no end to the number of teachers, principals, superintendents, and school board members who came forward to explain the new policy. Parents were told that most eighth graders could not read at their grade level and that many fourth graders could not add and subtract in any form of complexity whatsoever. The laments went on and on. Teachers and principals were tripping over one another to make it to the cameras where they told the public what a lousy job they had been doing for all those years.

For the most part, the coverage on TV and in the papers was "joyful event" sort of stuff. Ritualistically, first there was confession and then there was redemption. An apparently merciless terminology was applied in the confession—"educational malpractice"—and, in the same breath, the redemption was—"Abracadabra!"—unveiled.

People began touting "the Chicago Way." It was profoundly discussed on panels as a model. One envisioned a ceremony on the White House lawn honoring a school district that led us out of a national tragedy: the maleducation of our children.

The Chicago Summer School is, of course, promising. Not definitively ameliorating, let alone a solution, but promising. What got lost, however, was the candid statement: The organization of education in Chicago has been detrimental to the education of children for a number of years. How can the people responsible for a national tragedy confess without being shamed? The answer is: They work in a large organization.

In Chicago and so many other cities, the organization of education enables everyone to have someone else to blame. Teachers point at principals who point at superintendents who point at school boards who point at parents who point at teachers. What happened when everyone jumped at the chance to take credit for the Chicago experiment was a re-enactment of something John F. Kennedy said: Success has a thousand parents. Failure is an orphan.

A hundred years ago, a German philosopher-historian named Max Weber warned us that the large-scale organizations we were beginning to use to take advantage of industrial age technology were inevitably dysfunctional. One of the things he noted was that no one in large organizations is ever really responsible for what the organization does. These large organizations, Weber said, operate in ways and for reasons that no one really understands.

When he was publisher of The New York Times, Punch Sulzberger said: It is screamingly difficult to make any real change on this paper. It's equally hard to make a mistake. What-

ever you do, the paper comes out in the morning. I really think that I could take all the brass away and the paper would still come out the next day, and no one would know how or why.

Even when organizations admit to having problems and reorganize, the change does not eliminate hypocrisies; it substitutes new ones for the old. There often is a honeymoon period after change during which things seem better. Eventually, however, the enduring problems of organizations dominate.

In the following chapters you will have the opportunity to explore a number of hypocrisies that are found in most organizations. Each will be illustrated with findings from the behavioral sciences, newspaper and magazine items, literature and movies, and vignettes based on true incidents. In some cases the names of persons who were actually involved in the vignettes have been changed. Most of the stories are told by or about middle-level managers whom I know from traditional university classes, training seminars, and consulting experiences.

Before we begin, here is some advice about reading this book:

- Try to resist the temptation of skipping to the chapters on strategy and tactics. You will be able to make much better use of those parts if you read the earlier chapters. For example, many tactics are presented in only one form with, at best, one example. If you have read all the chapters, you will see broader applications for these tactics.
- Don't skip over something because it doesn't seem relevant to your situation. A true story about a CEO and an insurance company is told in the section following this one. Don't skip over it because you're lower in the hierarchy than a CEO. What happens in such instances affects the entire organization. Your skills at organizational survival will be sharpened by your understanding of what's happening up there in the executive suites. Eventually, hypocrisies lead to

mistakes that are so glaring that they cannot be hidden. Organizations want to fix blame for mistakes without destroying the credibility of the organization. That, alas, could be where you come into the mix.

- Don't think the real-life examples or the vignettes based on true experiences are exceptions or aberrations.

—Two—

The Myth of Management Wisdom and Productivity

So much of what we call management consists in making it difficult for people to work.
—Peter Drucker

The most forceful myth followed in organizations is that management knows what it is doing. Individuals, particularly those at the head of organizations, are very cunning at enriching themselves. But as managers—whether in the executive suites or on the line—these individuals usually do not know what they are doing.

You should understand this observation not to be critical of management, but rather to allow you to comprehend the ideology that managers foolishly, though unavoidably, share. In America more than in any other country except the old Soviet Union, managers derive their authority from a pretense that they have a science, a body of knowledge, which they adhere to as they make decisions and lead the organization. This pretense asks you to think of managers as you do engineers, doctors, lawyers, and automobile mechanics—people who approach a problem in terms of a knowledge base that has been tested and used for many years.

Managers do have successes, not many, but a few here and there. To be as precise as we can, 10 percent of new businesses succeed. That's a fairly reliable number, because the business sector and the government record keepers agree on it. It is so rare that those two sectors agree that you can trust it when they do.

While we don't have numbers as precise for management decisions, most observers would agree that a 90 percent failure rate is not an excessive estimation. Even the faculty at Harvard Business School would agree, so long as their grads were excluded from the 90 percent figure. There are two typical types of articles that appear in the *Harvard Business Review*. One type is about management failings; the other type is about new ideas for management success.

Are you feeling argumentative at this point, wondering "Well, then, what the hell keeps the economy going?"

Why can't a ten percent success rate be sufficient? No one knows, of course, what percent of management success would keep Frosted Flakes available at a price you can pay. So why couldn't it be ten percent?

Also, remember that there are non-management people, i.e., people who do the work in the organization. And there is technology. Those two, along with management's meager contribution, might play enough of a role to keep the economy going.

Some people attribute most of the economy's success to technology, which is seldom an artifact of large organizations. The second largest business in America during the late 1990s was the personal computer (drug traffic was number one), and that was developed by accident by some nerds who were having fun. In fact, big organizations are often detrimental to technological advancement. The VCR, invented by an American, was passed over by American business. It took a government agency—the Japanese Ministry of Industry and International Trade—to realize its potential. That agency then induced some Japanese companies to pioneer the VCR industry.

IBM got into the PC market late in the game. Its organization was too big to think of it before IBM representatives started noticing that their customers all had PCs on their desks.

Wisely, IBM kept development of the PC away from its own bureaucracy, farming that out to a trusted small group in Florida.

The 10 percent success-rate for management decisions is not due to a science or knowledge base, as the success of, say, your auto mechanic would be. Rather, it comes from: (1) having a lot of resources to gamble with; (2) making some good guesses; (3) being lucky; and (4) cheating, corruption, and other illegal acts. The scientific merit to the likening of managers to doctors and mechanics doesn't add up to a hill of beans, but there's gold in them hills. Many people make lots and lots of money maintaining the illusions of "management science." An upscale example is Harvard Business School; a downscale example is any of those pocket books on management wizardry found on the rack next to *Playboy* at the airport newsstand. They bear titles like *Overcoming Resistance to Change: A Manager's Guidebook, Manage Teams to Quality in Two Weeks,* and *The Seven Keys to Successful Managemen,* and are as ubiquitous as diet plans.

Nonetheless, I recommend Harvard Business School to anyone who wants to and can get accepted. It is a bargain at the price its students pay to learn from top notch mythmakers and soothsayers. High-paying companies dispatch headhunters to kidnap Harvard B-School graduates and treat them like royalty when delivered. (If you're thinking that those companies wouldn't be doing that if the graduates hadn't learned some knowledge that can be useful to the company, you are incorrigible because you've lapsed back into myth number one: Managers know what they are doing.)

The reader of an airport pocket book can also gain by learning how to use gimmick words like "reengineering," "quality processes," and "downsizing with heart." As we shall see, much of what management does involves words that have power because they don't mean anything. Skillful manipulation of the latest accepted words that don't mean anything pays off. Recently I heard a departing dean of a business school talk about his legacy. He had insisted, he said, that the graduates of his school be prepared to earn their keep by providing "value added." Later I saw a transcript of the speech. "Value added" was the phrase used for justifying everything about a B-School education, and "value added" was what that B-School graduate would bring to the business world. Does this mean that "value added" now replaces "efficiency," or is it "quality," or maybe "entrepreneurship?" Or is it "risk taking" or "innovation?" There's only one thing I can tell you for certain: "Value added" will not have to worry about aging.

I realize this contradicts an old saying about how ignorance cannot be learned. Ignorance, in the form of catchwords and slogans, is currency in the ridiculous world of organizations.

In the center of management's dilemma is the unpredictable universe. Managers have to pretend that they can predict with accuracy, and no one can do that. Forecasts and predictions about economic matters by economists, university teams, government agencies, and anyone else are normally way off the mark. Now and then, by sheer luck, someone guesses right.

Consider the Research Seminar in Quantitative Economics at the University of Michigan—regarded by the experts as one of the best forecasters in the country. That group reports that during the two decades of the 1980s and 1990s its Gross Domestic Product predictions were off by an average of 1.3 percentage points annually. So if they predicted 2.4 percent growth, actual GDP ended up anywhere between 1.1 percent (a bad year) and 3.7 (a great year).

Wall Street economists, especially the eminent ones, are usually off by around 32 percent in their projections on where the Dow Jones industrial average is going. CEOs are routinely off by a wide margin when they predict demand for a new product. Over the past fifteen years, the federal government has missed its forecast of the annual deficit by an average of $42 billion (around 22 percent). And, as *The Economist* noted: *While telecommunications experts in government and business ponderously planned an information superhighway with the*

Vice President as point man, a bunch of computer hackers, engi-
neers, and students scurrying about were actually building one,
the Internet.

On September 16, 2007, Alan Greenspan, the highly respected former chairman of the Federal Reserve, in a CBS *60 Minutes* interview, said that while he knew about subprime lending practices where homebuyers got very low interest rates only to see them later jacked up causing critical payment shock, he didn't have any hint of the harm they could do until late in 2005. There is general agreement in the financial community that the very low interest rates charged at the first stage of a subprime loan were possible only because the Federal Reserve, while it was under Greenspan's leadership, kept the banks' interest rates at unusually low, and unrealistic, levels for even the short-term long-term.

But be careful before you applaud the financial community for knowing what went wrong. They were the ones who made the loans, bought the mortgages, and traded in the mortgages that created the monster of failing mortgages. Can we let them off the hook of responsibility by saying "The Federal Reserve made us do it?"

As the post-mortgage-credit-crisis-dust was settling at the end of 2007, only one major investment bank had not been brought to its knees—Goldman Sachs.

Samuel Johnson said that "Tomorrow is an old deceiver." Nonetheless, managers are expected to be able to say with confidence that if such-and-such resources are added together in this particular way, there will be such-and-such a result. A good deal of organizational activity, including what you are doing and what you are advised to say, is a theatrical performance in which everyone pretends that the managers got it right.

There are strong forces at work to maintain hypocrisies both inside organizations and outside. In academia, for example, realities of organizations are objectively revealed in the behavioral sciences departments, while in MBA and MPA programs the hypocrisies are adorned with "scientific" status. Now and then the reality threatens the pretenses, as it did at the School of Organization and Management at Yale in the 1980s when a doctoral program was imparting some heretical views on the sacredness of *rationality*. Students were exposed in this program to the following view of rationality:

> *What are taught in schools of management as rational processes—such as hierarchical structures, task performance, and managerial decision-making—are in reality methods to serve emotional functions, including the need to protect organizational members against anxiety.*

This view was too threatening, so the School's dean terminated it. There can be no doubt about success for this *positive* approach. University programs in business and public administration thrive. There are plenty of applicants; the faculty usually receive higher salaries than the average faculty, to say nothing of the opportunities for consulting, and graduates find markets for their degrees.

This academic "think positive" is supported by an array of textbooks, "how-to" books, journals, and magazines. The rules that appear to be in effect for this support group are: Never speak ill, never question, never second-guess a management innovation unless you do so as an aside in praise of another innovation. These rules lead to publications that lavish praise on newness, always supporting the notion that management knows what it is doing. The only way you'll ever see criticism in this body of literature is when it is secondary to praise, as in the following example.

When AMR Corporation, parent of American Airlines, announced in 1988 it was revolutionizing the hospitality industry by creating a reservations system that would leapfrog existing technology, schools of business administration and the supporting print industry cast a big spotlight on that announcement. The spotlight said: "Here's the new leader. Follow the leader." And when powerhouse partners like Marriott, Hilton Hotels, and Budget Rent-A-Car bought in on the system, more spotlights showed us "the way." You will find nothing but praise—some of it lavish—in print. Five years later, the project was a disaster, costing AMR around $165 million in straight business losses. In addition, there were $500 million in lawsuit challenges. If you search the business literature for the years 1992, 1993, and 1994, you will find only one article referring to this debacle.

When projects fail, when things go wrong, the same managers who proudly took credit for the good times crowd out Pontius Pilate at the hand-washing bowl. The following case is an apt example.

For many decades prior to January 1994, 20th Century Insurance had been one of the premier insurance companies in America. Its low expense ratios were envied by its competitors, and in 1993 it was No. 1 in *Financial World's* ranking of insurance companies. CEO Bill Mellick was proud of his company's accomplishments: "I can tell you out of 100,000 homes within two-tenths of one percent how many thefts, fires, and total losses we'll have." The company was well within state and federal regulations, carrying $100 million in reinsurance. "Enough to cover the likes of the 1906 San Francisco earthquake," Mellick noted.

On January 17, 1994, the Northridge, California, earthquake translated into $1 billion claims on 20th Century. The company's stock went from $30 a share prior to the earthquake to $8 dollars a share six months after.

Experts now question Mellick's decisions. He should not have, they say, sold so many policies in one tremor-prone area, and he should have carried more reinsurance.

Mellick himself excuses the decisions. "I can't use statistics with an act of God," he protests.

Interesting. Do you suppose he attributed success to absence of God's acts during the good years? Not likely. Managers normally attribute success in their own doings to their acumen; but failure, they say, results from bad luck—unless it is someone else's failure. Most managers are ready with rational explanations for other managers' failures. Just as "the experts" explained the 20th Century financial disaster as management-decision shortcomings, managers, professors, and other experts are ever ready as "Monday morning quarterbacks."

Top managers commonly blame lack of success on bad luck, though they seldom attribute success to good luck. In a study covering a large number of company reports to stockholders, it was found that when the outcome for the year was favorable, management explained the success in terms of management decisions. Conversely, when the outcome was unfavorable, failures were attributed to outside forces over which management had no control. As one observer noted: when the unexpected happens, the self-proclaimed management futurists run around like so many Chicken Littles, crying "The environment's turbulent! The environment's turbulent!"

That's how Gary L. Tooker, CEO of Motorola, dealt with the sudden decline in his company's fortunes. In July 1996, the bubble burst for Motorola, which had been labeled "Corporate Golden Boy" during its windfall years of the early 1990s. Orders fell by more than 25 percent. Profits plunged, as did share value. The business world was "shocked." CEO Tooker blamed "circumstances beyond Motorola's control."

No one would deny that life is unpredictable and that none of us can ever hope to have control over what is going to happen, particularly in the case of large organizations. Yet it is part of American organizational folklore to picture top management as having such control. Enormous financial outlays and disruptions of lives are routinely invested in a belief that a manager knows what he is doing, as happened in the 1980s when General Motors (GM) spent billions of dollars and restructured virtually all of its operations on CEO Roger Smith's vision for a 21st century corporation. GM had just had its first year of losing money since 1921. Americans were buying Japanese cars.

Smith said he knew how to catch up to and get far ahead of the Japanese competition. He would beat them at their own game, computerization and robotization.

At the time—while Smith spent billions of dollars on computerized, paperless offices and robotized assembly plants—he was hailed in the business media as "a bold and visionary leader." The tone of all media coverage was, "Roger Smith points the way to the future for the automobile industry and probably for all American industry."

He failed. Spiderweb-gathering robots in defunct plant buildings are the testimony to his genius, along with an ocean of financial losses and unemployed workers. Management textbooks of the 1990s are filled with analyses to explain where Smith went wrong.

There is a vast market for such "Monday morning quarterbacking" because the American model for managers pictures composed rational actors who are always in charge. "They wouldn't be there if they didn't know what to do." Therefore, management failure must be explained in management terms. You can't say, "He failed because life is, say, a process of successes and failures over which we really have very little control." You must say, "He failed because, say, he misread the market" or "didn't bring in the right talent at the operational levels" or "applied the wrong technology" or any other explanation that suggests something over which he had control or should have known that was knowable.

In other words, the world of management must always be pictured in terms of rational action in a fully knowable world of happenings. There can be no accidents, no unaccountable events, no randomness, no chance. In those windows of truth when failure is admitted, the new management does not tell workers that their predecessors ran afoul of life in its reality; nor do they tell them that they, the new kids on the block, might also have bad luck. Rather, they say that they have answers to "the problems," implying that the problems and their solutions are known.

Frank Schnieder "knew the problems and the answers" when he took over ailing *Greyhound Lines* in 1991. He was highly praised for slashing costs, upgrading buses and facilities, and settling a bitter labor dispute that had pushed *Greyhound* into bankruptcy. But he didn't get people to travel on buses. After he was fired in 1994 (surprise, surprise), a number of analysts knew why he failed. The hubris of "management knowledge" has no limits.

Nowhere is the hubris more appalling than in management strategy. *Most so-called strategists,* writes Henry Mintzberg, *just sit on top and pretend to strategize. They formulate ever so clever strategies for everyone else to implement. They issue glossy strategic plans that look wonderful and take their organizations nowhere with great fanfares.*

So enthusiastic is this belief in knowledge and answers that middle- and upper-level managers are consumers for an industry that sells the answers, or approaches to find the answers. The industry revolves around universities, and consists of consultants, books, tapes, and workshops. "Every month," one middle-level manager said, "the senior management goes to some seminar and comes home with a new religion. We just hold our breath until they get over it."

Each of the new religions is peddled with, appropriately enough, an evangelical flair. If you've seen any of the management-improvement gurus on tapes and in books and articles and are presented as revelations, and have also seen Burt Lancaster as *Elmer Gantry* or any of the real evangelical "soul savers" on television, you have probably spotted the similarities. There is one tape of Tom Peters, one of the most notable gurus, sleeves rolled-up, pacing feverishly around the stage, throwing up his hands, sweating, and gnarling grammar as though to validate his sincerity, that is reminiscent of an old Billy Sunday film.

The lessons peddled on tapes and in books and articles are presented as revelations. Inspired by such revelations, managers can "lead" their organizations onto dry land after parting the rivers' waters. One of the best-selling management-inspirational books, *Reengineering the Corporation*, which is often proclaimed as the "theoretical basis" for downsizing, had, by the authors' proud admission, "an evangelical tone." A few years later, one of its authors wondered in print about failures in the reengineering movement. (Various studies set the failure rate of reengineering attempts at 67 percent.) "While countless managers have been persuaded to downsize," he wrote, "too many have had poor or disastrous results." Go tell *that* to the millions of downsizing's victims.

Will it come as a surprise to you to be told that you need not worry because the author of the regrets has the repair kit ready and available? After the laments he proceeds to provide answers, which is pro forma in the shell game of the organizational improvement literature. We are told that reengineering will not succeed if management does not "organize, inspire, deploy, enable, measure, and reward." Doesn't that in itself suggest that reengineering will seldom succeed? How many managers can have these skills? Probably few. It is simply too big an order. But that will not keep the majority of managers who are not up to bringing about this miracle from claiming they can.

Business books are often catechisms of the "Born Again" with a "this time I've really found it" message. After many years on the *Harvard Business Review* staff, including the position of Senior Editor, Thomas Teal left that prestigious wellspring of management teachings to write a book in which he said that management education was on the wrong track. "You can hardly swing a cat in the average workplace," he wrote, "without hitting several mediocre managers." Even after all the years of MBA degree-granting and the existence of journals like the one he worked for, he declared in 1995 that "mediocre management is the norm."

But do not despair. Just as the reengineering guru has the right answer *now* so does the "Born-Again" Thomas Teal. The reason for our failures in the business schools and journals, he tells us, is that "in educating and training managers, we focus too much on technical proficiency and too little on character." Does that sound a little like a proverb to you?

Around 50 years ago a prominent Nobel-Prize-winning social scientist, Herbert Simon, forewarned us to beware the proverbs parading in scientific costumes. Theories of organization, wrote Simon, developed a bad habit when they started using prescriptive language: *Prescriptive statements all too often are proverbs, having all the advantages and disadvantages of proverbs.*

If you're in search of a snappy, quotable phrase, a proverb is ideal, like *"Look before you leap!"* Sounds good and is good advice. But there is a contradictory proverb: *"He who hesitates is lost!"* Simon points out that most proverbs occur in mutually contradictory pairs, and that this is both an advantage and a disadvantage, depending on our purpose.

> *If it is a matter of rationalizing behavior that has already taken place or justifying action that has already been decided upon, proverbs are ideal. Since one is never at a loss to find one that will prove his point or the precisely contradictory point, for that matter—they are a great help in persuasion, political debate, and all forms of rhetoric.*
>
> *But when one seeks to use proverbs as the basis of a scientific theory, the situation is less happy. It is not that the propositions expressed by the proverbs are insufficient; it is rather that they prove too much. A scientific theory should tell what is true but also what is false.*

The challenge for any author who wants to lure you away from *Playboy* in the airport newsstand is to package proverbs so that they look original. Often, the opening chapter will reveal that all books preceding this one are full of proverbs.

One Man's Myth Is Another's Pink Slip

The Witch Doctors should be on your reading list. Its authors argue that the demand for "management science" is "created in part by the insecurity of corporate executives." All around them they see downsizing, rightsizing, restructuring—all those dreadful euphemisms for sacking people—and they want to improve their own performance. Burdened by their insecurity, managers overzealously mouth the proverbs and defend their "wisdom" by posing in suits and lavish office settings. Who will carry the buckets to mop up after their mistakes? Sometimes it's another guy in a suit and office; sometimes it's workers without offices. Seldom is it the one who fathered the mistake. Have you ever noticed how often managers say that while they have the answers, success requires "the 100 percent cooperation of everyone in this organization?" Doesn't that sound like a preparation for buck passing?

Or we might be exhorted to "put on a good face" no matter what happens to the "brilliant solutions brought by management." According to two eye witnesses, the following happened at The White House:

> *Vice-President Al Gore told his National Performance Review staff that they were about to reinvent government with a barrage of management improvement philosophy and techniques. Then John Daly, a motivational consultant, gave a pep talk. He told the group that "It doesn't matter how good you really are, but how you communicate how good you are." Then he led the group in a refrain from "Snow White and the Seven Dwarfs" ("Hi Ho, Hi Ho, It's Off to Work We Go").*

It will probably come as no surprise to you that in the end, workers are often blamed for the failures of "management knowledge." Either the dwarfs don't sing enthusiastically enough or demand more money than they deserve. Prior to the market-whipping taken by American automakers in the 1980s, management at the Detroit "Big Three" was venerated; after the defeats, the autoworkers were blamed because, you see, workers' unions had driven salaries and benefits so high that the American companies could not compete with "cheap Japanese labor."

In the 1990s, after a steep decline in this union power and the rise of Japanese autoworkers' salaries and benefits beyond what American workers receive, Japanese cars are still better, though American cars have improved. Many managers continue to blame workers for this second-best status in the auto, and many other, industries. American workers, we are told, are not properly educated and/or not sufficiently motivated to work hard in the new highly-technical workplace. Sometimes the workers are let off the hook a little, when American society and education are blamed. The point is that management is not the problem. How could it be? It's got a science and dresses well.

Overpaid workers are management's first favorite scapegoat; workers' inability to adapt to change is the second. When John Martin took over management control of an ailing Taco Bell in the mid-1980s, he said he looked around and found out that "the greatest enemies" of Taco Bell's success "are the tradition-bound ideas to which many of our employees cling." The fact that the tradition-bound ideas to which the employees clung were the ideas Taco Bell management had instilled via training programs and rewarded all these years conveniently escapes Martin.

"Change" is a hot word these days. Though empty of meaning because it can mean anything, it is another of those gimmick words that serves managers well. If you are a manager, you want to be full of ideas for "change" because, like "value-added," it rings of "modern management know-how." Once identified as what the new management science calls a "change agent" your 90 percent failures can be blamed on . . . workers who won't change. You have not only passed the buck, you have positioned yourself nicely for a headhunter's sales pitch to your next employer: "You'll love this guy, he's Mr. Change."

Managers sometimes drag absolutely absurd ideas around like security blankets. Their flights of fancy can be goofy, as when Roger Smith robotized at GM. In the novel *Martin Dressler*, make-believe eliminates reality:

> *Martin Dressler lives the America dream. The time is the 1890s, and Martin works his way up from cigar-store clerk to real estate mogul. He opens a chain of restaurants featuring the five-minute breakfast, then a chain of hotels, and Metropolitan Cafes featuring blue storefronts. In the end, the dream does him in. He realizes his most ambitious project, an enormous hotel with artificial lakes and forests, lit by mechanical moons, meant to supersede the outer world. This dream wastes his fortune. He hires actors to impersonate customers, then an actor to impersonate himself. Things appear to be going splendidly. Meanwhile, he, himself, wanders out penniless into the harsh sunlight.*

If you think that *Martin Dressler* is a pure fiction that bears no resemblance to the real world, consider Faith Popcorn, professional futurist, who peddles "trends" to a long list of big name companies and politicians. She's the source of the term "cocooning trend" (consumers are snuggling in with upscale take-out and a video) and, more recently, "pleasure revenge" (people are sick of being perfect, so they're lighting up cigarettes eating butter, not running, and buying furs). Though she's viewed as a sham by most people who write about her and her multimillion dollar business of selling these ideas, the business just keeps getting better and better. Her clients include: IBM, Philip Morris, American Express, Estee Lauder, Silicon Graphics, ConAgra, BMW, Reebok, Rubbermaid, Nabisco, Burger King, Chesebrough-Pond's, and Campbell Soup.

Popcorn is never wrong because, you see, her ideas "evolve." Thus, when sales of out-of-home food and beverages went to record levels, she did not say she was wrong about the "cocooning" trend. Rather, she explained that now the trend is *wandering cocoons. Cocooning*, says Popcorn, *is a trend that is evolving and evolving and evolving.*

Her problems with cocooning are typical. Her success as a guru is puzzling. William Lauder, President of Estee Lauder's Origins product line, says that what Popcorn achieves is something spiritual rather than practical or technical. (Translation: Yes, she's often wrong, but so what? She's uplifting.) A journalist who spent some time with Popcorn, her working associates, and her clients, concluded that *she succeeds not by selling a product of value, but by flattering executives' fantasies about themselves. She's selling a salve for executive insecurity.*

Even outright and indisputable failure for one of her ideas can not dampen her followers' trust in her. Heublein's hired her to design a new ad campaign for Smirnoff vodka using her "cocooning" idea. She came up with an ad campaign titled *Home Is Where You Find It.* Different scenes of people at home, often with a dog or cat, and Smirnoff vodka were run. Nothing happened to sales. The campaign was canceled. The executive who hired her said: *Faith's solution was too good. It was the right solution for the wrong people.*

Failure does not dampen enthusiasm for Faith Popcorn's visions in the hearts of the people who paid her. In the case of the vodka fizzle, the customers were blamed.

The Productivity Myth

Organizations pretend to be focused on productivity far more than they really are. Although there is no denial that productivity is a good thing for a business, Richard Farnsworth, President of the Western Behavioral Sciences Institute, says that *when it comes down to a choice between productivity and any number of other values and behaviors—such as maintaining the status quo or holding on to one's stereotypes—it becomes imme-*

diately apparent that productivity is seldom our paramount goal. If we were really interested in productivity we would, for example, find ways of making better use of women, who represent more than half of our talent.

There have been some increases of women in managerial positions, say two professors of psychology, Alice Eagly and Linda Carli, in a September 2007 *Harvard Business Review* article. Women now occupy more than 40 percent of all managerial positions in the United States, but within the C-suite they remain as rare as hens' teeth. "Consider," they say, *the most highly paid executives of Fortune 500 companies those with titles such as chairman, president, chief executive office, and chief operating officer. Of this group, only 6% are women. Most notably, only 2% of the CEOs are women.*

Preserving traditional power relationships—such as that between men and women—is only one of the considerations that are usually more valuable than productivity to the people who have the most power. Most managers will:

- opt to protect their positions every time those positions are in conflict with productivity.
- promote a person who will be loyal to them over a more productive person of questionable loyalty.
- place their own comfort (offices, limousines, secretaries, proximity to desirable locations) over productivity.

Much of what we hear about measured increases in productivity, says economist Richard Benson, *is purposely mismeasured and used as old-fashioned propaganda, or 'Psychological Warfare,' to help stabilize the [Credit and Stock] markets."*

Mismeasurement techniques vary from not including the dollars spent on computers and information technology, both of which often account for significant increases in workers' productivity, to ignoring the impacts on productivity caused by cutting wages and pensions. For example, when a company changes from a defined benefit plan to a defined contribution plan or makes workers pay a larger share for health benefits, productivity goes up.

These methods for increasing productivity do not support the notion that productivity rises when management finds a better way to allocate resources and/or organize the workplace.

—Three—

The Myth of Performance Evaluation

Assessing performance is fraught with ambiguities.
                                                    —Lee Bolman

If you want to see why it is a myth that organizational rewards are based on how well you contribute to your organization, start at the top. There is no correlation between executive compensation and executive performance. Study after study repeats the message: higher executive pay in corporation x does not mean that corporation x is showing a better bottom line. Indeed, sometimes the bottom line is going down while the executives' salaries are going up.

In 1996 the average salary and bonus for CEOs rose 39 percent, well above the 11 percent gain in corporate profits and the 23 percent rise in the stock value of their companies. On an individual basis, comparing executive compensations to how well their companies are doing in their industry reveals that the best compensations do not correlate with the best profits and stock value rises.

Even when there is positive correlation between a company's success on the bottom line and executives' incomes, the success may be dubious. Sometimes corruption, cheating and illegality enable an executive to boost the company's bottom line. American executives are unique examples of powerful people who know how to manipulate systems for private gain.

This has been known for a long time. At least since the late 1980s, American boardrooms have been trying to find ways to keep senior executives from increasing private gain at the expense of the shareholders. The three most popular reforms are recruiting more outside directors with whom the executives have no prior connection, linking pay to performance measures, and giving executives share options, to align their interests with those of shareholders.

The results have been similar to the results I have squirrel-proofing the birdfeeders in my backyard: cunning outwits control every time.

- Confronted with new faces on the board, Mr. Executive devotes most of his energy, time, and cunning to ingratiating himself to them.
- Confronted with performance measures, Mr. Executive focuses entirely on doing the things being measured, often to the detriment of overall performance.
- Confronted with the share-option approach, Mr. Executive concentrates on gambling to increase share prices. Common gambles are acquisitions and divestitures. This is a smart gamble because if share prices go down he has not lost much and has gained a "vigorous leader" image. "Vigorous leaders," failed ones as well as successful ones, are as much in demand by corporate America as seven-foot centers with a hook shot by the NBA.

In the public sector there is not even a rhetorical attempt to link pay to performance at the top executive levels. Public executive almost always take a pay cut if they come out of the private sector, which they usually do. Reimbursement is deferred to later, when the executive leaves public service and reaps the profits from the connections she has made in her government position. Furthermore, no one knows how to measure performance in the public sector.

In the not-for-profit, non-governmental sector, there is a lot of rhetoric about underpaid executives, but in fact they appear to be generously rewarded. Once a year, or so, you'll hear about a scandal at the top in one of the country's major charity organizations. Usually it involves a highly-paid executive and his staff overindulging themselves in the good life of limousines and private jets.

Unintended consequences abound in the not-for-profits. For example, do you think that the administrator of an orphanage should be primarily evaluated in terms of her placements of children in adequate homes, or in terms of her standing in the community? If, like most people, you choose the former, you might find it frustrating to learn that placement rates are not scored as high as standing in the community and find it exasperating to learn that the larger an orphanage is, the more likely it will be that its administrator will have standing in the community. There is, then, a motivation for an administrator to not lower the number of children under her care.

Administrators of foundations and institutions which gather contributions purportedly to help the needy are rewarded far more for the amount of money they bring in than for the amount that actually goes directly to the needy. As a result, administration of these organizations focuses on the kind of image that draws big contributions, is handsomely rewarded in salary and perks, and is more concerned with the appearance of "doing good" than with the amount of "good" that is actually done.

No matter where you look—in the private, public, or not-for-profit sectors—you'll not find much correlation between performance and rewards, and when you do find correlation it will be for reasons less than laudable. We should not expect a senior management that benefits from such a system to be vigilant in its reform. And they are not, though they fervently proclaim that they are. Reward systems in any organization, notwithstanding the public posturing of CEOs, bureaucratic administrators, heads of charities, and the Pope, are used to placate the powerful, inspire loyalty amongst a chosen few, and thicken the sinews of coalitions. Outstanding performance is sometimes rewarded for one of two reasons: (1) It is an accident in an otherwise consistent regime; (2) It is a byproduct. Some people favored by the regime are also highly competent.

Often, outstanding performance and qualifications are completely overlooked in favor of picking people of unquestionable loyalty. When Frank Bremer selected three top-level persons to guide the Iraqi economy toward privatization a few years after the U.S. invasion of Iraq, he bypassed available persons who spoke Arabic and had considerable experience in business in order to hire three young inexperienced persons who did not speak Arabic; however, his hires had no ties or loyalty to anyone else.

Sometimes the reward system works against the values it purports to support. For example:

> A *plane belonging to a major American airline was grounded one afternoon for repairs at Airport A, but the nearest mechanic qualified to perform the repairs worked at Airport B. The manager at Airport B refused to send the mechanic to Airport A that afternoon, because after completing the repairs the mechanic would have had to stay overnight at a hotel, and the hotel bill would come out of B's budget. So, the mechanic was dispatched to Airport A early the following morning, which enabled him to fix the plane and return home the same day. A multi-million dollar aircraft sat idle, and the airline lost hundreds of thousands of dollars in revenue, but Manager B's budget wasn't hit for a $100 hotel bill. Manager B was neither foolish nor careless. He was doing exactly what he was supposed to be doing: controlling and minimizing his expenses."*

If the people who have the authority to see and kill such penny-wise-pound-foolish policies were really paying attention these policies wouldn't exist. The fact is that the people with the full organization view—the men and women at the top—pay only lip service to their company's official policies on rewards for performance. The airline example probably resulted from a policy developed by a specialist—or maybe it was a consultant—on cost-cutting. It was ritualistic in the airline industry of the late 1990s to find ways to save money by rewarding managers who ran their own individual budgets frugally. If you're wondering why those specialists, or consultants, don't see the losses their savings cause, it's perhaps because I didn't tell you that specialists and consultants are included in the myth that managers know what they are doing. As with managers, one should not expect the wisdom of consultants to extend beyond self-promotional skills.

Hidden Agendas

Another flaw in reward-for-performance systems is the hidden agenda, which people like Marsha Downs usually learn from coworkers:

When Marsha Downs went to work as a claims adjuster for a national insurance company she was told by both the Director of Human Resources and her immediate supervisor, Monty Okun, that *around here performance is what counts. We reward the productive people and get rid of the others. Work hard and smart; we'll take care of the rest.* She liked the message. Today she'll advise you to search beyond the surface of such messages because her first annual evaluation was a disappointment.

After twelve months of receiving no feedback on the quality of her adjustments, Marsha received a computer printout that indicated the amount of time she spent on each adjustment plus the dollar settlement, and then compared her numbers to those of the other adjusters. The highest-ranked adjusters were those who spent the least *amount of time and had the lowest dollar settlements.*

Although her supervisor did not invite her to discuss this ranking, she did so on her own initiative. What did it mean? Monty told her that she should not pay much attention to it. *Just some numbers game the people up there like to play,* he said. She was perplexed: *But I'm seeing myself ranked near the bottom of a list that's titled 'Annual Evaluations'!*

That's not what I look at when I make my recommendations, he replied. *In fact I've recommended you and all of the adjusters in this section for raises. You're all doing a terrific job.*

Though still perplexed, Marsha just nodded and left his office. In a few weeks she found out that raises had been given to a few adjusters. She was not one of them. Those who received raises had been at the top of the evaluation list. So, she discussed it with Monty again. *I'm going to level with you, Marsha, I don't know what's going on. I did all I could. I guess the best advice I can give you is to cut down on the time and dollars in your adjustments.*

She argued in vain about how each case is different. He simply agreed with her. *It's not fair,* she said. *The results have more to do with the types of cases I'm dealing with than with my performance.* He agreed with her. *It's the system,* he moaned, throwing up his hands.

Months later, Marsha stopped off at a bar after work with another adjuster and found out how experienced adjusters played the system. *Every time you have an obvious low-dollar case,* she was advised, *settle it over the phone. Mail the form, let the claimants do the work. So long as they see that you're going to pay them, they'll be glad to do it. The company doesn't audit the small cases because it's not cost-effective in terms of an auditor's time. So, no one is going to second-guess your decisions on those. Claims that'll obviously involve bigger dollars must be investigated, but just cover your ass in case of an audit. Your real goal is to settle for a relatively lower amount of money in a short amount of time. Claimants want to get things done yesterday. So work that angle. Find the quickest way to the smallest dollar amount.*

Hidden agendas are a problem for you because you have to find out about them and also because if you get caught doing something punishable, and someone is in a mood to mete out some punishment, you can't use the "following orders" defense. Usually higher-ups confronted with hidden agenda behavior will get that real sincere look on their faces and say something like "That's certainly not our policy." Consider an incident at Prudential Insurance Company.

What Marsha learned is an age-old truth about organizations. *People will find ways to give the appearance of performing according to the organizations' methods of performance evaluation and reward.* As we will see when we discuss people in the next chapter, playing these kinds of games in the organization is entirely natural. "Everybody does it," and it often leads to reward rather than punishment. Now and then the organization is compelled by outside forces to do something about it, as happened in 1996 when Prudential Insurance was fined and sued because its agents were acting illegally.

Management at Prudential had set up some nice rewards for certain insurance renewal policies which under some circumstances were illegal. An internal audit in 1982 warned management that some Prudential agents were using deceptive practices. Management ignored the warning. Rewards continued to go to agents who double-talked elderly policy holders into renewals advantageous to the company but disadvantageous to the policy holders. Eventually a required outside audit in 1994 exposed what was by then a widespread web of customer deception. Nonetheless, Prudential management took the position that *we were unaware that practices contrary to the historical philosophy of this company were occurring. Such practices have no place at an institution that has long served Americans honorably and responsibly. We have taken steps to correct these misguided practices.*

Avoiding the $ Word

In the millions of words filling the unending pages of all those books and lectures-on-tape which tell managers how to motivate workers, you will seldom find the word *money*. The standard pitch is to "inform" the manager that workers *are not motivated* by money. What does motivate workers? Things like participation, self-actualization, and empowerment.

Well, the pitch is a little more sophisticated than that. You are told that workers are in need of a certain amount of money, as they need a certain amount of physical security. But if you want to get more productivity out of your workers, give them a sense of ownership, of belonging, and of participating.

This message is for persons who have very little if any capability of paying people more money. Since the late 1980s, the prevailing organizational ideology is that productivity must be increased without increasing the costs of labor. Top management will not hire a consultant who suggests motivational techniques that involve paying workers more money. Managers will not attend a *"How To . . ."* seminar or pick a *"How To . . ."* book off the rack at the airport if it mentions the $ word as a reward system for workers; it's OK to financially reward managers, especially top managers.

The guru of all this is a psychologist named Abraham Maslow whose "hierarchy of needs" is found on at least one page of every book published on management. Maslow's hierarchy looks like a pyramid. The most basic need—security—is at the bottom. At the top is self-fulfillment. Money is one of the basic needs. According to Maslow, as we satisfy each need, we move upward to higher needs. Once we have a decent salary, we start looking for socialization, approval from others, things like that. When we have enough of that we move upward toward self-fulfillment.

Maslow advised managers to listen to what he called the quality of employee grumbles. "I don't get paid enough" is, by Maslow's designation, a low-order grumble. "My talents are not being fully utilized" is a high-order grumble. You should judge your effectiveness as a manager by the quality of grumbles from those you supervise.

Management theorists like Maslow have decent enough intentions. They want to bring more dignity and self-satisfaction to the workplace without requiring increases in money costs to management. Unfortunately, there is no chance for utopia at the workplace. Managers will take these ideas and try to exploit them. Values of human development cherished by the Maslows become false pearls management throws to real swine.

Study after study has shown that these notions are alien to the workplace. Workers from the lowest to highest levels always want more income. There is no such thing as a level at which people are so satisfied with their income that they wish no more. The drive for self-achievement is indeed important to most people, but not if it means less income.

When the Maslows acknowledge the differences between their theories of who people are and what the studies say, they have an ingenious explanation. They tell us that their theories deal with the potential of the human being. Our institutions twist the human being out of shape, creating a money-grubber where there is potential for a self-actualizer. What we need is a complete overhaul of our societal ethics.

This provides a basis for thinking of organizations as moral training grounds and managers as moral leaders. Such leaders save us from ourselves. We are back to being worshipers in Henry Ford's temples. Picture the manager in flight, airport pocketbook on management wizardry in hand, break into an angelic smile. Now you know why.

Mission Statements, Bizspeak, and Bromides

In a 2006 study by Bain and Company, 85 percent of large companies worldwide have mission statements. As pointed out in a *New York Times* article by Kelley Howard, *As the use of mission statements has spread, some have become so filled with jargon and bromides that many employees now dismiss them as window dressing.*

To give you an idea of how bad it can be, consider this one from Howard's piece: *It is our responsibility to assertively administrate timely deliverables in order to solve business problems.*

—Four—

Not in *This* Organization!

I believe in looking reality straight in the eye and denying it.

—Garrison Keillor

If you sit down with the average management person and talk about these things, she will nod knowingly. If you ask her if that's the way things are in her organization, she'll probably say: "Not here." She might volunteer that prior to her incumbency things were that way. She might talk about what a rough road it was to eliminate that stuff. Or she might tell you that "we haven't gotten rid of all of it, but we're well on the way."

Most top executives talk about these things as "people" or "communications" problems, and they add, pridefully, statements like: *Our people give it to us straight. We have very open relationships between and amongst our people.*

In a study of 165 upper- and middle-level managers in six companies (an electronics firm, a manufacturer of a new innovative product, a large research and development company and a small one, a consulting-research firm, and a producer of heavy equipment), it was found that managers, particularly those at higher levels, live in a world of pretenses, even keeping themselves confused about the truth as they know/don't know it.

The actual behavior of these managers contradicted their professed attitudes and prescriptions about effective managerial action. Whenever they discussed effective management and/or how their organizations operated, they talked about the vital importance of innovation, risk taking, flexibility, trust, and openness. Risk taking, in this study, meant risking self-esteem, as, for example, when one speaks the unwelcome truth to his superiors ("I understand that you're enthusiastic about this idea you've come up with, but I must tell you why I think it's a bad move.") or when one risks putting millions of dollars in a new investment.

Their behavior contradicted their stated beliefs both in how things should be and are in their organizations. They were rarely observed taking risks or experimenting with new ideas or feelings; they seldom encouraged others to do so; and disagreement with a superior was limited to suggesting alternative ways of accomplishing small and insignificant aspects of the superiors' proposals.

Though these managers insisted that their subordinates enjoyed a work environment filled with trust and openness and knew they would not be punished for failures resulting from risk taking, an interview of 25 such subordinates painted a picture of low openness to uncomfortable information, low appreciation for risk taking, little trust, emphasis on conformity, and dislike for conflict.

This indicates, as do so many studies, that managers live in a "Let's Pretend" world regarding their relationships with subordinates. If you interview managers about these matters, they will tell you, usually emphatically so as to be in step with their self-image of decisiveness, that their subordinates do "just about everything I ask for willingly," and that they and the subordinates talk together frequently and openly. Interviews with "the subordinates" consistently point us in the opposite direction. The subordinates find their bosses vague and not eager to be pushed for clarification, unable to accept criticism, unaware of difficulties at the subordinates' levels, and uninterested in knowing about them. When asked "Do you give the appearance of doing things willingly?" the answer usually is: "Sure, I want to survive."

The "Let's Pretend" characteristic of organizations is often depicted in organizational behavior studies through quotes from *Alice in Wonderland*. What a contrast to the logical, rational, practical and orderly visions of organizations broadcast by top management, wherein though chaos reigns all around us, we, the managers, are maintaining order and progress in a logical and practical way.

"Let's Pretend" is complicated further by the phenomenon of "We must pretend very hard because we know deep down inside that we are pretending."

In the study of those 165 managers, all interviews were either taped or carefully recorded in notes. Analysis of the tapes brought out a fairly consistent pattern of contradictions. In the early stages of the interviews, the managers tended to articulate the party line. In later stages, they contradicted the party line, describing situations more consistent with what the researchers observed and with subordinates' descriptions of those situations.

To put it another way: Early in the interview stage managers stuck to the pretense; later on, they spoke realistically. Here are some examples. The first statement, in bold print, is what a manager said early in the interviews; the second statement, in italics, is what the same manager said later in the interviews.

We say pretty much what we think to one another at all levels and between levels.

We are careful not to say anything that will antagonize anyone.

We understand one another. Relationships are close and friendly, based on years of working together.

I don't know how people feel about me.

When we have executive meetings, we tackle all issues.

At executive meetings, we tend to spend too much time talking about relatively unimportant issues.

Now and then organizations stop to study themselves. The results can be surprising, as it was to top-management at Capital Holding Corporation's Direct Response Group (DRG) in 1988 when DRG went through reengineering. According to the DRG Vice-President:

> *We had been told—and now we know it's true—that before you can effect any significant change, you've first got to understand your company's culture. Therefore, the first thing we did was to conduct a cultural audit, which helped us discover and understand our employees' attitudes.*
>
> *We put together a team to get the real dirt on us as a company by means of interviews with frontline employees. We wanted to find out the unwritten rules in the organization. The team asked questions such as, If your younger brother or sister came to work here, what would you tell them about getting ahead in this organization? The results were unpleasant. We thought we had a customer-focused organization, but in interviewing more than a hundred people in the organization, the team heard the word 'customer' just twice. In our employees' minds, pleasing the customer had little to do with getting ahead in the company.*

Reforming Performance Evaluation—Again?

Every so often an organization announces it has learned from the mistakes of the past and has now fashioned a proper performance evaluation system. The nagging truth is that each new performance-evaluation method is based on solving the problems of its predecessor; in time, the reform will be found to be full of problems as well. No one is ever going to "get it right" because of interpersonal psychological limitations. One or a combination of the following errors will haunt every attempt to achieve objectivity in performance evaluation: attribution, the "halo effect," leniency, strictness, central tendency, and recency.

You are already familiar with attribution errors, from the discussion on how a CEO will attribute good times to his genius, and bad times to bad luck. When a supervisor evaluates a subordinate, he will not allow "bad luck" as a factor in failures, as he does for himself. And he will tend to praise those aspects of his subordinate's performance for which he can take some credit.

The "halo effect" happens when a supervisor concentrates on only one of several things and rates everything according to it. A supervisor who is convinced that being on time for work and being there all the time you are supposed to be at work might rate you high on everything, or low on everything, if you are, in his eyes, dependable or not.

Some supervisors give super ratings to everyone (leniency error) and others do the opposite (strictness error). In contrast, supervisors might lump everyone around the middle (central tendency error), while others rate employees according to the employees most recent behavior. And, of course, there is no small amount of racial, age, and gender bias in the system.

These errors have been common knowledge for a long time. Research strongly suggests that most evaluators will fall into one or more of them, no matter what the organization does to change it.

You can't change it either. Fairness and objectivity will only rarely command your performance reviews because even if the system allowed it people just aren't up to it. What you can do is use this knowledge of the system to your own advantage. For example, if your supervisor is a "halo effect" type of evaluator, find her Rosetta stone. The chapters on strategy and tactics give you a number of other ways to succeed because of flaws in your organization's performance evaluation system.

"Mirror, Mirror, on the wall, who's the fairest of them all" asks the wicked ol' witch, knowing full well which answer she'll accept. No less of a fairy tale is the claim that organizations select the best-qualified applicants for positions. Whether the position is to be filled by a new person or someone already in the organization there is no way that "the best qualified" can be known. Behind this facade, you will find that "the best qualified" means scoring higher on a test or interview or other evaluation technique. The relevance of those tests and the other techniques to the job in question is always shaky at best. That's how the American court system, most personnel specialists, and your common sense see it.

While it is possible to make distinctions between the "totally unqualified" and "very qualified," it is very difficult to make distinctions between the "very qualified," and usually impossible to find the "most qualified." All screening devices— tests, educational degrees, certificates, interviews, in-basket exercises, and so on—are imperfect ways to identify ability to do a particular job.

Before a person actually performs on a job for a period of time, there is no way to know how she will do. Screening devices can point out totally unqualified persons—a chauffeur must be able to drive—and they provide organizations with the appearance of objectivity in decision making.

This latter function of screening techniques, providing "appearances," is significantly practical. Throughout this book the intention is not to deny the importance of techniques and ideologies that help organizations create facades, which are needed in the day-to-day real world in which organizations operate. The theme of this book is to help you recognize facades and arbitrariness, to keep you from being swept away by the rhetoric of organizations.

What degree of driving skills are necessary for a chauffeur? It's not difficult to know how to set up, carry out, and grade applicants on tests of driving skills; but, how do we know which level of the tested skills is appropriate to the job? Usually the standard set is arbitrary, though there will be a lot of huffing and puffing to make that standard look as though it is absolutely indispensable for the job to be done right.

The facade of "choosing the best qualified" was brought down in public by the U.S. Supreme Court in a 1987 case involving the promotion of a woman instead of a man, even though the man had scored slightly higher on tests given for the position. Quoting from a brief submitted to the court by the American

Society for Personnel Administration, the Court said that *it is a standard tenet of personnel administration that there is rarely a single best qualified person for a job. Final determinations as to which candidate is best qualified are at best subjective.*

In government employment, where the facade of "selecting the best qualified" becomes a legal requirement, there now are standard techniques for manipulating the system. The most commonly used are tailoring, provisional appointment, and bridging.

Tailoring goes like this: Wynona, Director of Field Office Operations for the Agricultural Extension Services, has a new budgeted position to fill in the Sioux Falls office. The title for this position is "public relations coordinator." The job description is based on the need to publicize agricultural services available for the Sioux Falls region.

Wynona thinks that Margie, who has worked for Wynona three years as an administrative assistant, would be perfect for this new position. She works with the Agricultural Extension Service personnel office to write the job announcement so that the "preferred skills" listed in the announcement are very similar to Margie's skills. Certain skills that Margie has and the other applicants will not have are included, such as "experience in the Director of Field Office Operations' office."

When the selection committee meets and the applications are reviewed, Margie is clearly the winner.

Provisional appointment goes like this: Wynona either cannot contrive with the personnel office to tailor the preferred skills, or Margie doesn't have any unique skills to list. Wynona appoints Margie to do the job as a provisional appointment, pending development of a new test for the new job. In the meantime, bureaucratic foot-dragging delays development of the new test. Six months later the job is publicized, with a listing of preferred skills that only Margie has because she's been doing the job for all that time. Sometimes a new test is never forthcoming; eventually, the provisional appointment is rolled over to be a permanent one.

Bridging is the technique Wynona could use if she had requested, but had not yet been given the new position. She would appoint Margie on a temporary line to do the job. In a year or so, whenever she felt it would be accepted, she would withdraw her request for a new position and submit a request to bridge the temporary line into a permanent position.

We Care About Our People

Perhaps the greatest organizational hypocrisy lurks in the phrase *Here at the Goodparts Company, we care about our people.*

Organizations are genuinely concerned about "their people" as workers and will have an interest in doing what is possible to improve "their people" as workers. American organizations have never had an interest in "their people" as individuals who have needs that are different from the needs of organizations.

There is a big pitch made about organizations being concerned with "its people," "the total person," "the needs of workers," and so on. There is a growth industry called Human Relations (sometimes, Human Resources) which produces hundreds of books and articles every year. You find it at universities in separate courses; you can earn a doctorate in it. And you can be fooled by it, into thinking that it is humanism in the workplace rather than what it really is: techniques to improve people as workers for the organization. One reason you can be fooled is that the rhetoric can be alluring. For example, this is typical:

> *We hunger for community in the workplace and are a great deal more productive when we find it. To feed this hunger in ways that preserve democratic values of individual dignity, opportunity for all, and mutual support is to harness energy and productivity beyond imagining.*

There is nothing intrinsically wrong with trying to improve people as workers. But it is phony to present that as a concern with humanism, i.e., people as people.

Human Relations was invented seventy or so years ago after some researchers found that if management appeared to be interested in the individual human-being side of their workers, the workers worked harder. This was a bonanza for management. Improved productivity at little, if any, cost. Learn the first name of a worker and something about his personal life. Next time you pass him, smile, call him by his first name and ask him "How're the kids?" This will produce a little more spring in his step, a little more eagerness to work for you and the company.

You can hear a lot of denial about this. Managers will swear to you that they are really concerned about "their people" or "the people around here" and that they are insulted by this negative judgment on what is a noble intent. A few of them probably really do care about people. And a few of them don't but have talked themselves into thinking they are. But whatever they say, you should never assume that anyone in your organization really cares what happens to you other than in your capacity as a worker in that organization.

In the late 1980s, there were a few serious attempts to provide work-family benefits, most notably in hospitals. Those pioneering efforts are fading in the glare of "competition," a word that along with "globalization" has taken on a religious status equal to "the Father," "the Son," and "the Holy Ghost." Consider these numbers: In the late 1980s, there were 1,200 child care centers in hospitals; in 1997, there were 600.

In recent years a number of advocacy groups have formed to promote "the family" in the workplace. Helping employees balance job and family has become a hot topic. But how family-friendly are the employment policies at some of the prominent advocacy groups that say they are pro-family?

A *Washington Post* survey found unevenness. At the Rutherford Institute, a religious liberties defense group in Charlottesville, Virginia, there are paid maternity leaves, free medical coverage for employees' families, and many young mothers regularly work from home or bring their babies to the office. On the other hand, at Concerned Women for America, a conservative advocacy group in Washington, pregnant women are told, "Congratulations! You've just gotten a promotion in life: being a full-time mom." At Concerned Women for America there is no paid maternity leave and almost all new mothers never return there to work.

Overall, the survey found "family-friendliness" in family advocacy groups about the same as one finds it throughout all American organizations. Some do only the minimum required by law, others do more, and some are outstanding family supporters.

It is useful for you to never drop your suspicions because an organization pursues a worthy, even highly commendable, cause. Organizations to "feed the hungry" are still organizations.

Though management-with-a-heart champions are often disingenuous, there are refreshing bursts of honesty now and then, as when in 1994, Robert Haas, CEO and Chairman at Levi-Strauss said that worker participation and empowerment policies are important at his company *because we believe in the interconnection between liberating the talents of our people and business success.* If Haas were to go sentimental, get serious about being nice to people because they're people, he'd be in trouble with his board of directors. Speaking for the board, F. Warren Hellman worries aloud that a worker-orientation approach could deteriorate into touchy-feely stuff. He and the rest of the board have approved all of the Haas management innovations. "We're behind Bob," says Hellman, *he's made a fortune for everyone. Still, the fundamental challenge for Levi's is to be sure that decisions enhance shareholder value.*

Both Haas and Hellman can be tough on people when profits are involved. In 1994, for example, a Dockers factory in San Antonio was shut down and the work shifted to a Costa Rica locale where labor costs are a bit lower than in San Antonio. My research tells me that no matter how high-sounding the talk about caring for the workers, if a company can find cheaper labor it will show its present workers the door and move to where the cheaper labor is.

A few years ago, a management-improvement training film was produced that unintentionally depicted blatant hypocrisy. The film shows us how at Patagonia the working environment is designed to enable workers to reach their full potential. Employees are just as likely to be found playing volleyball as working on projects. They go mountain climbing with the owner and top executives. They have generous maternity leaves. There is child care. Everything is worker-centered. The owner-CEO says on-camera that "we have a familial atmosphere around here."

Later in the film we witness an "agonizing experience" for the caring Patagonia management. The economy declines, people are buying less. So Patagonia has to get rid of large numbers of employees. Nothing is said about what Patagonia does to ease the new financial burdens of the laid-off workers. Rather we are told how Patagonia management cleverly works to recapture the commitment of the workers who are left.

Notice that Patagonia did not decide to take some serious losses, maybe cut back on executives' and other managers' salaries in order to maintain at least a modicum of salary level for the workers. As is almost always the case in the American organization, when times get rough there are a few, always at the top levels of the organization, who decide which of those at lower levels are to bear the sacrifices.

In general, Japanese and German organizations do not do this. In those countries, it is considered either unethical or unlawful, or both, to lay off workers with no more than a "sorry, but times are difficult." By custom in Japan and by law in Germany, companies must have a plan for how they will protect the incomes of their full-time regular employees in hard times. Sometimes the company will go into new activities to find work, other times they will train and place their workers with other companies in different occupations, and seldom will a Japanese or German company protect profits while sacrificing workers.

When Japanese and German practices of worker-protection are proposed to American managers, the response is usually predicated on the "value of individualism in America." Here in America, you see, we are rugged individualists. We do not expect to be taken care of by the organization "from cradle to grave as in more socialized countries." The same American managers who claim that our workers are our most important asset will justify disposing of the workers when times are tough in the name of "the American way."

There is no reason for us to splash around in the philosophical whirlpool of individualism versus collectivism. This is not the place to debate the merits of those competing values. However, in the spirit of this book on how to survive in an organization, we should take note of the fact that when the chips are down you are told that life is a struggle, and it is up to the individual to learn how to struggle if she is to survive. It's the American way.

A Vice President of Philips Petroleum Company wrote a thoughtful article about all this for *Harvard Business Review.* He began with the observation that lack of workers' commitment is behind much of the behavior blamed for high costs and poor service, and then explained why the very structure and purpose of organizations make it impossible for that commitment to develop.

Power to do any of the things that matter to workers—hiring, separations, changes in duties, transfers, penalties, promotions, pay, location of where work is done—belongs to the organization. Power is an inherent possession of the organization.

Therefore, power is seen as something belonging to the organization and opposed to employees' interests. What else is power for if not to control employees?

> *Power, to the employee, is clearly the differentiating quality between the organization and himself. The organization has it; he does not. He senses unpleasant implications. If the organization needs power to deal with him*

in order to secure its purpose, then his interests must
somehow be at odds with the organization's interests,
and vice versa. The objectives of the organization must
not be his. As he sees it, therefore, it is a case of 'them and
us'—or even 'them and me'. Rejected by the organization,
the employee rejects it. He 'decommits.' He perceives him-
self as excluded and subordinate.

This Vice-President/author then comes to a most insightful conclusion. In his observation, he says, employees accept these conditions as a price for earning one's bread. Work becomes a means to an end instead of a worthy end itself. The worker makes no commitment either to the work or to his organization because it is not in the nature of people to make commitments to means; people commit to ends. What we are left with are employees who view jobs and wages as commodities which are interchangeable with one another. Employment opportunities resemble one another. There is simply no basis for loyalty to the organization.

Blessed Be the Motivated

The organization's search for motivational techniques can be reasonably compared to the search for the Holy Grail. As anyone who has conducted management seminars and workshops will tell you, there is no question asked more than "How do I get an employee to do what I want him to do?"

Organizations "with heart" are usually organizations using the appearance of "we care" as a motivational technique. This technique is one of the more recent in a long line of techniques that have been proposed and tried since the early years of industrialism in America, the most recent and popular of which are *job enrichment*, *teamwork*, and *empowerment*.

Job enrichment is an expansion of the job to include some of the planning for and evaluation of it that was previously done by management or other specialists. According to the theory, this increases motivation because increasing a person's responsibility increases her commitment to the job.

Teamwork is a small group of people with complementary skills working together to achieve a common purpose for which they hold themselves accountable. Devotees of this theory carry through with sports' lingo by calling supervisors of teams "coaches."

> *Some time ago, Mahmood Mohajer, a production supervisor at a Digital plant, realized that his work group was two weeks behind in an important production run. In the past, Mahmood would have immediately put everyone on an overtime schedule. This time, he did things differently. He first met with the production teams and outlined the problem. He then asked them to come up with a solution.*
>
> *Mahmood got the team's response the following Monday. Everyone decided to work the entire weekend to catch up. They had accepted responsibility for meeting the production goals and came up with a way of doing so that would meet their needs as well as those of the firm. Because it was their idea, team members were highly motivated to make their solution a real success. Mahmood says his approach to employee involvement is a 'coaching' rather than a 'policing' role.*

This motivational technique has two theoretical bases. First there is the theory that people become committed when they have a sense of ownership. Second is the theory that group commitment is stronger than individual commitment.

Empowerment is another name for job enrichment.

Our purpose in this book is to enable you to cope with organizational strategies and techniques, so we will focus on your awareness of them for what they are rather than delving into their theoretical deficiencies. However, you might now or in the future be a manager who is using these techniques; coping, for you, requires that you understand why these techniques have short shelf lives.

The major problem with these techniques is that they are not backed by the full support and sincerity of the organization. Organizations cannot be what they are not. They can never relinquish power; they could not exist without it. They can delegate little bits of it—*You can decide how you're going to get this job done*. And, of course, they can orchestrate a symphonic language of employee importance.

Try this: The next time you hear a supervisor or higher-up saying something about empowerment ("My people make all the decisions and do all the work. I'm almost superfluous around here.") ask her if you and the other employees at your level can decide salaries and other benefits for yourselves and for her. You can be assured of a hasty retreat by her, both verbally and physically.

Organizations cannot, will not, really give up their power to make the important decisions. Eventually, if not immediately, employees see through the facades of motivational techniques. You, as a user of those techniques, must learn to cope with the "rock and a hard place" features of your situation—on one side a suspicious workforce, on the other side a group of supervisors who want you to tell them that the workforce is enthusiastic about these motivational techniques. In the chapters on strategy and tactics, we will provide guidelines for survival in such situations.

Legal Rights in the Workplace

Another reason for the popularity of motivational techniques is the growth of employees' legal rights in the workplace. Prior to the 1950s, courts viewed jobs as a privilege, not a right. Employers could legally place virtually any conditions upon employment. Only unions stood in their way of absolute power over employees. The judiciary played an almost invisible role in this area.

Beginning in the 1950s, the federal judiciary began establishment of "rights" of employees. Over time the following doctrine emerged: Citizens retain all their constitutional rights in the workplace. Only compelling reasons for doing so can justify the violation of any of these rights.

Today, courts will not allow employers to do what they want with employees. Aware of the legal costs and the public image losses resulting from employees' charges of unfair selection and promotion practices, sexual harassment, and other violations of individual rights, organizations have practical interests in maintaining their employees' satisfaction.

Being Unethical About Being Ethical

One of the biggest scams going on these days in large organizations is the pretense about ethics. Organizations in the private and public sectors are supposedly seriously instituting ethical guidelines as a response to broad public demand. Tough language accompanies announcements of new ethical commandments: The U.S. Navy, Astra, Mitsubishi, and many other organizations have proclaimed "zero tolerance for sexual harassment." Orange and Rockland Utilities warns that anyone who engages in financial improprieties will be shown the door and maybe a jail cell. And so it goes. To underline the seriousness of this new wave of reform, it is often noted that schools of business and public administration have added courses on ethics to their curricula.

What usually happens is this: (1) there is a scandal, (2) the guilty agency or company reacts indignantly, vowing to "get to the bottom of this," and (3) the agency or company brings in an "independent" investigator from the outside or appoints one internally.

Surprise, surprise, surprise. The worst that the investigators can find is one or two guilty parties, who are summarily dismissed. However, to ensure against anything like this ever happening again, the investigators recommend institution of ethical guidelines and training programs in ethics. Yes, of course there are consulting companies ready at the door to provide, at a good price, pamphlets on "How to Institute Ethical Guidelines." Training courses are also available, but that's a little more expensive.

Gerald Meyers, former CEO of American Motors, is one of many who question the sanctity of this so-called ethical movement.

Some companies, he says, have less than honorable motives in mounting an outside investigation. First, the probe instantly produces good publicity. It also buys time with regulators, whose chronic understaffing often makes them willing to consider cutting back their own probe if the company's looks reasonably thorough. And doing even a cursory investigation on its own helps the company's legal position. The reason: An outside attorney's findings are generally privileged. Consequently, a company can get a grip on how badly employees behaved and begin assembling its defenses with little risk of disclosure.

As for the other side, the "investigators," *Business Week Online* refers to it as "Ethics, Inc."—a billion-dollar industry "laundering images of soiled companies."

These "independent" investigators have a built-in conflict to be scrutinizing. And as suppliers of interest because they are paid by the company they are supposed lucrative services to Corporate America, the law and accounting firms that usually run the probes are well aware a reward may be in store if they put the best face on the bad news.

What happens after the best face is put on? A few people, if any, are fired, a code of ethics is installed along with a training program and a whistle-blower hotline? Senior management communicates throughout the organization that all the rhetoric should not embolden anyone; there are no clear signs given that if you blow the whistle you will go unpunished.

Surveys find that if you work for an agency or company that has an ethics policy, there will be just as much pressure to compromise standards for the sake of the organization, and you will witness just as much misconduct as you would if you worked in an agency or company that did not have an ethics policy. An expert on ethics in public agencies refers to whistle-blowing as a "lonely and hazardous initiative."

American businesses can have a tasteless hunger for profits, and will engage willingly in chicanery if there's a possible profit to be made. For example, as journalist Anthony Faiola points out:

> *While the natural rain forest might be disappearing rapidly from the globe's Southern Hemisphere, in the United States the business version is proliferating. U.S. companies have caught jungle fever, bottling and selling, packaging and re-packaging just about anything with a rain forest theme, capitalizing on the apparent soft spot in the American consumer's heart for protecting habitats—and for preserving enough oxygen for future shoppers to breath.*

The rain forest theme is a branch of the 1990s' green marketing movement, in which companies stress that their products are environmentally friendly. The theme *taps into consumer interest in the environment that's become big since the 1990s,* said Jason Clay, a former marketing executive. *People often feel they're making a positive impact on the environment when they purchase these products.*

Federal officials say that's not always the case, Faiola notes. In 1997, for example, *the Federal Trade Commission charged Benckiser Consumer Products, maker of EarthRite household cleaners, with falsely claiming that a portion of its profits was being channeled to rain forest preservationists. Benckiser settled the case.*

There is unquestionably rampant greenwashing going on. says Randall Hayes, executive director of the San Francisco-based *Rain Forest Action Network.*

—Five—

What Are People . . . Really?

I contradict myself. I am large. I contain multitudes.
    —Walt Whitman

There is now a large body of evidence on how inept organizations and their leaders can be, as well as on how leaders can be corrupt and, in general, sometimes downright toxic for their organizations. You find it in business, the military, government, churches, and non-profit charity work.

The harm done is incalculable. Workers lose jobs, pensions, and hope. Stockholders watch their wealth disappear. The public loses confidence.

So why doesn't anyone do anything serious and meaningful about this? Beyond slaps on the wrist and pious declarations of indignation, we don't appear inclined to punish anyone. And, more significantly, we accept bad leadership. We make excuses for it. We even praise it with indulgences like "It could have been so much worse had he not been at the helm." It is common to find in surveys of organization members contradictory views. The same persons who say that their organization's leadership is a disaster often say that they support the continuation of that same leadership.

It's absurd. It's irrational. But it's us.

Is there an explanation that would help you and me survive in an organization? I think so. The following reasons are often given as the explanation. In each of them there is something constructive for us to mull.

One reason: We are frightened people frustrated by our inability to find authority figures to be what our parents were supposed to be. For some of us they were, for others they weren't. In either case, we hesitate to reject flawed authority figures, even sometimes when they appear to be incorrigibly bad because our need for authority figures can transcend our knowledge of their wrongdoing.

I believe knowing this tells us something very useful: expect colleagues in the workplace to withdraw from criticizing leadership to the point where they would question that leadership's right to its authority. It tells us to beware logical arguments aimed at undermining authority.

Another reason: We have a need for human community. The workplace is not the only opportunity for human community but it is certainly the most ever-present one on an everyday basis. We can't go to church nor play golf or bridge with friends all day five days a week. Expect people to tolerate their organization's shortcomings so long as their needs for community are satisfied by the organization's existence and activities, no matter how sordid the activities might be.

Another reason: We need security, physical and emotional. Even up to the moment an employee is discharged as part of cost-savings, he may well believe that the organization is his best chance for physical and emotional security.

Another reason: We feel powerless. (One of the reasons I wrote this book.) I wanted to lessen your feeling of powerlessness.

A final reason: There are people in the organization who gain from the organization's flaws and incompetence. They'll work at keeping the status quo. You'll want to keep this in mind should you be put on a committee to improve one of the flaws or areas of incompetence.

The illusions of organization discussed in previous chapters are, in part, designed to deal with our need for authority, human community, and security, as well as our feeling of powerlessness. They are myths intended to keep us all hanging in, and good ones, given our human needs. A rational man in a classroom situation might say, "But there are alternatives to the organizational illusions." (Union organizers have and continue to work that angle.)

The perhaps less-than-rational man says, "But I've got a job and an income and a community of fellowship at work and physical protection. The alternatives are too vague, and somewhat scary. So, my boss is stupid. So what?"

The reasons why your organizational colleagues endure incompetence, corruption, and abuse of power are one of the things I think you need to know as you prepare yourself to be a survivor. Another thing is role playing.

Role Playing

On a pleasantly warm October Friday morning, the British troops set up their monitoring stations. Each time a "colonial" would try to pass that line, she or he would be challenged to show authorizing documentation. It went well enough for a few hours, until a young man lacking authorization was arrested. He struggled with the two British soldiers who grabbed him by his arms. They wrestled him to the ground and were holding him there when another young "colonial" threw himself into the struggle. This attracted a few more British soldiers, which, in turn, brought in some more "colonials." In minutes there was a brawl. The street was filled with it. The fighting was ferocious.

That incident took place in 1997 during a reenactment at Colonial Williamsburg. All of those involved in the brawl were reenactors; but the brawl was not in the script. The actors had gotten carried away playing their roles.

Organizations give us roles to play. Requirements of the position we hold are powerful influences on who we are, what we believe, how we think, and the values to which we are committed.

Gladys Danter was Director of Academic Programs at the Guantanamo Bay Naval Base, Cuba. During her first two years at the job, there were more applications than there were classroom spaces. Only applicants who met strict requirements were admitted. Once in the program, students were graded according to tough and strict academic standards. Gladys was known as a champion of academic standards. Whenever she spoke publicly about the program, she referred to the rigorous standards with pride.

In 1994 the Guantanamo base was downgraded, and the number of naval personnel at Guantanamo decreased by a third. Because of that and because there was considerable uncertainty regarding those personnel who were left, class enrollments plummeted to a point that was financially unsound for the program. Gladys advertised her program on every bulletin board and personally promoted it wherever she could. She also decreased enrollment requirements. Late in 1994, the program was rebuilt to a break- even point.

Then the instructors began complaining about the low quality of students. But Gladys had become a champion of "the late bloomer" and "the disadvantaged." She had redefined the program as *an opportunity for the 'desiring-though-unprepared' as well as the prepared student.* She lambasted the instructors as *a snobbish elite with tunnel vision of academic purpose.* She equated lowering standards with *the eternal and true meaning of democracy in America.*

When you are dealing with a Gladys, it is difficult to know if she believes in what she says. We like to think that people are both sincere and reasonably consistent. We do not like to think that people shape their values to fit their job-survival needs. We particularly like to think that people with strongly-held views have strongly-held beliefs, and that these strongly-held beliefs are unrelated to paychecks. Yet we know that jobs and careers do influence our principles, maybe more than we want to admit, maybe more for some people than others.

It is tempting to judge Gladys, to denounce her discovery of *the disadvantaged;* but it is a mistake to do so for she is trying to survive, and your denouncement will inflame her. Most people like to think they are sincere most of the time. Perhaps it is the gap between that and what they know to be the case, which explains why people reach for their dueling pistols when you question their sincerity. As important to you as is knowledge of people's true nature, it is equally important to join them in hiding it from themselves if that is what they want.

Inconsistency

Gladys Danter acted inconsistently because she is a human being. Human inconsistency has been explained in many ways, all of them theoretical and none of them provable. Perhaps the best explanation comes from evolutionary biologists who point out that the human species developed both selfish and social genes for survival. Selfish genes seek only to reproduce themselves; social genes cause us to seek the good will of others. In the real and complex world, these genes sometimes work against one another. One's attempt to retain the good will of others can lead him to limit his own chances for success.

People tend to dislike suggestion of such inconsistencies. We want to dance in a world where altruism is consistent with our own good, where pursuit of our interests enhances the public good. We dislike being thought of as inconsistent in how we present ourselves. Inconsistency is something we can attribute to others but not to ourselves. Tell someone that in your experience people are inconsistent and she will nod enthusiastically. Then tell her that she might also have some difficulties with consistency and she will deny it. She might even be insulted.

Honest People, An Oxymoron?

Creative memory is one of the reasons why people don't always tell the truth. They sometimes simply do not know what the truth is. At other times people lie. The lie is something for which you must develop a taste and appreciation. Like myths, they are part of the glue that holds a society together. *The lie,* says Quentin Crisp, *is the basic building block of good manners.* That may seem mildly shocking to a moralist—but then, what isn't?

Despite its value to the civilized world, never accuse a person of lying. Although honesty is overrated as a virtue, people want the mantra of *being honest.* So, be careful when you spot or suspect a little dishonesty. Do a lot of affirmative nodding while processing skepticism in your mind. Of such paradoxes is society constructed: although lying can be a public good, few want to be known as a liar; although honesty can be disastrous for the public good, most of us want to be an honest person.

If you think I am building cocoons for people who tell lies so that I can give you honorable and safe passage through that dimension of organizational behavior, please take the time to read a marvelously unique book by Harry Frankfurt, a Professor of Philosophy Emeritus at Princeton University. The book has a catchy title, *On Bullshit.*

Frankfurt tells us that we have no clear understanding of what bullshit is, why there is so much of it, or what functions it serves. And we lack a conscientiously developed appreciation of what it means to us. In other words we have no theory. What I think can be helpful to you is Professor Frankfurt's way of distinguishing between a person who tells a lie and a liar. While the lie must be judged on its individual merit, this judgment should not be confused with a judgment that the person who told it is a liar.

It's not easy to doubt the truthfulness of others. We have a desire to believe what others tell us, especially our friends and loved ones. We equate their telling us the truth with their regard for us. To admit that people are telling us lies introduces a threat into our lives. Therefore, the first thing you must do is to steel yourself to be able to deal with the self-delusions intertwined with the concept of truth. In addition to that you must bluff naiveté, pretending to believe when others need that. The major thing to keep in mind is that it is not in people's basic interests to always tell the truth, and that people often think they are telling the truth when they do not know what the truth is.

When the Ethics Resource Center in Washington, D.C., surveyed 100,000 U.S. workers in 1996 about workplace ethics, the results came out like this: 56 percent saw employees lying to supervisors; 41 percent viewed records being falsified; and 35 percent observed stealing.

In 1997, another study was done by the Ethics Officer Association which concluded that, *despite a booming interest in corporate ethics in the last decade, Boy Scout honesty in the workplace seems as rare as a dress-up Friday. Nearly half of the 1,324 workers surveyed said that they engaged in unethical and- or illegal acts in the last year. The most common behavior included:*

- Taking credit for a colleague's idea.
- Lying to a superior or an underling on a serious matter.
- Lying to a customer.
- Cutting corners on quality.
- Covering up incidents.

Some managers claim to be working diligently to discourage lying and other disreputable employee behavior patterns. Some are straightforward about it, admitting that it's undesirable because it hurts the bottom line (which is not always true), while others take a pretentious and highly disingenuous high ground approach. In either case, management often encourages and rewards lying and other such habits. Psychologists who study lying point out that society in general and organizations in particular often punish you for telling the truth and reward you for lying. If you arrive late for a meeting because you overslept, you know that telling the truth can lead to punishment, whereas a nice little lie will not.

Psychologist Bella DePaulo and colleagues had 147 people between the ages of 18 and 71 keep a diary of the lies they told during one week. Most people, she found, lie once or twice a day—almost as often as they snack from the refrigerator or brush their teeth. Both men and women lie in approximately a fifth of their social exchanges lasting 10 or more minutes; over the course of a week, they deceive about 30 percent of those with whom they interact one-on-one.

Some types of relationships inspire more lying than others. Authority relationships—such as those between children and parents, or supervisees and supervisors in organizations—are virtual magnets for deception, says DePaulo.

Lies are difficult to notice. Lie detecting machines are only slightly more reliable than your insights into the mind of a poker-faced opponent across the card table. Psychologists have studied theories based on speech-tracking and body language, but there is little confidence in any of the theories. Lies appear to be safely undiscoverable, at least at the moment they are told.

Lies abound in the marketplace. There is an inelastic demand for them. Donald Trump bragged: *The final key to the way I promote is bravado. I play to people's fantasies. People may not always think big themselves, but they can still get excited by those who do. That's why a little hyperbole never hurts.*

I'm Not In It for the Money

In the same way that we have difficulty with the honesty mystique, we have difficulty admitting that we cannot find perfect matches between our stated values and what we do at work. We want to believe that we are following certain norms in the workplace regarding reasonable acquisitiveness, generosity, decency, unthreatening behavior towards others, and fair play; norms given us at home and in church. We can't do it because of human nature and because organizations wouldn't let us even if we could. So, therefore, as it is with lying, we learn how to live in denial of what we're doing. We have to fool ourselves—which includes the requirement that others play along with our pretenses—with illusions about not being in it for the money, about refusing to work where fairness, decency, and fair play are not in observance, where we can not be proud of the product or the service.

The *work ethic* is a triumphant example of our denial. I agree with whoever said, *Personally, I have nothing against work. I just don't happen to think it's an appropriate subject for an ethic.* We have made it so because we need something high-sounding to drown out the sounds of reality gnashing at our denials. It was invented by Confucius, and made popular in the Western world by John Calvin. Calvin said that if you follow the work ethic, you're obviously in God's good favor. I've always appreciated the observation that if work were such a splendid thing, the rich would have kept more of it for themselves.

Our need to take pride in the outcome of our labor is another problem for us. Only the extraordinary suppleness of our value systems can account for how we justify some of the things we do. The cigarette industry, unsurprisingly, comes to mind.

Nancy Brennan Lund was vice president in charge of Marlboro, the flagship brand of the Philip Morris Company. At Philip Morris, she says, people don't just tolerate their work, or rationalize it. They are proud of themselves and their company.

Those comments were made to a *Washington Post* staff writer, who tells us that after spending some time with Ms. Lund and her colleagues at Philip Morris, it became clear to him that they believe they are fighting for something more than just life spans or cardiopulmonary health—something as deeply American as you can get: freedom.

The reporter goes on to say that the Philip Morris executives and others he interviewed insist that the real issue is not health, but choice. They see themselves as defending the right to make one's own choices, not just for smokers but for all Americans. Perhaps, he says, they have always believed these things. Or perhaps they have repeated the concepts over and over again to the point where they have come to believe them. It doesn't really matter. What's clear is that they do believe—truly, deeply, perhaps even madly. One of them said that, in her eyes, an adult's right to choose to smoke is as important as a woman's right to choose whether to have an abortion.

Values and morality are sometimes like ready-made suits people put on to cover something else. It is possible, for example, that magazine moguls like Hugh Heffner and Robert Guccione really do come to believe their own rhetoric about how lurid nudity is really all about freedom, changing life styles, and social maturity. But one wonders if that is what motivated them in the first place.

Why is there a market for what appears to be sheer hypocrisy? Why do people listen to, applaud, and feel good about bullshit?

One of the reasons is romanticism. People usually prefer a romantic rendition to the actuality of events. Horace may spend most of his life in the office and with colleagues because he is bored at home, but we don't want to hear that. We want to hear that Horace is a super achiever, dedicated to his work. We like simplistic versions of life in which good triumphs, at least eventually if not immediately.

Our passion for romanticism leads to both good and evil consequences. It leads us to do heroic unselfish acts; it also inspires us to slaughter one another. I advise you to avoid both of those extremes, and the gullibility that hangs around with romanticism. You don't want Donald Trump winning you over by playing to your fantasies. Or if you do, at least you want to know what's happening.

I don't see Donald Trump as an aberration. He represents all the things I read about in books on leadership. There is a difference, however, between his bluntness and the artful euphemisms of those books. Rather than say "play to people's fantasies," the leadership rhetoric says: "People need causes. Inspire them with one." So, one man's Barnum is another man's Moses.

Sometimes People Are Better Than They Say They Are

Inconsistencies between people's beliefs and actions have some pleasant outcomes, as Richard LaPiere, a *Stanford University* sociologist, found out on an unusual cross-country drive. In 1930, at a time when there was considerable prejudice expressed about the Chinese, LaPiere began a two-year cross-country trip with a young Chinese couple. They visited 184 eating establishments and 67 hotels, auto camps, and tourist homes. In these 251 encounters, LaPiere observed racial discrimination only once.

Six months after visiting each establishment, LaPiere sent the proprietors a survey that asked a wide variety of non-prejudice oriented questions and one question on prejudice:

Will you accept members of the Chinese race as guests in your establishment? He received responses from 81 restaurants and cafes, and 47 hotels, auto camps, and tourist homes. Of the 128 responses, 118 indicated that they would not accept Chinese guests.

The Good Samaritan Doesn't Come Along Very Often

People in organizations do not always dupe themselves in highly self-serving ways of questionable morality, nor are they always untrustworthy, greedy, nasty, and incompetent. People are sometimes trustworthy, unselfish, altruistic, and competent. People are complex combinations of characteristics that are sometimes good for you and sometimes bad for you. They are enigmas in motion, as difficult to predict as it is to paint a moving train.

Throughout history man has been aware of his intricacy, his capacity for evil as well as good and his tendencies to often mistake error for truth. Mythology, literature, religion, and philosophy are filled with revelations of man's permeable and imperfect character. They are also based on hope for a better world, which is psychologically significant but also potentially hazardous.

The Good Samaritan in the *New Testament* does help the man on the roadside who has been stripped and beaten by robbers. But remember that before that happened many pious priests and Levites passed by without helping. And the study of Good Samaritanism done by the psychologists Darley and Batson suggests that altruism has still not infected human behavior.

Darley and Batson set up an experiment in which some divinity students were placed in a situation where they had to move quickly from one building to another to deliver a sermon on the parable of The Good Samaritan. They were told that in one building they would have an opportunity to rehearse the sermon until they were called to appear in the other building to deliver the sermon to a group of faculty members and other divinity students. What they were not told was that the experimenters would plant an indigent-looking person lying on the ground, groaning, between the two buildings, and that when they were told that it was their turn to go over to the next building and give the sermon they would also be told to hurry up because the audience was waiting. Every one of the divinity students ignored the man lying on the ground, rushing by him, usually not even "noticing" he was there.

How We Can be Trained to be Unfit

In the previous chapter we saw that organizations play an interesting game with the word "rationality." Though rationality is assumed to be a sterling characteristic of organizations, "satisfycing" is a more appropriate label for what they do. Organizations set up procedures that are acceptable to the major power players and can be accomplished in the given time frame. These procedures—ways of doing things—are somewhat rational for the problems at hand, but can be frightfully irrational for something that might come up tomorrow. Once the procedure is in place, it cannot know when it is being stupid. And the people applying it are "just following orders." Or, just doing what they have been trained to do.

A sociologist named Robert Merton said that this is the way things always will be in large organizations and labeled it *trained incapacity to act rationally.*

Merton said that large organizations are usually low-risk cultures. The managers usually play it safe by doing things as they were trained and according to the current rules and regulations.

No training, no set of rules and regulations, can provide a rational basis for action in all situations. There will be times when a person must improvise to serve the organization's goals, when "by the book" is dumber than dumb. A famous old case, regarding a Norwegian explorer named Bernt Balchen, is illustrative.

Balchen, a native of Norway, declared his intention to become a citizen of the United States a few years before he went on the Byrd expedition to the Antarctic, at the special request of the Admiral himself, who needed his skills.

When he returned, Balchen applied for his citizenship papers; the required five years from his date of application had passed. The Bureau of Naturalization ruled that he did not qualify because he failed to meet the condition of five years' continuous residence in the United States.

The Admiral and others appealed stating that Balchen had been on a ship carrying the American flag, was an invaluable member of the exploration team, and when not on board the ship was in a region, *Little America,* to which there was an American claim. *Sorry*, said the reply, *the Bureau cannot proceed on the assumption that Little America is American soil. That would be to trespass on international questions where it has no sanction. The appeal is denied.*

If you're one of those who think that this would not happen in the private sector, think again. A few years ago, IBM Credit Corporation had a revelation about how company policies had led to a "trained incapacity" that was costing the company many lost sales. IBM salesmen were storming the walls of company headquarters because their requests for financing took an average six days to clear, too long a period of time, leading some customers to change their minds about buying a computer or fall prey to a competitor's lures.

The IBM Credit procedures were at that time considered state-of-the-art. The procedures for decisions went like this: First, a specialist checked the potential buyer's creditworthiness. Then, another specialist tailored the loan agreement to fit the particular circumstances of this loan. A third specialist determined the appropriate interest rate. Finally, an administrator sent a quote letter by Federal Express to the field sales representative.

They tried various ways to fix it. So long as they worked at improving the process they were stymied. Then someone suggested that perhaps this process and these experts were the problem; perhaps the process was rational for everything except making quick decisions, and perhaps the experts were experts at taking a long time to make a decision. An entirely new process was put in place using one person as a generalist with some expert-systems computer programs at her fingertips. The waiting period for loan approval was cut drastically.

A significant reason why companies find it worthwhile to replace experts with computerized expert systems is because you can change the expert system much easier than you can the human expert. As much as we talk about the need for life-long training and retraining, the fact is that humans find it very difficult to escape from the treadmills of their training. What were once regarded as well-trained experts can become unfit just because they are what they are.

One of the reasons I want you to understand these things about people is because you might be one of those IBM salesmen who was losing sales because of the trained incapacities of credit approvers. You should know better than to wait until your company corrects the problem. Companies are so mesmerized by their own hypocrisies most of the time that they seldom get around to correcting things just as IBM in that case.

You'll be better able to deal with that kind of frustration if you understand the reasons. Too often people in situations like that think the persons thwarting their success are doing so because they're stupid or mean-spirited or petty bureaucrats. That's inept problem analysis. You have enough to deal with in the real world; if you misread the road signs you'll end up lost in circles of your own doing.

Where One Stands Depends On Where One Sits

Lt. Marjorie Dabney looked in the mirror one morning and wondered if she had the nerve to tell her boss, Major Ray Rusek, that he was the author of his own displeasure. The day before he had been furious about her memo indicating that the department had exhausted its office-supply funds for the year, three months before the end of the year. *How,* he asked aggressively, *can we be expected* to *do our job on such a flimsy budget allocation?* He glared at her as though she were the culprit.

She just shrugged her shoulders. She didn't have the nerve to tell him that last year, when he was in the budget division, he was the one who had drastically cut all departments' office-supply funds' allocations. His explanation was that he had done a study of other army bases and found that they spent less on office supplies. Now hoist with his own petard the Major seemed unable to recall what he did the previous year.

Marjorie smiled sarcastically at herself in the mirror, deciding to not refresh the Major's memory. Better, she thought, to use some petty cash funds to buy supplies. It wasn't exactly in accordance with the rules and regulations, but she had learned the hard way that it's less risky to bend a rule than to embarrass a boss.

One's commitments are at least partially molded by one's job. From the benches at the bottom to the wall-to-wall-carpeted executive suites, one's work helps create one's principles and commitments. A change in the work situation or moving to another organization can change a man's principles so completely that one is tempted to start a Rent-A-Principle Company. The following newspaper commentary makes the point:

> *At the national education summit, its co-chairman, the CEO at IBM, said 'It's time to stop making excuses. It's time to set standards and achieve them. There must be accountability. We need educated people for consumers. We need them to be thoughtful.'*
>
> *Such words, coming from his lips, should have evoked a national belly laugh. Today he is the self-proclaimed pope of education. Yesterday his job was to keep America dumb. Today he wants to teach kids to read and think. Yesterday his job depended on brain-washing young adults to buy an addictive product that kills them.*
>
> *Today he is a CEO of computers. Yesterday he was a chief executive of cigarettes. From 1989 to 1993, he ran RJR Nabisco, [where] cigarettes accounted for 57% of its' $15.7 billion in revenues.*
>
> *Under him, RJR unleashed its Joe Camel advertising campaign, with a cartoon camel in roles of adventure and glamour. By the middle of his reign at RJR, Camel had become the most highly identified cigarette among children.*
>
> *In 1993, the American Medical Association published several studies on the effects of the campaign. The studies found that 90% of teenagers, 90% of 6-year-olds and 30% of 3-year-olds linked Joe Camel with cigarettes. Camel zoomed from less than 1% of the illegal teen cigarette market to 32.8%.*

It would be consoling to believe that this phenomenon is limited to chief executives of greedy corporations, particularly the cigarette industry. If only it were true. Consider our educational institutions, where we hope for the finest hours in American organizational honor and integrity. A newspaper columnist has the following report:

Two weeks ago I wrote about social promotion. Since then I have learned a lot about the different ways that teachers and school administrators see their classrooms and interpret their policies.

A middle school teacher called to say that teachers often recommend that up to 50% of their students repeat the grade, but that the teachers' recommendations are overridden by school principals.

The principals, teachers believe, work on a kind of quota system because the performance evaluations, and thus the pay raises, of the principals are affected adversely by the number of students who are not promoted each year. You won't be surprised to hear that the Schools Superintendent sees things differently. "There are no quotas," he says flatly.

But he also acknowledges that, in the past, schools have not done a good job of showing students the relationship between success and effort—that's an educator's way of saying that students who didn't learn have been promoted to stay with their peers. That's why it's called social promotion.

Sometimes people are quite aware of how they change values or switch allegiances to protect themselves. In the movie *The Outlaw Josie Wales,* a disreputable geezer who poles a dilapidated ferry across a river takes pride in his survival skills as he sings southern patriotic hymns when taking southern troops across, and northern patriotic hymns when taking northern troops across. But many of us pretend even to ourselves that our value positions are made of sturdier stuff than self-protection.

In the movie *The Bridge On The River Kwai,* a British military officer who is in a Japanese prisoner of war camp along with a number other officers and enlisted men directs the British prisoners in construction of a bridge for the Japanese army.

When a small group of British commandos arrive to blow up the bridge, this British officer tries to stop them, at the risk of his life, from blowing up his bridge.

While that story might be an extreme case, man's need to mentally go beyond the purely functional aspects of work is part of his nature, and you will find him capable of amazing flights of the imagination at all levels of the organization. Perhaps he will go only far enough to relieve the boredom of simple-repetitious tasks by playing pranks and engaging in other fun-type activity with coworkers, or perhaps he will convince himself that his job is a sacred trust.

In the 1920s, when psychologists first studied industrial man, they marveled at how workers could create something of emotional significance out of an extremely boring work situation. The psychologists came to the conclusion that it is impossible to deprive any kind of work of all its positive emotional elements, that the worker will find some meaning in any activity assigned to him, something of significance to others or something that can satisfy, after a fashion, the instinct for play and the creative impulse.

Forty years later a sociologist's recollections of his days as a factory machine operator illustrated that initiative, that urge to defeat the beast of monotony, with his own experience:

> *I stood all day in one spot beside three old codgers in a dingy room looking out through barred windows at the bare walls of a brick warehouse . . . leg movements [were] largely restricted to the shifting of body weight from one foot to the other, hand and arm movements confined, for the most part, to a simple repetitive sequence of place the die, punch the clicker, place the die, punch the clicker, and intellectual activity reduced to computing the hours to quitting time.*
>
> *I developed a game of work. It was quite simple, so elementary that its playing was reminiscent of rainy-day preoccupations in childhood when attention could be cen-*

tered by the hour on colored bits of things of assorted sizes and shapes. The basic procedure of this game I created at the clicking machine could be stated in the form: As soon as I do so many of these, I'll get to do those. If, for example, production scheduled for the day featured small, rectangular strips in three colors, the game might go: As soon as I finish a thousand of the green ones, I'll click some brown ones. And, with success in attaining the objective of working with brown materials, a new goal of I'll get to do the white ones might be set. Or the new goal might involve switching dies.

Workers at higher levels and in more technical jobs also play games, as did a group of computer engineers at Data General playing what they called *tube wars:*

One day Alsing came back from lunch and went to work on his terminal. Everything looked right, all his files seemed to be in place—until he tried to do something with them. Then, to his surprise, he found that all of them were vacant. It was like opening a filing cabinet and finding all the drawers empty. They were dummy files. It took me an hour to find the real ones. So now one can never be sure, when one logs on the system, that what one sees is real. Alsing struck back. He created an encrypted file and tantalized the team: 'There's erotic writing in there. If you can find it, you can read it.'.

—Six—

The Human Condition

It has been said that man is a rational animal. All my life I have been searching for evidence which could support this.

—Bertrand Russell

People think that they see things independently and objectively. They believe that when they remember those things, they remember them as they saw them. Actually, perception is selective and subjective, and what we remember is a creative process involving the original subjective perceptions plus things that have happened since. "Memory," said Walter Benjamin, "is not an instrument for exploring the past, but its theater."

This puts you in a difficult position when dealing with how people remember the past. They will believe they are remembering something correctly when they are not. If you need to correct their recollections, you must do so delicately. You never know how important that particular version of the past is to them.

In the Japanese movie *Rashomon*, three people involved in a rape and murder give three different accounts of what happened. A non-participant eye witness to what happened gave a fourth account that was completely different from the other three. Each of these four persons insisted that he or she was telling the truth. One of the clever aspects of this classic film is that you, the movie viewer, see the rape-murder at the beginning of the movie. Then, as you see it through the eyes of each of these four persons, each version takes on a life and meaning of its own that so intensely seeks believability that you cannot simply dismiss it as a lie.

Rashomon displays memory as theater. Each witness' version is provided a staging. Everything that is said is plausible, though self-serving to the narrator. It is a valuable lesson for you. When we discuss tactics, you'll be advised that vividness is more important than factualness when you are trying to influence someone. People trust their imagination. Capture mine and you can get me to remember things in a lot of different ways.

In an experiment that set out to reveal that memory is reconstructive, 45 persons were asked to view seven different driver education films depicting traffic accidents, and then they were asked to guess the speeds of the cars. The guesses varied according to how the question was asked. Those asked: About how fast were the cars going when they contacted each other? made an average guess of 30 miles per hour. Those asked: About how fast were the cars going when they smashed into one another? made an average guess of 41 miles per hour.

In another similar experiment, the viewers were sent home and then brought back for questions a week later. Some were asked: Did you see any broken glass when the cars hit one another? Others were asked: Did you see any broken glass when the cars smashed into one another? More than twice as many persons saw broken glass when the cars smashed than when they hit.

Another useful thing for you to know about memory is that people tend to remember things as being better than they probably were. In memory, Tennessee Williams said, everything seems to happen to music. You can often influence a person's thinking about a present situation by contrasting it with the past. It's not even necessary to paint the past your color. Just say, "Things around here are not the way they used to be." The other person will usually fill in rosy adjectives for the past, and be ready to join you in your assault on whatever aspect of the present you are assaulting.

Airbrushing One's Past

Ferdinand Waldo Demara, whose life was portrayed in a movie, *The Great Imposter*, hoodwinked people by impersonating a professor, a monk, a prison warden, a surgeon, and a schoolteacher. There are few persons capable of pulling off that many big hoaxes, but many get away with fudging resumes and application forms. Experts on personnel recruiting say that falsifications in presentations of oneself are easy because checking on references is slipshod.

One reason for the failure to carefully screen applicants' claims is that matters such as educational degrees are taken for granted. Another is the fear of lawsuits. Another is the fact that there are usually no rewards in doing that kind of checking. And, there are rewards for hiring people without carefully checking out what they say on their applications, particularly when there is a shortage of qualified people in particular occupations. That's probably why agencies that do research on this subject report that in 2006 the largest increase in lying about education and work experience was in the health services industry.

The National Transportation Safety-Board (NTSB) shocked many people with findings about the American Eagle crash in 1995 near the Raleigh-Durham airport. The findings indicated that though many people at the pilot's former employer, another commuter carrier, were uncomfortable with his cockpit skills, no one told American Eagle. According to the NTSB report, the prior employer's standard response for employment history would not have included meaningful information on training and flight proficiency despite the availability of such data. The Raleigh-Durham crash happened because this pilot failed to follow established procedures. He, the co-pilot and thirteen passengers died in the crash.

Most employers give only "name, rank, and serial number" type information when asked to furnish information about previous employees. This keeps them safe from the anger of the former employees and from lawsuits. Why take a risk when there's no gain? Concealment of "problems" can even bolster a sense of humanitarianism: "The guy deserves a fresh start to have another chance."

What this means for you is that some of the people with whom you work are sailing under false flags. Their behavior can be influenced by their attempts to keep you and others from discovering the secret. It's amazing how cleverly some illiterate people can keep others from knowing that they cannot read. Many people who have no foreign language fluency get jobs which supposedly require a certain foreign language fluency. And they keep those jobs! One of the reasons bluffing works is because others are benefiting from the bluff or would be embarrassed by its uncovering. So, when you come upon a bluff, find out who else is gaining from it before you develop your way of dealing with it.

Virtuousness

After the Republican and Democratic party conventions in the summer of 1996, you might have thought it would be a tough choice deciding which was the more virtuous party. One writer described the conventions as "virtue fests." Candidate Dole talked about taking the country back to "old values," and President Clinton promised "to protect our values." But not only politicians got on the "virtue" bandwagon that year.

Charlie Sheen made tabloid headlines by running up a $50,000 tab with the Heidi Fleiss escort service, then declared himself a born-again Christian. Geraldo Rivera, who, as one reporter put it, ". . . pioneered the craft of filing video dispatches from the primordial ooze . . ." became a passionate opponent to filth on daytime TV. A public relations executive, whose past clients included Michael Jackson and numerous other non-candidates for Boy Scout Of The Year Award, led a campaign to build a 'Statue of Responsibility' as counterpoint to the Statue of Liberty.

In the chapter on strategy, I will advise you to not be virtuous. But, since it's safe to assume that not everyone is going to read this book and follow my advice, there will be a lot of virtuous people on the elevator with you tomorrow morning. Some of them will have just discovered virtue the night before; some will have long memories of themselves as virtuous people. The newly virtuous are the ones saying good morning to everyone; they want to prove to themselves that virtue brings joy, and joy wants to be shared. The veteran virtuous are extremely polite but often pinch-faced; the burden gets heavy over time.

Since Freud, psychoanalysts have suspected that virtuousness is a kind of penance. Keep that in mind. There may be a guilt-ridden soul inside the display of moral rectitude.

Self Perception Theory

Managers who have had a lot of experience, and learned from it, will pass on a valuable piece of information if they like you. They'll tell you: If you want a group of workers to do things a new way, and they're opposed to it, ask them to "give it a try for just a little while." No one can get people to do things easier than the people themselves.

This well-experienced manager is revealing the secret of manipulating self-perception theory, according to which people infer their beliefs from watching themselves behave and hearing themselves speak, then inferring that their actions and words are manifestations of their attitudes and beliefs.

What the experienced manager is telling you is that if you get people to do something for awhile, they may very well come to believe that they like doing it.

People bring this disposition with them when they enter organizations. The organization gives them things to do, along with instructions. As time passes, the people have a tendency to come to believe in how they do things. I remember a group of workers in a Louisiana unemployment insurance payment office.

At the time, I was a consultant with the U.S. Department of Labor on computerization of unemployment insurance services. The goal was straightforward: change over from a manual to a computer system. I am not a computer expert. My role was to help management accept the change.

My clients in Washington thought it would be a good idea to clean up data while we were at it. One example was the category "veteran." Different local offices used different definitions of "veteran." Some included military service of less than a year, some did not. Some required honorable discharge, some did not, and so it went.

A universal definition was worded in Washington. No problem was anticipated in its implementation because it was assumed that the people who had been working with forms for many years would not care one way or another how the category "veteran" was defined. A meeting I had with the staff of a local office in Baton Rouge proved otherwise.

The Baton Rouge staff was convinced that a mistake had been made about a serious matter. The definition of "veteran" which the office had used for more than thirty years—and same of the staff had been there that long—was to them the legitimate one; therefore, the universal definition which we intended to use had to be illegitimate. Their logic was that if the Baton Rouge definition had worked for all these years, if people had been paid unemployment benefits partially based on the definitions used, then the definitions must be legal, and any change in a definition would require at least legislative action.

I saw this as a self-perception problem, that the staff had come to believe in these definitions because they had classified people and made decisions affecting these people based on the definitions. I thought the legality issue was a smokescreen. To test this, I spent two hours explaining to the staff that all of the definitions with which they worked were administrative decisions that carried no definitive legal authority. An administrative decision can be unmade by the people who made them.

Although they could not argue with that, I could tell they were not buying it. The next day I heard the same objections about changing definitions. It was important to have their positive participation in the project because when you are making large-scale changes in data systems, you must avoid antagonizing the persons who will be making the data transfers. Disgruntled people can make a lot of mistakes either to deliberately sabotage or just because their heart is not in what they are doing.

We discarded the universal definitions and stayed with what had been used in the past. The advantages of "cleaning up data" were overwhelmed by the need to avoid any possibility that the data would be distorted in the transfer to a computer database.

How Different Can One Be?

Teamwork has been a basic value in organizations for a long time. In 1951, David Riesman wrote, "what matters about the individual in today's economy is less his capacity to produce than his capacity to be a member of a team."

Organizations will accept, even relish, a certain amount of originality from us, so long as it goes along with a cooperative team spirit. The others in our work groups also have a restrained acceptance of individuality. We will be discussing in greater detail, below, the power of group norms on individual behavior; for now, it is sufficient to note that groups in which we work and socialize allow us some, but by no means unfettered, individuality, and that popularity of the individual in the group is the critical variable for deviation from group norms. In other words, the more popular you are, the more you can get away with behavior that is not usually approved by the group; and, vice versa, lack of popularity dooms you to a conformist role unless you are prepared to incur group wrath.

Aggressiveness

The best in-depth analysis of success, the Grant Study, followed the lives and careers of 470 men for 25 years, beginning with their early years as students in a prestigious Northeastern college. Socioeconomically, these students were in the privileged class, and in every conceivable way they were "winners."

When they were 45-years-old, the subjects were classified as Best Outcomes and Worst Outcomes. Characteristics of the former were: steady career progress, income higher than father's at same age, a continuing satisfying marriage and friends, light use of alcohol, and children who are socially and emotionally stable. Characteristics of the Worst Outcomes were the opposite: sporadic or no career progress, lower income than father's at same age, and so on.

The Best Outcomes were aggressive in the workplace; the Worst Outcomes were passive in the workplace. Almost all of the Best Outcomes had a "take charge" attitude about their work and their organizations. Many spoke of how they worked at their appearances so that they would not be viewed as "obnoxiously aggressive". One recalled how he had in high school organized a political clique that had "ruthlessly run the school," and how he had learned in college the social skills that enabled him to survive and rise in the "hurly-burly struggle" of organizations without offending or unnecessarily intimidating people.

The principal investigator on the Grant Study refers to that person as representative of the Best Outcomes. He, at least at 45, was very successful in his career, in his family life, and in his social life. His people-skills were crafted through experience. He had learned that he could have a happy marriage along with his aggressive style because his wife knew he always loved and respected her. At work his aggressiveness was a positive force in his career because he always showed respect for the people with whom he was dealing, and because he put in a lot of thought and effort on style.

The Grant Study suggests, as do many other studies, that aggressiveness combined with a viable style underlies much of the success we see in organizations, despite the idealistic and naive notion that aggressiveness is dangerous to one's career. So long as aggressiveness is not viewed as "obnoxious" it helps one climb the ladders. Unfortunately for women, female aggressiveness is less acceptable than male aggressiveness.

Usually People Prefer the Easy Way to the Hard Way

Values that are easy to live by have longer life spans than values that are not. People will, for example, do what's easy to do for their children and avoid or put off the difficult, no matter how eloquently they protest otherwise. A journalist in Washington, D.C., who attended the district school system as a child and watched it deteriorate as an adult, has the following thoughts about her fellow black district dwellers:

> *O.J. Simpson . . . rolled into a Washington church on Wednesday evening to play the prodigal son before a crowd of 1,500, who plopped down $10 a head to take his confession. The large turnout made me wonder: What does Orenthal James have that 80,000 District school-children apparently don't? After all, the homage paid to him is the kind of care and attention that D.C. public school supporters would die for.*
>
> *What on earth does it take to get that kind of backing for the city's schools? Where, oh, where, for instance, are the crowds when principals and teachers sit in nearly empty school auditoriums on PTA nights waiting for parents who never show up? Where were the thunderous crowds when the city's elected leaders turned their backs on urgent pleas for substantial funds to repair school buildings or when the mayor and council decimated the school system's budget?*

How is it that some people can drop everything and attend to O.J. Simpson's personal needs, yet are nowhere to be found as public education in the District slides down the tubes?

Maybe the reason O.J. draws a crowd while the schools draw empty space is because O.J.'s event is a lot easier on the mind. After all, what does it take to leave home for an evening of news media bashing?

On the other hand, fixing a broken educational system that is shortchanging an overwhelmingly African American student body requires long-term commitment, know how, patience and follow-through—all of which are a tad more demanding than experiencing the gratifying joy of issuing rhetorical taunts against external enemies, real and imagined.

That same night, at the Democratic Party Convention in Chicago, the Vice-President of the United States soulfully told the delegates and millions of TV viewers that he had dedicated himself to fighting the smoking of cigarettes the day his sister died of lung cancer in 1984. She started smoking at 13 and died at the age of 45. As his mother took off her glasses and wiped tears from her eyes, Mr. Gore brought the audience to a stunned silence as he gave what one reporter described as *an excruciatingly detailed description of that visit to his sister's deathbed while delegates sniffled.*

Unfortunately for Mr. Gore, the next day he was confronted with some uneasy truths. Was it true, he was asked, that after his sister's death he had continued to receive annual checks from his family's tobacco farm? Was it true that he continued to accept campaign contributions from the tobacco industry after his sister's death? He acknowledged that these things were true and that perhaps he should have told that to the delegates. Why had he accepted tobacco money if it were indeed the case that his sister's death had the effect he claimed? Sometimes, he answered, *you never fully face up to things that you ought to face up to.*

Most of us most of the time find it very difficult, maybe impossible, to live up to all the values we espouse. Maybe the problem is that we have established standards that are simply too high for people to follow.

How Cruel Can People Be?

To be cruel is to be disposed to inflict pain or suffering on others. Cruelty is built into humanity. All we seem to need is a reason, and we will, often with lofty rhetoric and inordinate pride, inflict pain and suffering.

The Milgram Experiments in 1961 are an example of how our need to conform can spark our cruel streak.

A sample cross-section of the adult (aged 20 to 50) male population (blue-collar workers, engineers, salespeople, schoolteachers and others) of Bridgeport, Connecticut, were selected at random and participated in a study of obedience at the Yale University Psychology Department. It was an experiment to determine how much punishment one person would inflict upon another when so ordered. The participants were told that they were engaging in a study of learning techniques and were paid a modest few dollars for their time.

The subjects were told they would play the role of teachers in a study of how punishment induces learning. Each "teacher" was first taken by an experimenter dressed in a gray laboratory coat to a room in which a "learner" was strapped to a chair with an electrode attached to his wrist. The subjects did not know that the "learners" were confederates of the experiment trained to play certain roles.

Then the experimenter took the "teachers" to an adjoining room, from which they had no view of the "learners." The experimenter, deliberately looking seriously stern, instructed the "teacher" to read a series of word pairs to the "learner" over a speaker system connecting the two rooms, and then to reread the first word along with four other terms. The "learner" would indicate which of the four terms was in the original pair by pressing a switch that caused a light to flash on a response panel in front of the "teacher."

When a wrong response appeared, the "teacher" was instructed to administer a shock to the learner through the electrode and to increase the intensity of the shock each time a wrong answer was given. The "teacher" controlled switches that ostensibly administered shocks from 15 to 450 volts. The switches were labeled Slight, Moderate, Strong, Very Strong, Intense, Extreme Intensity, Danger: Severe Shock, XXX. The "teachers" were given a test shock of 45 volts to mislead them about the authenticity of what they were about to do. Though there was no actual shock, the "learner", as trained, deliberately gave false answers, and when the "teacher" pushed the switch he heard a taped recording of murmurs, gasps, pleas, and shrieks matched to the ascending voltage.

When the "teacher" balked at administering the punishment, the experimenter prodded him, using the following sequence: (1) Please continue; (2) The experiment requires you to continue; (3) It is absolutely essential that you continue; (4) You have no choice, you must continue.

If the "teacher" was still unwilling after the fourth prod, the experiment was ended.

How many of the 40 subjects do you think stopped, and where? If you had not known of this experiment before reading about it here, you probably guessed on the very low side. Everyone, including those who designed and conducted the experiment, was surprised and frightened by the results:

Twenty-six (65 percent) continued to the end of the experiment and shocked the "learners" to the XXX level!

None stopped prior to 300 volts, the point at which the "learner" pounds on the wall and begs to be let out.

The Milgram experiments shocked everyone involved in them and everyone else as well. Other experiments have supported the Milgram findings. At Stanford University, when a group of faculty and students simulated a prison, it was not long before those playing the roles of guards were willing to punish the prisoners with physical and psychological pain.

Experiments such as these can no longer be performed. The official reason is based on the principle that they violated common ethical codes. Many of us wonder if the real reason is that these studies took us too close to an aspect of humanity we dread to see, a horrible flaw in our souls. Taboos haunt open discourse in the social sciences. It would seem that there is general agreement with Lionel Trilling's admonishment that the contemplation of cruelty will not make us humane, but cruel; that the reiteration of the badness of our spiritual condition will make us consent to it.

The conclusion reached by most of those who have analyzed studies such as Milgram is that when we are placed in organizations, given a role, and put into contact with authority figures, we will follow orders to perform harsh acts that seem to us to be out of character when we think about ourselves independent of such roles. Becoming a person involves being conditioned to accept authority. We are taught to get out of the store if told to do so by someone working in the store, or maybe even by an adult customer. Bus drivers, policemen, teachers, the postman all have an authority in their realms, which we are taught to respect.

Organizations are built around authority positions, usually pictured on a hierarchical chart. Salary, office, manner-of-dress, and privileges improve as you go up the hierarchy. This makes it easier for us to accept authority, because, deny it as we might, we are impressed by such things. In the early 20th century, successful Americans were attracted to Calvin's claim that God reveals his satisfaction by providing wealth and social status in life on earth. There's more than a touch of Calvinism that lingers in all of us. We are, at least, closet worshipers of the material indications of success, and we will do some loathsome things to follow authority.

We will even risk the lives of others when it is not necessary to do so, if there is sufficient threat to our jobs and organizations, as did managers of the tragic last liftoff of the space shuttle Challenger in 1986. On the day before the scheduled launch, engineers at Thiokol Corporation warned that the O-rings in the rocket motors provided NASA by Thiokol would probably fail in the unusually cold temperatures predicted for the following day, add that the result would be explosion of the motor and craft. The crew would be doomed. Thiokol's top management hesitated to pass on the warning to NASA because the agency's support in Congress was waning. The public had lost its enthusiasm for space, and NASA was falling behind on scheduled launches. A lot of political support was involved in launching Challenger on schedule.

When Thiokol recommended canceling the flight, NASA was furious. Thiokol requested time to reconsider; its senior managers huddled and then, still against the advice of their engineers, recommended the launch. The O-rings failed almost immediately. Challenger and its crew were destroyed.

Performance of harsh actions that are inconsistent with our self-images are often excused with "my hands are tied" reasoning.

My Hands Are Tied (Don't Hold Me Personally Responsible)

How often have you heard phrases like "My hands are tied," or "Due to circumstances beyond my control," or "I had no choice"? Usually you heard it in conjunction with something happening to you that you didn't like.

Most of us want to appear personally blameless, telling you why you did not get the promotion, the pay raise, the desired transfer, and so forth. The "my hands are tied" rationalization is very important to us as human beings. Therefore, you should allow it as a defense mechanism, unless your tactic is to discredit the person using it, which can be a self-destructive reaction.

Interviews with large numbers of persons in a variety of work settings reveal that if people come to believe someone is being less than forthright when he uses the "my hands are tied" excuse, they will be extremely suspicious of him in all future relationships. When you or I hear about an organizational decision, we usually have to just trust the reasoning we are given for it. We cannot know precisely how the decision was made. Normally we trust these procedures. But if we have reason to think we've not been told the truth, we bristle.

Nowhere is this more salient than in promotions and pay raises.

It's Not What You Do But How You Do It

Nick Grote is a supervisor of 30 packagers in a mail-order company. He applied for a promotion to director of shipments. The company hired an outsider, Bill Wheatley, for the job. Nick was told by the company's head of personnel that Wheatly got the job because of his experience as a manager of shipments in another company. Nick accepted the decision. The process, he told himself, had been fair.

Two months later Nick got to know Bill as a fellow member of the company bowling team and found out that Bill had never worked in shipments prior to this job. Now Nick was furious. Not as much about the fact that he didn't get the job as with his perception that the procedures for filling the position had not been fair.

In this case, Nick's trust had been violated; his expectation of procedural justice ignored. It is from such experiences that people walk away saying "I'll never trust those bastards again." Although everyone seems agreed that trust is vital for cooperation, individual human defense mechanisms lead us to use techniques that destroy trust. We tell less than the truth to avoid uncomfortable confrontations. Sometimes it works, so we are encouraged to stay with that tactic. We often don't know when it is not working because those who suspect us keep that suspicion from us.

Loss of trust, then, is hidden from us. We see only the results of it, and usually misinterpret what's going on because we do not know the source. Something called "the zone of indifference" is the first casualty in the breakdown of trust. This is the willingness of others to do what we ask them to do without raising questions or objections. You need to be very aware of this as you fashion your strategy and practice your tactics. The moment someone senses that you are manipulating him, he will distrust you, but probably will not reveal his feelings. The mistrust will be manifested in other ways that development and your ability to discern what is going on will be seriously limited.

Being concerned with trust in terms of strategy should be clearly separated in your mind from your natural sentimental need for trust. Trust in others, and theirs in us, makes us feel good about ourselves and is therefore an important human need. Our discussion of trust as strategy should not be confused with trust as sentiment, except insofar as knowledge of the human need for trust helps explain why people have a natural disposition to trust you.

How We Get To Be Who We Are

Carl Jung, the founder of analytical psychology, wrote that *development is learning to be that which is possible.*

For Jung, each of us struggles in our early formative years to find a social being, a person accepted by others. While we have choices, we are forced to limit ourselves to that which is attainable. Jung stressed the significance of the result: *To win for one's self a place in society and so to transform one's nature that it is more or less fitted to this existence, is the ultimate psychological achievement for every individual.*

It is useful, therefore, for you to think of the masks and screens you encounter as significant achievements, as methods of adaptation that have worked. If you respect them you can deal with them better than if you fret over their lack of congruence with "reality" or "truth." Later in this book you will be advised to share peoples' illusions, to even nurture them, in order to get what you want.

Humor

Life, says a comedian, is like an onion. The outer layers are a joke, and when you peel them away, there's another joke underneath. And underneath that, yet another joke, and underneath that, yet another. When you get to the core of the onion, however, it's no joke.

Catch-22, One Flew Over The Cuckoo's Nest, Murphy's Law, and *The Peter Principle* are examples of how we use humor to make the hypocrisies of organizations tolerable. Hypocrisies are more sufferable when softened by wisecracks and derision. "So long as we can laugh about it, we can live with it."

For example, the wisecrack that in organizations "people rise to the level of their incompetence" softens the common observation that so many people serving in higher organizational positions are misfits. How, common sense asks, do people get to those positions, given the organizational myth that people and their records are carefully screened in a well-designed process which guarantees "selection of the fittest"? The wisecrack gives us an answer without threatening the ideology.

It might appear at first glance that humor undermines authority; usually, it supports authority. Studies of humor have all concluded that joking about "the boss" normally reaffirms his authority. Perhaps no group of workers kid more about hypocrisies and "ridiculous" rules than do the military. Yet, there is a remarkable willingness to live with the hypocrisies and follow the rules.

Humor can also relieve boredom, which is important in many organizational situations because it helps to maintain the attention of the worker. An adventurous sociologist who went to work incognito at a monumentally-boring job tells us how his fellow workers played out silly games to find relief from tediousness.

> *My work group had developed various 'themes' of verbal interplay which had become standardized in their repetition. These topics of conversation ranged in quality from an extreme of nonsensical chatter to another extreme of serious discourse. . . . Serious conversation could suddenly melt into horseplay, and vice versa. In the middle of a serious conversation on the high cost of living, Ike might drop a weight behind the easily startled Sammy, or hit him over the head with a dusty paper sack. Interaction would immediately drop to a low comedy exchange of slaps, threats, guffaws, and disapprobation which would invariably include a ten-minute echolalia of 'Ike is a bad man, a very bad man! George is a good daddy, a very fine man!'*

Kidding themes were usually started by George or Ike, and Sammy was usually the butt of the joke. Sometimes Ike would have to 'take it,' seldom George. One favorite kidding theme involved Sammy's alleged receipt of $100 a month from his son. The point was that Sammy did not have to work long hours because he had a son to support him.

Unfortunately for persons who are targeted, humor can be nasty. Employees do not only kid-around about rules and other organizational norms; they also make fellow employees the victims of humor. "In-groups" chortle over individuals and other groups; sometimes elaborate, clever patterns are followed. In the chapter on tactics we will suggest you take an "audience" role in humor, particularly when you are a "new kid on the block," and always when the laughs come from laughing at someone. Humor is a complex social phenomenon with pitfalls that you are better off avoiding. People who are the butt of humor are expected to learn to live with it. So they deny or contain a fury that might let itself loose at any time. You'll never be able to control all the potentials for trouble; but you can minimize some of the potentials for yourself.

Some people appear to ask for others to make fun of them. They'll refer to themselves in self-deprecatory terms, kidding about their fatness, accident-proneness, lack of prestigious education, inelegance in speaking, or something else. In many cases, these people are trying to hold off criticism by saying "Hey, I know I'm bad. You don't need to tell me." While it may seem that you are being invited to join in the bashing, and these people may even laugh heartily when you do, there is always a large risk that you are offending them.

—Seven—

Groups and Jobs
Shape Our Attitudes

Without friends no one would choose to live, though he had all other goods.

—Aristotle

Two heads can be better than one; or twice as bad.
—Source Unknown

People at work form into small social groups. Sometimes, as in the case of the machine-operators group discussed earlier, how the members of a group relate to one another, even in the kidding-around relationships, is a very serious matter to them.

There came a time when the sociologist working incognito with this group tried his hand at a group humor theme that was based on George's daughter's marriage to the son of a professor. Now and then George would comment on having seen the professor here or there; Ike would then kid about George knowing a professor. "I made a suggestion to Ike," the sociologist reports: "Why don't you tell him you saw the professor teaching in a barber college on Madison Street?" Madison Street was in a disreputable part of town.

Ike did. The result was surprising and disappointing. "George reacted to it with stony silence. . . . He was sore. He didn't say another word the rest of the morning. There was no conversation at lunch time. A pall of silence had fallen over the room. A very long, very dreary afternoon dragged on. Finally, after Ike left for home, George broke the silence to reveal his 'feelings' to me: 'Ike acts like a five-year-old, not a man!'

What went wrong? As the sociologist explains it, the professor theme had been one in which George gained status, so much so that he had to be kidded about the status. The sociologist's variation downgraded the importance of the professor and, therefore, George's status.

The sociologist had violated a subtle aspect of in-group humor that is illustrated in an old joke about prison-group psychology:

At the beginning of his first night at a state prison, an inmate hears other prisoners yelling out numbers and laughing. He asks his cell mate "What's goin' on?" The cell mate says: "We're tellin' jokes. We know 'em so well we just have to say the numbers." The new inmate asks if he can tell one. "Sure," answers the cell mate, "try 23, that got a great laugh last night." So the new inmate yells out "Twenty three." No one laughs at all. "Well," says the cell mate, dismissing the newcomer's ineffectiveness with a casual wave of his hand, "some people just don't know how to tell a joke."

The significance of groups in the workplace was academically discovered around eighty years ago in the now-famous Hawthorne studies. A team of Harvard researchers were surprised to find that norms and bonds established in small work groups could be more powerful influences on individuals' behavior than rational self-interest. For example, even when increased output led to higher wages, workers would produce below their capability if group norms dictated that they do so. Furthermore, what each worker produces can be determined more by group standards for that individual than by the individual's native ability.

Inasmuch as the operators were agreed as to what constituted a day's work, one might have expected rate of output to be about the same for each member of the group. This was by no means the case; there were marked differences. At first the experimenters thought that the differences in individual performance were related to differences in ability, so they compared each worker's relative rank in output with his relative rank in intelligence and dexterity as measured by certain tests. The results were interesting: The lowest producer in the room ranked first in intelligence and third in dexterity; the highest producer in the room was seventh in dexterity and lowest in intelligence. Here surely was a situation in which the native capacities of the men were not finding expression.

From the viewpoint of logical, economic behavior, this room did not make sense. Only in terms of powerful sentiments could these individual differences in output level be explained. Each worker's level of output reflected his position in the informal organization of the group.

From these studies flowed a wealth of information about workers. In addition to seeing a worker as an individual trying to gain financial and personal rewards from his job, a new perspective was added, in which the worker was seen as a person seeking acceptance and recognition by his fellow workers. Social importance within the small working group can be as significant as the paycheck, even more so.

What surprised everyone the most about these findings was how emotions and the need to belong could overrule rationality. Further studies supported and embellished on what had been discovered at Hawthorne. We found out that soldiers put their lives at risk—hardly a rational act—not for patriotism, but to stand tall with the others in their small fighting unit, that real physical illness can result from being separated from a small working group in which one had been a member for many years, that small groups will conspire to act illegally to protect themselves from "others," and many more things, some of them quite remarkable.

For many years, it was thought that this phenomenon was limited to work groups at the lower ends of organizational pyramids, particularly where the workers were rather uneducated and not well paid. Then, in the late 1960s, a social scientist named Irving Janis introduced us to Groupthink. How is it, Janis asked, that a group of highly intelligent, well-informed people at the highest organizational levels can make blatantly stupid decisions. The Bay of Pigs fiasco was his favorite example.

In 1961, about 1,500 Cuban exiles landed in the Bahia de Cochinos (Bay of Pigs), Cuba, with the mission to oust the Communist regime of Fidel Castro. The operation was planned by a National Security ad hoc group of the most knowledgeable and prestigious civilian and military leaders available to the American government. The Cuban exiles had been trained by the CIA and supplied with U.S. arms. With few exceptions, they were either captured or killed by the Cuban army. The operation was a disaster.

The old saying about two heads being better than one is challenged by Groupthink. Each member of the group that sent those Cuban exiles on a doomed-from-the-start mission was personally selected by President John F. Kennedy to ensure that planning and execution of the operation would be guided by the very best expertise available. So, what took place in the group meetings that can account for such blundering on a large scale? What is the answer to the question Kennedy blurted when told of the results: "How could we have been so stupid?"

Janis, who pored over hundreds of relevant documents relating to the group's formal and informal meetings, found that although this group comprised one of the greatest arrays of intellectual talent in the history of American government, it was nonetheless, in the final measure, just another group that fell prey to the albatross of Groupthink.

Specifically, the individuals in the group became "groupies" and elevated the value of consensus above all other values, including, especially, the value of dissent and argument. All groups expect their members to reinforce the group's norms in what they say and do; some groups go so far as to almost forbid (implicitly, of course) dissent from the group's consensus or behavior at odds with the group's norms. The "Bay of Pigs

Decision" group, says Janis, became so obsessed with the goal of reaching agreement on how to accomplish the invasion that when it got to points of agreement, it had no tolerance for criticism of that agreement, even when the criticism consisted of no more than a realistic appraisal of alternative courses of action.

Another significant point to draw out of this example is the weariness of groupie pressures as well as the hazards. There's a lot of talk about the happy work group, and not so much about the oppression of individuality that is often an imperative aspect of these happy work groups. William F. Whyte, lamenting the inordinate number of studies and case histories on how to fit the individual to the group, called for studies on *the tyranny of the happy work team! The adverse effects of high morale!*

Group rivalry and feuding is another feature of group behavior you'll want to know about.

Maydeen Willis, supervisor of an eight-person accounting section for a manufacturer of kitchen cabinets in Kansas City, knew she didn't like Gloria Partee the moment she laid eyes on her, which was the morning Gloria reported to Maydeen as a new accountant in that section. Gloria looked and acted like a swinger, which did not go over well with Maydeen, a back-to-the-fundamentals Baptist who did not drink, gamble, dance, or play cards.

After three months, there were no doubts about two things: Gloria was an accomplished and hard-working junior accountant, and Gloria loved all the things from which Maydeen religiously abstained. Maydeen did not hide her disapproval of Gloria's lifestyle. The other junior accountants in the section followed Maydeen 's lead, so Gloria found her at-work social life with the ten women who worked in the nearby procurement section, who enjoyed Gloria's earthy sense of humor, which had come to include a repertoire of 'Maydeen jokes' along the lines of 'Maydeen is so up-tight that she. . .'

Tensions mounted both between Maydeen and Gloria and between the accounting and procurement groups. Maydeen's

supervisor realized she had to step in when Maydeen declared
Gloria as unsatisfactory on a performance evaluation without
being able to justify it. So, Gloria was transferred to the procurement section; in a few more months, group identity for both
groups became hostile towards the other. Today, new workers
in either group either join in on the hostility or are ostracized.

Feuding Groups Often Sabotage One Another

Hedrick Collendale, a sales manager for a West Coast paper
company, will tell you that hostilities between groups can ruin
you. A few months ago, when he first came on the job, he
launched an ambitious yet realistic campaign to increase sales
25% in six months. He discussed it thoroughly with the manufacturing manager, so he thought all of his ducks were in order.
Then he found out, in an interoffice memo, that the credit manager was tightening up on credit.

His superiors told him that the credit manager's decisions
were final in such matters unless the company treasurer or the
auditors overruled him, which they did not want to do. Other
people in the company told him that the credit manager could
have waited to tighten credit, but it wasn't surprising to see him
make his move just as the sales department announced an
aggressive campaign because *there's always been bad blood
between credit and sales around here.*

Hedrick watched helplessly as sales declined.

People Want to Keep Their Jobs

*The idea was to create a mirage in the Everglades, so
seven congressmen would hail the Immigration and Naturalization Service for its expertise in managing South
Florida's tide of undocumented foreigners.*

*So just before the delegation arrived, Miami INS offi-
cials, with an assist from the regional director's office, got*

rid of more than 100 detainees from an overcrowded detention center by releasing 59, including nine criminals, shipping 61 more off to different facilities and warehousing 19 in distant jails.

Then they laid on overtime help at Miami International Airport to keep the usual logjam at Customs flowing freely, and took criminal aliens out of holding cells and let them sit in the waiting room until the delegation finished its tour.

This description of agency behavior, as contained in an INS Inspector General report, tells us something that we know happens frequently, though we might not want to think about its full repercussions. People will go to great lengths to protect their jobs.

Private sector admirers will say that what the INS officials did in Miami cannot take place in the private sector because of competition, lack of unfettered job security, and other blah, blah, blah. Human resource consultant Brian Becker provides an interesting view of job protection in the private sector. He recalls a discussion he had with a human resources manager.

Bob reported that during a ceremony to celebrate the integration of five manufacturing units in his company, a final separating wall was to be demolished. Proud of their total quality management (TQM) environment and with senior management present, the integration team cracked open a wall and out fell $200k of faulty product that had been hidden in the wall. Bob reported that he was stunned by the ingenuity workers used to conceal mistakes. . . . I then asked him, if he were in manufacturing's shoes and concerned about paying his mortgage or if a promotion rested on the perception of his or his team's performance, would he consider hiding the error in the wall? He thought for a minute and said, 'I see your point.

Right now I'm trying to figure out how to minimize the perception that our TQM program is in trouble.'

Studies of both workers and managers in the private sector tell us that they try to hide errors.

Molehill Men

A molehill man, said Fred Allen, *is a pseudo-busy executive who comes to work at 9 am and finds a molehill on his desk. He has until 5 pm to make this molehill into a mountain. An accomplished molehill man will often have his mountain finished before lunch.*

Bob Trent, an associate market analyst for a large clothing-distributing company, has a molehill man for a boss. George Willoughby, Bob's boss, is both chief market analyst at the Chicago office where Bob works and marketing staff consultant at the company headquarters in Seattle. George is a whirlwind of activity. He is always on the run with an overflowing briefcase, lunches and dines only in a business-setting, and complains that modern communications technology ruins his vacations.

Bob "works hard" too, but in less of a frenzy than George, who advises Bob, "Don't get yourself into my hellhole. This company depends too much on me. One sacrificial lamb is enough for one office. After I die from stress, I hope you play it smarter than I did."

George says things like that somewhat seriously and somewhat kiddingly. Even though he appears to be openly and honestly sharing his feelings with Bob, and though the words sound caring and concerned, Bob does not feel comfortable in his relationship with George. If he tries to discuss a different way of doing things, George's busy schedule gets in the way. *God, I'd love to have time to discuss things like that with you, Bob. Maybe one of these days, things around here will settle down and then you and I can really do some brainstorming. It's certainly needed.*

If George asks Bob to do something out of the ordinary, he always prefaces his request with something like *I hate to ask you to do this, but we're in a bind here. . . .* . Every so often George will tell Bob a company success story, and add something like *We're making it happen, Bob. When I see things like this I decide that all the sacrifices are worthwhile.* He often comments on how much he envies the lives of the 40-hour-a-week employees. *If only I had it all to do over again, I'd stick with that life!*

George has put Bob in a very difficult position. He has assumed a role of indispensability and forced Bob to relate to that role. Not only is George "indispensable," the way he plays that role is necessary. He tells everyone "If I don't bust my butt around here, my job doesn't get done." Furthermore, he plays the "helluva regular guy" because he wants to spare Bob his suffering. George is a martyr. It's not easy dealing with martyrs, though probably easier than dealing with molehill men.

Lazy-Susans

Molehill men have opposites—Lazy-Susans—who avoid work at every opportunity.

Patsy Clyde is Section Chief for Garden Supplies at the Trenton outlet for a nationwide house and gardens franchise. Her boss, Susan Midkiff, who is supposed to keep Patsy's inventory up-to-date, has a vast array of ways to avoid doing her jobs. Susan's desk is always covered with paper in a way that deceives you into thinking she's working on it. If you walk by her office without entering, the computer reflections suggest serious activity; if you enter, you see design patterns (colored balls, etc.) running routinely across the screen. People who have caught on tell you that Susan comes into her office on a regular basis to move some of the paper around. Where she is when she's not in her office is anyone's guess. Meanwhile, Patsy's inventories suffer.

There are various reasons why the Lazy-Susans get away with their pretense to work. One is that organizations are not always set up in ways that enable them to catch such things; though, of course, the illusion is that they do. Another reason is that people like Susan sometimes have power relationships with the persons who are responsible for policing her work; we'll discuss that in the next section when we deal with power and influence. For now we just want to establish "Lazy-Susans" as very real players on your work stage. You'll have to deal with them.

Dangerous People

I have never been in a work situation where there was not a mentally deranged person. The more I talk with others, the more I know that this is the norm. These persons are kept on for various reasons, one of which is that people are afraid of them.

Let's Be Fair

> *In America everybody is of the opinion that he has no social superiors, since all men are equal, but he does not admit that he has no social inferiors.*
> —Bertrand Russell

Americans love to talk about their passion for fairness, particularly when it affects themselves. After all, in this country everyone is equal, well, except for those who aren't. The phrase "a fair day's pay for a fair day's work" is sufficiently protean to serve all of our consciences, as Janet Schrader discovered in her job as a welfare caseworker:

> *On a Monday morning in late April [1996], about 20 women assemble in a conference room for an orientation on the state's new welfare law, which has just taken effect*

in Northern Virginia. Some of the women have just applied for AFDC [Aid to Dependent Children] benefits, others have been receiving public assistance for years. This morning, they will 1earn that their benefits are temporary (24 months), that they must sign an agreement of personal responsibility in which they agree to abide by the rules of the new program; that they will receive no additional benefits if they give birth to another child while receiving AFDC; that they must search for a job in the next 90 days and that they must participate in 20 to 32 hours of community service per week for six months if they fail to find a job.

I am giving the welfare reform presentation this morning, and I've decided to use transparencies and an overhead projector. That way, the grim and sometimes angry faces in the crowd will be focused on the writing on the wall instead of me.

When I get to the part about community service work, I give an example: 'For instance, you might be asked to shelve books in the library.'

This notion of community work experience gets the most mixed reaction. A woman in the audience comments loudly, 'You mean we have to work for nothing?'

'No,' I say, 'you're getting your AFDC benefits and food stamps. That's not nothing.'

She mutters again that community service is working for nothing. Others, not so vocal, nod in agreement.

Some of the welfare mothers in the group said they saw the point and welcomed the experience of community work. But not in front of those who are the most vehement about working without pay. Group norms are powerful inhibitors of dissent, particularly when the prevalent group complaint is led by a highly dedicated-to-the-cause individual or group Not all people—but enough to justify your attention—have highly self-serving notions of equal-

ity and justice. Because fairness is a holy word in the American religion of democracy, we are obliged to at least listen when a claim to its violation is invoked. And, oh, how some people can use it, from the lowest to the highest levels of organizations.

The woman who complained about working for nothing has her counterpart in the CEO who lobbies for tariff protection on the basis of "fairness," or those who, like AT&T chief executive Robert Allen, say that it's fair for them to pocket $16 million in salary during a year that 40,000 workers are laid off. When C. Vin Prothro, CEO for Dallas Semiconductor, was accused of overpaying himself (around $10 million for three years) he shot back: *It's unfair to put a value on my services.*

While it is practical to recognize that fairness is in the eyes of the beholder, it is important to be seen as a fair person. Sometimes just talking about how significant fairness is goes a long way to establishing and maintaining the image of being a fair person. People have a need to believe that others are dealing with them fairly; therefore, just telling them you are concerned with fairness and applying it in your dealings with them is sufficient.

"I'm Going To Be Frank With You"

Next to the cult of fairness stands the popular but dubious religiosity about sincerity. The journalist and broadcaster Daniel Schorr said that *if you can fake sincerity, you've got it made.* Some people work hard at faking it, as they do with fairness, because there is indeed a big payoff. Your chances of success with people are very much dependent upon your ability to appear sincere and fair.

Who's Picasso?

My final observation about people is contained in a TV drama that appeared more than thirty years ago. I'm not sure of the title. It went like this:

Four couples are having dinner together. The four men are junior executives at a large Midwestern company. The conversation has been ranging from comments on little league baseball to recent best-selling novels. Right now it is on a Picasso exhibit at a local art gallery.

Sarah Wilson, a newcomer to the group because she just recently married Howard Wilson, says: *I have heard that so many times. Who is Picasso?*

The silence that follows is thick and awkward. Edith, hostess, says brightly, *Sarah, I'll take you to the exhibit tomorrow. Julia, did you notice I stole your recipe for the salad oil?* then Julia answers. The tension left from Sarah's question lingers.

That scene fades into the "Thank you for such a wonderful evening" departure scene, which fades into a scene of Sarah and her husband driving home. Sarah says, *Honey, I'm sorry. I'm such a klutz. I really wanted to find out who Picasso is and embarrassed us.*

Howard replies, *Sarah, you're missing the real point. George, Henry, Phil and I are all in a situation where getting further up the ladder is all we know how to do. We're all running scared. We don't know if we're up to it. Hell, we don't even know if we're up to where we already are.*

We have a big house, two cars, money for the kids, all of that. But do we really have that stuff, I mean own it? I don't think any of us feel comfortable about that. The insecurity carries over to our wives.

You violated a rule that all of us observe, at work and when we socialize. If someone starts to talk about something, you say anything except you never ask the person to answer a question that they might not have the answer to. That would be too threatening.

Hell, Sarah, none of us knows who Picasso is.

In junior executive and other organizational circles, theatrical staging and role playing carry over to social affairs. Just as one knows that she is not supposed to ask a peer or a superior a question that might reveal ignorance at work (it's ok to do that with an organizational inferior; in fact, that's part of your job), she also knows that this etiquette carries over to a dinner party.

Conclusion

While at all times you should observe the rules of etiquette at the masquerade ball, don't wait until the stroke of twelve to find out who's who.

—Eight—

Power

His father, self-hauled to the pinnacle of produce manager for a supermarket chain, preached a sermon illustrated with his own history—I had to haul wheelbarrows of sand for the stonemason when I came here. And so forth. The father admired the mysteries of business—men signing papers shielded by their left arms, meetings behind opaque glass, locked briefcases.
—E. Annie Proulx, *The Shipping News*

Power is the organization's last dirty secret.
—Warren Bennis

Mary Foster is still remembered at Potswana Power Company as "the favor exchange center." She was secretary to the Manager of Operations who passed on to her the unpopular job of deciding how requests for emergency service would be scheduled. When storms hit the Potswana area, the requests piled up as red slips on Mary's desk. No matter how she arranged the service, it always seemed like 90% of the customers were furious and the other 10% indifferent.

She also found herself on the phone with, at first, persons who worked at Potswana and wanted her to respond favorably to "a friend." Eventually she was discussing such favors with political and business notables in the area. One day she even received a call from her boss who was out-of-town. He had been called by the City Manager looking for one of those "emergency" considerations. So he called Mary and asked her: *Do you think you could help him out on this, Mary?*

Over time Mary came to the realization that she had an opportunity to make a good thing out of a thankless job. The approach was simple and classic. If you want me to do you a favor, what can you do for me, or for another person who can do me a favor? She constructed an elaborate influence network, parlaying one connection into another, building a system that involved almost anything: getting hard-to-find tickets to an official event, fixing traffic tickets, getting appointed to the city's policy advisory boards, providing home owners with renovation permits, getting a job with the city, and much more.

Mary accomplished a Grand Master finesse in the power game. She took an undesirable task and built an empire out of it. The reason she could do that is because organizations abound with opportunities to advance one's interests by gathering power and using it with skill. You have seen that organizations are not driven by their own engines of rationality. Rather, they are driven by the self-serving forces of individuals and groups. Power is what makes things happen as they do in organizations.

You look at the organization's chart and you see who has the authority to tell whom to do what. As your eyes go up the hierarchical line, you see increasing authority. But anyone who works in the organization will tell you that "the real power around here" is only partially revealed on that chart. Whereas authority is the right to influence others, power is the capacity to influence others.

You have to learn how to learn about the power structures and the powerful people in your organization if you're going to be effective for yourself, and you won't find that on the organization chart, or in the organizational mission statement, or in the budget, or in any written statement. You also have to learn how to get power and, even more important, how to use it. The following item appeared in *The Washington Post* about a woman who is trying to do that:

Sharon Flynn Hollander, the new chief executive of Georgetown University Hospital, usually likes to read books that take her away from the daily concerns of her work in health care. But Hollander's current bedside reading—The Generals' War: The Inside Story of the Conflict in the Gulf—*deals with battles not unlike those she faces in the rapidly changing medical industry.*

'I'm interested in how the generals crafted strategy, how they thought ahead strategically,' she said. 'That's something I have to do.'

Why would Sharon have to go to military books for help? Why aren't there mainstream business books available to her?

Power has an aura more mysterious than sex nowadays. There was a time when both topics were not spoken of in polite circles. Now that sex is a commonplace subject, only power remains in the shadows. Here and there Sharon will find, at best, some paragraphs, maybe a chapter, and a few books on power in the organization and business literature. So, she goes to the literature on war, where the focus is on power and conflict, and where winning is the most important thing because the only alternative is defeat.

Readers like Sharon inevitably find their way to Sun Tzu's *The Art of War*, Machiavelli's *The Prince*, and Musashi's *The Book of Five Rings*. These three writers deal directly and honestly with the phenomena of power, conflict, and warfare. In a popular edition of Sun Tzu's writings, James Clavell says that the truths taught by Sun Tzu, Machiavelli, and Musashi *can equally show the way to victory in all kinds of ordinary business conflicts, boardroom battles, and in the day-to-day fight for survival we all endure—even in the battle of the sexes. They are all forms of war, all fought under the same rules—his rules.*

These three men had in common a commitment to developing prescriptions and a moral code for the use of power. Like Nietzsche they recognized that a morality fitting for ordinary affairs was dangerous when the affairs involve power and conflict. Whereas humanity and justice have a place in some of our dealings with one another, opportunism and flexibility are the virtues of preference in conflict. Think of it this way: Picture a courtroom. You are the judge. So you should be guided by principles of justice and humanity. Now picture yourself as a lawyer in that courtroom. Your role is to win in your conflict with the other side. Opportunism and flexibility are far more relevant principles for you now. You owe that to your client and yourself.

You must believe in what you are fighting for, of course, but don't shackle your instincts and your skills with beliefs appropriate for another situation. Sometimes, in conflict situations, the ends will justify the means. Sometimes, in conflict, the use of violence is appropriate in order to minimize the total amount of violence that will be used. Timing and deployment of resources become opportunistic factors of great importance.

As those words suggest, to be responsible in the arts of conflict draws upon a morality that stresses winning. And that is what you want to do.

This is not meant to suggest that every event for you in the organization is a battlefield, but many are, and for those, you should be prepared by understanding power, knowing how it can be gained, and becoming skillful in its uses. The last point— skills in using power—will be discussed in the chapter on tactics. In this chapter, we deal with understanding power and finding out how it can be gained.

Most of us are curiously fascinated by power, as the father in Proulx's novel was in awe of men carrying locked briefcases. Even while we denounce power and its uses, novels and movies that include very powerful people are more popular than novels and movies about ordinary not-so-powerful folks. The three ingredients for a blockbuster novel or movie are power, wealth, and sex.

A successful executive wrote a book on power in which he concluded that the ultimate symbol of power in an organization is the appearance *that one has no time for mundane details and that one's comfort and convenience are the responsibility of other people.* Have you ever noticed how this becomes increasingly true as one ascends an American hierarchy? It is like rising in the nobility of the *ancien regime.* Each step brings more care and attention from others.

The usual reason given for this is that as a person climbs the ladder she needs more time to think and analyze in preparation for the decisions she will make. Her time becomes too valuable to waste on making her own coffee. Yet, there is also a considerable literature on techniques for managerial relaxation—also available at airports. I once suggested in a seminar for middle-level managers that doing things for oneself, like making your own coffee, could be a form of relaxation from management stress. The discussion brought out clearly that most managers want to keep those things as they are because they enjoy being served like minor royalty.

This is one of the more intoxicating aspects of power—literally lording it over others—and it explains why we should never expect those above to go very far in the empowerment of those below. Barely any of the plans to empower workers at lower levels get much beyond the distance words travel, and those that do don't last. If rationality reigned in organizations, the argument that empowerment of workers increases productivity at the same time that it leaves more time available to the manager would be triumphant. But power is far more of a driving force than rationality, and people rarely surrender power willingly.

For males, power can also provide another benefit—women. Henry Kissinger said that when he was asked by the Chinese Premier how it was that an unattractive middle-aged man like he got so many pretty young girls, he answered: *Power is the ultimate aphrodisiac.* If women ever really shatter the glass ceiling, they will probably also find "getting handsome young men" as one of power's fringe benefits.

All of those aspects of power are evident, and you have seen them. It is more important that you learn about the less obvious because it is from the less visible that you will gain the insights necessary for survival and success.

In the obvious world, power in organizations flows downward from the top. Up at the top, bosses establish policy and goals. These policies and goals are handed or shouted out to people on level two of the organization. So it goes until orders reach the bottom of the organization where there is obedience. All of this is constrained by a formal system of authority that distinguishes legitimate from illegitimate uses of power.

In the real world, informal coalitions of individuals and groups, which usually include the authority figures, establish policy and goals after considerable maneuvering and bargaining. The formal system of authority makes official what the informal system decides. Thus, the appearance of "obvious power" remains intact. It is said that a leader finds out the direction in which people are going, and then gets in front of them.

A CEO at Honeywell defined leadership as a kind of partnership with other key persons below the top levels:

> *You can't just say, we're heading for this place or that with an immediate buy in. We're apt to end instead with a bunch of people reacting with something like 'listen to that smart bastard.' What you've got to do is constantly engage in reiterating what you say and what they say is possible. And over a couple of years the different visions come together.*

When visions come together in this way, there are winners, the individuals and sections that formed the coalition supporting the final vision or policy, and losers. It is not the case that all the different interests expressed at the beginning of the process find a way into the final solution. For example, increases in workers' salaries may be in the game at the beginning, but not at the end. As the various parties bargain and negotiate, interests with the strongest power base have the most to say about what the final vision will be. Currently, workers' interests and some areas of middle management have weak power bases.

Coalitions are mercurial. The one leading to the final vision at Honeywell was disappearing as the decision was announced. You don't find them on organization charts, and only a careful observer could tell you who makes up a coalition as it is forming. Coalitions shift with issues and often cross vertical and horizontal organizational boundaries. For example, they can include people at several levels in the organizational hierarchy and from different product, functional, and/or geographical divisions or departments. The coalition leading to the Honeywell vision is but one type.

Coalitions are always power bases, but not all power bases are coalitions. If a power base has an agenda, that is, it wants to affect the policies of the organization, it is a coalition. At least, that's the difference I use in this book when I refer to them. It's important for you to recognize the difference. If you're in a situation that involves a power base, you're dealing with individuals and the people protecting them; if you're dealing with individuals who are part of a coalition and the issue involves policy, you're also confronting the protection of that coalition's desired policy.

Here's an example of a power base at work:

When Rick Farnsworth became head waiter at a four-star restaurant in Richmond, Virginia, he puzzled over the way Henry Cortland, the maître d', treated customers. Henry was downright rude to them. When Rick commented on this to one of the waiters who had been with the restaurant for years, he was told *Yeah, that's ol' Henry*. Why, Rick asked, didn't one of the managers spot this as a problem and do something about it. The other waiter laughed and walked away.

Management was one of the reasons Rick had taken the job at this restaurant. It impressed him as being first-rate. How, then, was Henry getting away with treating customers as though they had come for a free meal at a soup kitchen? Why didn't management get rid of him? There were plenty of complaints from customers. But nothing came of them.

It took Rick months to learn what was going on. Over the years Henry had done a lot of favors for management. He participated in fudging reports for the local fire and police authorities (*No room in the restaurant had exceeded the legal occupancy limit during the year*), lied for them when they were not where they were supposed to be (*Mr. Hardaway is not in his office at this moment. He is returning something left by a customer last evening.*), and pretended to be unable to find reservations when management wanted a table at the last minute (*You're simply not on the list, Mr. Beck. Perhaps, as you say, you called. But I can only give you a table if you are on the list I have in front of me.*).

What Rick found is fairly common in organizations. Research reveals large numbers of people who say they are pressured by their supervisors to sign documents containing lies, overlook mistakes, support incorrect decisions, and do business with the supervisors' friends. The favor-doers gain power over the supervisors who are applying pressure. In the example, the supervisors became part of Henry's power base.

Power gained by underlings for these reasons has implications for all the rest of us because, for example, the way that management treats Rick could be affected by what Henry wants, but management can't tell that to Rick. So, not only do we suffer the consequences of these informal power arrangements, we are often ignorant about the real reasons for what's happening to us.

Furthermore, because power relationships are not posted on the bulletin board or published in the monthly newsletter, they are the subject of speculation and rumor.

Another way that subordinates gain power over their supervisors, or others higher up in the organization, is by doing the "dirty work" that administrators and professionals don't want to do.

When Lee Iacocca took over at Chrysler in 1979, he found that Chrysler management, in a misguided effort to free itself for what it called *policy thinking*, had delegated far too much of the nitty-gritty to subordinates. One of the results was that subordinates were able to conceal from top management how poorly the company was doing. Promotions and bonuses were flowing to these subordinates despite mediocre or even poor performance.

In a study of mental hospitals, both administrators and physicians were found gladly yielding control of behavior in the wards to the attendants. Because the administrators and physicians were required to go into the wards to carry out some of their responsibilities, they became highly dependent on the attendants' good will. An "unhappy" attendant could make life miserable for the "visiting big shot." The administrators and physicians also delegated a number of their own responsibilities to the attendants, particularly responsibilities involving direct physical contact with patients.

These "arrangements" enable attendants to use ward life as they wish to use it. Some run protection and/or provision rackets, some gain sexual favors, others satisfy needs for power and control. Eventually everyone views such arrangements as "the way things are," and they are considered legitimate, even when they are blatantly illegal.

How secretaries gain power by doing things the boss doesn't like to do is legendary. And, like the hospital attendants, they will use their power in different ways. Some keep it limited to getting what they want from their bosses; others extend their power to other parts of the organization.

Delegation of power along with tasks is inevitable. The larger the organization, the more prevalent it will be. Those whose names are found at the top of organizational charts, as we saw in Chapter One, often do not "know what they are doing," nor do they have the capability to oversee all that they supposedly oversee. A well-known lament by a college president went like this: *You see me ceremonially. If you really saw me, you would know that my real job is to provide sex for the students, parking for the faculty, and football for the alumni.* That may be a slight exaggeration, but the point is a good one—heads of organizations must delegate and then work with the realities that are left as a consequence. It is not at all rare to find a high-level administrator who says he is like the pinball on a pinball-machine board, going wherever the initial thrust and the bumps send him.

Most of the delegation that matters and the unofficial power that results is not publicized, so you have to work at finding out about it. An interesting case in point:

Thomas Wyman, Board Chairman, CBS Television, went to Washington in 1983 to lobby the U.S. Attorney General, Edwin Meese. When he arrived at Meese's office, he was met by Craig Fuller, who introduced himself as one of Meese's advisors. Meese would be late for the appointment and might not have much time for it when he arrived, Fuller explained. *I know something about this issue,* he said, *Perhaps you'd like to discuss it with me.* Wyman waved him off and sat ruffling through magazines until Meese arrived. The Attorney General was apologetic, but, nonetheless, had no time for a real meeting. *Did you go over it with Fuller?* he asked Wyman, who said he had not. *You should have talked to Fuller,* Meese said. *He's very important on this issue. He knows it better than any of the rest of us. He's writing a memo for the President on the pros and cons. You could have given him your side of the argument.*

Just as underlings can have unofficial power, those at higher levels can have unofficial power in addition to what they have because of their position. In fact, struggles for unofficial power are an abiding characteristic of life at those higher levels. In *Men and Women of the Corporation*, a classic study by Rosabeth Moss Kanter, we find:

> *Somewhere behind the formal organization chart at Indsco was another, shadow structure in which dramas of power were played out. An interest in corporate politics was a key to survival for the people who worked at Indsco. This had both a narrower, more personal meaning (how individuals would do in the striving for hierarchi-*

cal success) and an important job-related meaning (how much people could get done and how satisfying they could make their conditions of work).

When you're dealing with a coalition, there are distinct disadvantages and advantages compared to when you're dealing with power base. The main disadvantage is that you might not know what the coalition's policy agenda is, and because of that ignorance you might say or do something about a policy that alienates persons in the coalition. The advantage is that when you know the coalition's policy agenda, you can work that angle.

Consider the following example:

Philip, an associate professor in economics at a leading city university, wanted to offer a course on how the inadequacies of most poor African countries prevent progress and economic development. His department chairman, Sophia, rejected the proposal. Henry insisted that the rules required a faculty vote prior to the chairman's decision. The item was put on the agenda for the next faculty meeting.

Philip knew that Sophia had friends in high places. Now he experienced it. He had a call from the dean in which the dean told him he was pushing the envelope, openly challenging the chairman. *We don't have much tolerance for that,* said the dean. Then Philip had the chairman of the political science department in his office. *Even if you get the economics department green light,* he said, *Sophia will reject it and most of us* on *the review committee will support her.*

There were a few more telephone calls and visits to his office, all to deliver the same message.

Philip had coffee with a senior member of the faculty, Arthur, who had "been around forever." He asked Arthur to tell him what was going on. *Why these high level confrontations?* he asked Arthur. *Is her power base ready to throw down a gauntlet over a disagreement over a new course?*

Oh, said Arthur, *that bunch is OK when they're not carried away by their sense of mission. Years ago they started to slowly meld into a fiercely dedicated group with the mission of saving Africa from those who say we should desert it. Didn't you notice the introduction of an African Studies Program last year? How could you expect to be anything but opposed when you say you want to teach a course in which you analyze the reasons why Africa is doomed to mediocrity, at best? Underneath the warm and fuzzy stuff are important interests. The Dean likes the publicity and cash flow of the university's foreign aid contracts with the government. The chairman of the political science department likes the involvement of his public administration faculty in those aid programs, as does the chairmen of public health and agricultural departments. All of these people are a coalition when it comes to blocking something as threatening as your course.*

Philip revised the description of his course. All the readings and lectures remained as they had been. He added to the description that the purpose of the course was to identify solvable problems that kept Africa from developing faster. The dean and the chairman in the coalition praised the course and recommended it to students.

Democratization of Organizations?

Not only do organizations pretend to have heart, be communities, and even be families, they also claim to be democracies when it is convenient to do so, i.e., when they are trying to win that ever-elusive commitment from you. What you're told is that this organization has thrown away all the dictatorial crap. You know, you're told to jump, and all you say is "How high?" We're a democracy now. The CEO is like a president of the country, and the board of directors is the legislature. People around here are equal and have rights.

Conveniently, nothing is said about periodic elections, a staunch pillar in any democracy. In organizations, supreme power is vested in the chief executives, period. The leadership of

American organizations is never elected by the people of the organization, and almost never are the masses of an organization even consulted about changes in leadership.

The phrase "we are democratizing things around here" employs a misleading and self-serving meaning of the word "democratizing." "Enlightened despotism" or "benevolent dictatorship" would be more accurate terms for characterizing what is usually meant by the phrase "democratic organization." But since the purpose of such a phrase is to lull you into commitment by getting on your good side, you should not expect your organization to use an accurate label.

Nor should you expect your organization to even carry through with the lip service about delegating power and all that. A study of over 800 employees in organizations noted for doing a lot of huffing and puffing about sharing power between management and labor came to the conclusion that *for most workers, sharing power is just an Olympian ideal*. When asked to rate the willingness of their managers to share power and authority on an "A" to "F" scale, 65% of the workers gave grades of "C" or lower. Only 12% gave their organization an "A."

Those findings are consistent with all the major studies that have been done on worker involvement in decisions. Perhaps the most definitive was a University of Michigan survey which included 2408 workers—covering an occupational strata from low-level service workers to "knowledge workers" and middle managers. In this group, 42% trust their organization's commitment to involving workers in decisions only "somewhat," 21% trust it "only a little" or "not at all." A mere 17% of this group said they would feel comfortable offering to their managers an alternative way to do their jobs.

Do not misunderstand the point being made here. It is not being said that organizations should be democracies. Rather, the point here is that organizations are not democracies. This is true especially in the United States, where workers do not participate in the making of important decisions as they do in many Scandinavian countries, and to a lesser extent in Germany. Also, the practice of participation itself is not being attacked here. Benevolent dictatorship and enlightened despotism are preferable to dictatorship and despotism.

Are There Organizational Genes?

American organizations are probably incapable of genuine concern for their workers; benevolent dictatorship is probably as good as it is going to be for employees. Organizations seem programmed to extol themselves while berating employees. Consider the debate over what is to blame for the fact that worker compensation has stagnated since 1979. Many experts, including the Secretary of Labor, blame organizational greed and lack of conscience about workers. The National Association of Manufacturers (NAM) weighs into the debate with the observation that although worker anxiety is a problem, the solution is for workers to accept the responsibility for their plight. *Workers have a responsibility to help themselves by acquiring skills and enhancing their own proficiency*, says the NAM.

No one would want to deny the NAM their own viewpoint. But it is striking that this viewpoint would see only worker improvement as a solution to what many believe to be one of America's most serious problems at the beginning of the twenty-first century. What about the possibility that poor leadership of America's private sector is maybe a little at fault? Could greed have a little bit to do with it? There are at least three respectable schools of thought among leading economists that the NAM knows about. The hypothetical explanation they chose is one of them. But of equal standing is the explanation that owners and top management are taking advantage of their position in the balance of power between owners/management and labor.

The NAM explanation of the problem is typical of the party line. Could it be in the genes? Some historians of labor relations in America find a clue to the disdain for workers in the early years of American industrialization, when ignorant immigrant labor dominated the workforce. The simple, common sense reason might be the entire explanation: there's profit to be made in cheap labor.

You won't find much criticism of greed and cheap labor in any of the management literature. Sometimes it's praised, as when Donald Trump wrote that *The point is that you can't be too greedy.* Because greed and the search for cheap labor are such basic ingredients in the business world, government often goes along, even when ranting and raving against them.

Before and during the 1996 Olympic Games in Atlanta, for example, illegal aliens—tens of thousands in numbers—worked at private-sector sites, restaurants, hotels, and other service-industry businesses. At the same time, the President and congressional leaders were pontificating against illegal aliens in general and illegal aliens working at the Games in particular. Yet there were only 52 Immigration and Naturalization Service agents working the four states involved in the illegal movements (Georgia, Alabama, North Carolina, and South Carolina). Tips from angry American workers spurred most of the INS raids. But the political constraints on interfering with the search for cheap labor were obvious, as is indicated in the following news report in June 1996:

> *Last year an INS raid on the Olympic Village construction site netted 37 illegal construction workers but left behind dozens of others who managed to hide. Since then, there have been no raids on Olympic-related construction projects, some of which have fallen behind schedule and are being rushed to completion in time for the opening games next month.*

In addition, though the arrested illegal aliens said that their employers knew that they were illegal, no government action was taken against the employers. Let The Games Begin!

Let's Pretend to Have Employee Participation in Organizational Decisions

A less-than-masterful, but nonetheless optimistic solution to the problems of organizations has been declared: Let Them Participate. This solution is based on a recognition that management does not always know the best course to follow in making decisions about organizational direction and the evaluation of personnel. Some of the platitudes offered as profound revealings are:

- If you want to know what's wrong with an organization, ask the workers.
- Workers can tell you better than a high-paid consultant how to increase productivity.
- When workers participate they become owners of decisions. Owners work harder than non-owners.
- Empower your subordinates.
- Leadership is good followership.

The truly reborn acceptors of this salvation will take the pyramidal figure of organization and turn it upside down with an enthusiasm smacking of religious revelation. *See!* They shout passionately, *That is what I mean. That is the solution. Workers on top. Middle management in the middle. Top management on the bottom. On tapes about organizations claiming to be following this reformation, managers inform you that their job is to 'get out of the way of the workers. Help them do what they feel should be done.'*

People in power have about as much interest and commitment to passing their batons on to the workers as they have to taking pay cuts, and they do associate the two. With so few exceptions that they bear no significance, the record of this new catechism in action is one of lip service only.

Organization watchers will tell you that "participation" is an old reform theme. Every once in a while it gets a new suit and fanfare. Management By Objectives (MBO) is an earlier variation on the "participation" theme; it's still around, so you should know about it. In this variation, you and your boss together decide on the performance criteria by which she will evaluate your work. You talk things over and mutually agree on a set of objectives that will be achieved within a certain period of time.

Research and common sense tell us that your boss is much more influenced by what her boss thinks should be your performance criteria than what you think. So, you're bound to be a little skeptical when your boss tells you it's between her and you. In one study a group of middle managers said that MBO in their organizations was MBT: Management by Terror. They said that they were manipulated into agreeing to unrealistic goals and then punished if they did not reach them. That was bad enough. Insult was added to that injury when they were reminded that they had "set these goals for themselves."

The odds are that you will not be subjected to MBT, because most managers never get beyond the first meeting. Traditionally, "the boss makes a big thing out of it when the two of you meet. At the end of the meeting he tells you to write it up. You do. You give it to him. That's the last you ever hear of it." Organizations could not function without unofficial power

Unofficial power is almost always needed simply to get one's job done. Most large organizations are so labyrinthine that work cannot be done unless one can "get around the system." Even CEOs and vice-presidents find that they can do little if they rely entirely on their formal authority, proving a point made many years ago by one of America's greatest organizational theorists: *Authority is the willingness of people to do what you ask or tell them to do.* If someone does not do what you tell them to do, then you don't really have authority over her. It is naïve to say that authority includes the power to fire those who fail to obey legitimate commands. In the tortuously complicated large organization, there are many things that prevent such a seemingly obvious aspect of authority from being possible.

As Dwight Eisenhower said, *Leadership is the art of getting someone else to do something you want done because he wants to do it.*

Sometimes unofficial power is used as a means—for good and bad purposes—and sometimes it is an end in itself. George Orwell said that *One does not establish a dictatorship in order to safeguard a revolution; one makes the revolution to establish the dictatorship.* For Orwell, power was never a means; it was always an end. Surely he is partly correct, notwithstanding the hesitancy we have to agree that our favorite leaders are at least partly motivated by intoxication of power itself.

We also have a seemingly infinite capacity to believe in the innate goodness of power when we associate it with a temporarily good usage of it. We watch a mother breast feeding our loved one, and we put out of mind the fact that, as George Bernard Shaw observed, *mother's milk nourishes murderers as well as heroes.*

For all of these reasons, you should not make moral judgments about power or people's motivations in seeking and using it. Here is what to keep in mind:

- People rarely join organizations to advance the organization's goals.
- Official and unofficial power is to organizations what energy is to physics: a constant and consistent presence that determines the direction of everything.
- To some extent, people will talk about power, but there will always be hesitancy to discuss it fully.
- Moral judgments are made about uses of power based on how one views the purpose for which power is used. There will always be great differences in these moral judgments because of differences in viewpoints on the uses of power.
- People are in awe of power and find its uses fascinating.
- You must learn to analyze power and its uses in your organization. Never judge it. Become skillful at gaining and using it.

—Nine—

Sources of Unofficial Power

It is said that power corrupts, but actually it's more true that power attracts the corruptible.

–David Brin

Official Power

A professor has official power to grade her students. If she chooses to she can use this power to influence some students to do things unofficially. Their need for good grades and anxiety about what she might give them leaves them vulnerable to her persuasion. Most bosses are aware of this power. Some use it extensively, and others are more selective. Some use it to promote the effectiveness of their work units. Others use it to enable corruption.

Chester Barnard, arguably America's greatest organizational theorist, called what I call illusions, "belief systems." These belief systems are powerful inducements for workers to participate willingly in the organization's command structure (i.e., to follow orders). Therefore, the chief function of the executive is to instill in workers the belief systems—management knows what it's doing, productivity can be measured, individual workers' contributions to productivity can be measured, and so forth.

Notice that all of the organizational illusions not only support the leadership of organizations; they also discourage a sound-minded person from challenging the illusions or leadership. Jean Lipman-Blumen calls these illusions *control myths*, and says they are the first thing one should think about when wrestling with the question: *Why do members of an organization tolerate toxic leaders?* Or, to put it another way, *How do toxic leaders get away with what they do?*

The control myths work so well because they satisfy both the followers' needs for certainty and security and the leaders' needs for order and control. Control myths operate very effectively because the leader does not have to waste a moment's time imposing constraints on our behavior. We do it to ourselves.

From the Interactivity, Interdependence of Work

A French sociologist studying a cigarette-making factory was surprised by the results of his research team's interviews with women who ran machinery. His working hypothesis was that these workers would manifest their hostility toward management in certain ways. The research technique used is a familiar one: subjects are asked to talk about things that make them angry on the job. Surprisingly, the women interviewed never mentioned management, but they were furious with the men who repair their machines because "they are not dependable," "they take care of it when they get in the mood," and "they deliberately take longer than is necessary."

It didn't figure. The operators had time off to read, smoke, do anything they wanted within the building while their machines were repaired. There was no loss of pay or bonus possibilities. All the women were on a fixed weekly salary. Why should they be so angry?

Then the sociologist remembered something about power: *I will resent it when another person flaunts his power over my ability to function, even if the consequences are minimal and not harmful to me.*

It would be difficult to think of an organizational work situation where this kind of unofficial power relationship did not exist. Small and inconsequential as it may seem, it can have inordinate consequences. No matter how independent you might like to think you are, from the moment you arrive at your workplace you are very dependent on the actions of others. For example, who opened the building, provided the heat and electricity? Who provides your equipment and repairs it? Who picks up what you are sending, brings what you are receiving? Who has to approve what you are sending? Whose output do you wait for before you can do your job? For the same reasons, you have unofficial power over others.

Most unofficial power originates in activities rather than in individuals. Considering that organizations are intricate networks of activities, it is obvious why they are such fertile ground for power relationships. Of course, not all working interrelationships become power relationships. Your working relationship with another person becomes a power relationship when three conditions are met:

- That person's work is in some way dependent on what you do.
- What you do is significant to him. (If you show up late to unlock the building, he is kept from doing something that is important to him.)
- He must deal with *you*. (He cannot get around the problem by having someone else open the doors, nor can he fire you and hire another person to do the job.)

Experts on organizational power use words like *interdependency*, *salience*, and *scarcity* to name these three conditions. There is considerable subjectivity in all of this; with, perhaps, salience (significance) being the most subjective, as we saw in the case of the French women who operate cigarette-making machines. If Charles is unable to complete a report due at 10:00 in the morning because I do not show up on time to unlock the building, the significance is objective. If the timeliness of the report is not affected by my lateness, but Charles is upset because he resents being kept waiting, the significance is subjective.

People who understand the subjective aspects of power are able to manipulate other people, gaining more influence than one would think possible given the objective situation. Two examples are:

- Modern-day courtiers gain power over their bosses when the bosses become dependent on their flatteries.
- Once I realize that your sense of salience is highly subjective, I can gain power from a job as trivial as opening the building door in the morning.

You have to keep an eye out for objective power. Subjective power is more hidden. You have to probe and analyze to discover it. More on that when we get into strategy.

Expertise

Expertise is the knowledge and skills that enable us to be unique in solving organizational problems. The unofficial power we gain from it works in ways similar to how interactivity power works; it depends on interdependency, salience, and scarcity. It is often asked why the George W. Bush White House did not use the Iraqi experts in the State Department for advice on the occupation of Iraq when it began in 2003. None of the three conditions under which expertise has power prevailed. The President was not dependent on State Department participation. The viewpoint of the State Department's experts were not relevant to him. There were other middle eastern experts whose views were more consistent with his own who were available.

Doing the Work of the Organization and Sabotaging

The easiest way to explain this point is to give two examples, both from real life:

- A payroll clerk who feels he has been unjustly terminated prints out and distributes throughout the organization previously-secret salary listings with names
  attached.
- A chain of drugstores doubles the profit margin on some
  generic drugs. A pharmacist at one of the chain's pharmacies comments casually to customers as he hands
  them their order for a generic drug, *We're sorry we can't
  keep our prices lower to be competitive with most of the
  other pharmacies in the city.*

Opportunities for sabotage abound in any organization.
Merely by adding a twist or wrinkle to her daily task performance, the worker can strike back at the overwhelming power
advantage held by the organization.

Examples of this are the use of tactics like *work to rule* by
school teachers, *Blue Flu* by policemen, and *Red Rash* by fire-
men. Each is an attempt to get around the legal ban on strikes
by public employees by disrupting the flow of services to their
publics.

Personal Power

Some people, we've all known them, are charismatic. They have
energy, determination, negotiating skills, they speak well, they
articulate visions we can all understand, even identify with,
and we trust our futures with them. These people are their own
source of power.

Loop, Loop, Who's in the Loop?

Being "in the loop" means being one of the players in the power
game. When someone says "no one makes a move around here
without asking Mike about it first" he is saying that Mike is an

important player, a dominant figure in "the loop." When someone says "They're not going to undergo any big changes without getting some input from Phil," they are saying that Phil is "in the loop."

Power and Space

Where people are tells you something useful about their power. The most valued space is corner offices on top floors, and the status of corners carries over into informal organizational activities. This is most easily seen at office parties, as a publishing house CEO tells it:

> *Sitting at this type of social function is a kind of defeat, not only because it projects fatigue and a general lack of energy, but also because it prevents movement and puts the sitter at a disadvantage in terms of height. Participants in the power game will remain standing even when they have one leg in a cast and are obliged to lean on a cane, as I myself have frequently witnessed!*
>
> *One can easily assess the relative importance of senior executives by watching their behavior at parties. Those who are most sure of themselves find a corner; those less sure of themselves place themselves in the middle of the traffic stream; the least secure players circulate around the room, avoiding the corners, which are already occupied, but attempting to form a circle of followers large enough to give them a visible constituency of their own.*

Study these patterns and learn from them.

Arrangement of Office Furniture

You should understand power implications of office furniture so that you can arrange your office to suit your own needs, and so that you are more aware when in others' offices.

If you have a small office, it is best to place your desk so that there is the maximum available room for you sitting behind it and the minimum necessary space where a visitor will sit. Your desk should be between you and the visitor. The visitor's chair should be as out of view from the door as you can place it. Thus, when a passerby looks into your office the visitor will be out of direct view and you will be seen sitting with as much space around you as possible.

If you have a large office, do the opposite so that the visitor has to walk the maximum distance possible within your office before getting to your desk. Many executives divide large offices into two sections: the formal desk-meeting section and an informal-meeting section consisting of a couch and a chair or two. Usually there is a message being sent when the visitor is invited to sit at the desk (This is official and/or is decision-making time.), whereas being invited to sit in the informal area means different things to different people. Over time you will become familiar with the tactics being employed by persons who invite you to sit one place or the other.

For your own tactics, I suggest you use the informal area when you are negotiating, or just chatting, and the formal area when you have your decision made and have the other person there to communicate that decision. The people you deal with will appreciate this consistency. People tend to accept power imposed in a straightforward manner; just as they resent power imposed in what they regard as a pretext of informality. People do not like to be openly tricked. Keep in mind this axiom of power usage: People do not like being surprised by the exercise of power. If they are anticipating it, they accept it far better than if they are not.

If someone does not accept your suggestion for seating, you should assume she has a power reason for doing so. As one executive explains these matters:

> *A certain tug-of-war is often evident when the two parties have different goals in mind, the 'host' trying to push the visitor toward the sofa, with the plea that he*

will be 'more comfortable' there, the visitor obstinately making his way toward the desk, or vice-versa, of course.

Some people are past masters at this game. When he comes to visit my office, a well-known lawyer of my acquaintance always manages to sit on the sofa between me and the telephone on the end table when he wants to persuade me to do something I would just as soon not do. In the first place, he has trapped me in a semi social position, by getting us both on the sofa; in the second place, he has effectively cut me off from the telephone, so that I can't be interrupted by a call. . . .When he wants to sell me on something, he sits on the chair in front of my desk, then gradually works it around until it's beside mine, so that he's moved to my side of the barrier, so to speak.

Keep file cabinets, or plants, or anything next to the two sides of your desk to prevent people from being able to move to that position. Unless it is to your advantage to do so, never sit in the informal area when pressured to do so. Just stay in your desk chair. It is important in your own office to be in charge of such things. If your will is being tested subtly, just as subtly make sure you win.

Never let anyone sit on your desk. There are some bosses who will do this in order to bluntly deliver a power message. They will only do it when you are sitting in your desk chair. With them, get up from your chair and stand facing them. With anyone else, tell them where you want them to sit.

Sources of Conflict

Power is spread around in any organization. For you to navigate safely, you'll need to understand the sources of conflict. Seldom will anyone tell you what's really at stake for them. Normally you'll get an earful of the organizational rhetoric. People are not going to say to you, "I'm going to fight that because it diminishes the status of my work unit. I don't give a damn about how good you say it will be for the organization. My work unit is the organization."

The sources of conflict begin with the fact that resources are usually scarce in any organization. There aren't enough promotions and pay raises to give them to everyone. If space is not cramped today, it will be tomorrow. There's never enough equipment to satisfy all needs. Not every person or unit can be put in charge of every project. There isn't enough time in which to do things. Not everyone's idea can be followed.

Where resources are scarce, there will be conflict over who gets what, when, where, and how. You soon learn in an organization that while your formal position and the soundness of your ideas are important in this conflict, you seldom win with them as your only power assets. So, you learn to deepen and expand those assets.

Values are another source of conflict. For example, marketing's and production's values are often in conflict. Suppose the marketing division wants to expand in a certain geographic area and wants to do so quickly with what it regards as an insignificant decrease in quality, but the production division wants to block the expansion because it regards the quality decrease as significant. Both divisions fervently believe they are in the right for the company. Someone above both divisions must decide which side to pick. There is seldom, if ever, an objective, scientific basis for making such a decision. Power coalitions will decide the argument.

Power is itself a source of conflict. People do not wait until the day of battle to build their power assets. They do so in anticipation; and when the day of battle arrives, they look around for their natural allies. As they gain power, most people find it intoxicating.

Interdependencies between jobs are also a lively source of conflict. Organizations put you in situations where you cannot do your job without coming into conflict with others, which forces you to develop power resources. This is not an aberration of some organizations; it is the norm for all of them.

In less than a week after he became night dispatcher for Town Taxi Service in Phoenix, Maury Babkins found that he could not avoid running into scheduling conflicts with Bea Monroney. Bea handled all the airport "runs." Maury started his shift at six in the evening. At six-thirty Bea would call him and give him her airport schedule. His job was to get cabs to all the people on Bea's list. On his first night, he went over with her conflicts due to commitments he had made prior to her call. There just were not enough cabs to handle both Bea's and his commitments. *That's your problem*, she told him. *I've given you the airport schedule. You've got to make it work.*

Maury tried to talk about this with his supervisor, but was dismissed with the comment that it was his problem to deal with, but to remember that the company always preferred to do long airport "runs." On the other hand, his supervisor said, *don't leave me or anyone in top management with a complaint from someone about our not showing up when he expected one of our cabs. You're paid to schedule*, the supervisor said, *deal with it.* Now Maury knew why the company had such high turnover in the night dispatcher position. The situation was impossible, unless he found a way around it.

He considered what power he had and decided to use it to his own advantage. His power resided in his being the only person who knew what happened on the telephone when people called him with requests. So, he took matters into his own hands. Anyone who called him before Bea Monroney's call at 6:30 was told that *due to the heavy demand for cabs at that time we can't guarantee service until 6:30. If you'd like I'll take your number and call you back then.* After he had the airport runs list he arranged the cabs he had available, giving first priority to the airport runs. He had persons who were going in directions compatible with the airport runs share the ride with the airport riders. If he had more cabs available he assigned them to the other callers. Callers left on the list were told there were no cabs available.

Over time Maury gained an unplanned power base amongst the drivers who liked the increased tips gained when they carried the extra passengers who were doubling up with the airport passengers. Drivers wanted to be "in" with Maury because he had discretionary power over who was assigned the doubling-up fares, so Maury could ask them to do him favors. For example, he was frequently called by Bob Tinker, one of the owners, to provide a cab for Tinker himself, someone in his family, or someone else. If he had no cabs available he would say *Mr. Tinker, I'm running on empty right now. How important is this to you.* Tinker invariably said it was very important. Maury then said *I'll get it done.* He then called a driver at home who was glad to do a favor for Maury. Maury's power base continued to expand as he learned to interconnect needs and his pivotal position.

A long-standing and major complaint the company had heard from the drivers was that after they arrived at the airport they often had to hang around for hours before picking up a passenger. There was even talk that the drivers' union would demand hourly pay to the drivers for that slack time when the time came for a new contract to be negotiated.

Maury spoke privately to Tinker about this problem. *I have this idea, Mr. Tinker, that might save the company a lot of money. Suppose I try to provide extra passengers on the airport runs. The drivers would make more money. So they might not mind sitting around that time so much.*

Tinker thought it was a brilliant idea. *But let's, keep it between us*, he cautioned Maury. *Yessir*, answered Maury.

Maury knows well the axiom that when you control resources for which there is more demand than supply you have power. After hearing about "Maury" in a seminar, a student asked: *Did Maury get promoted?* The professor replied: *Not yet. He's made a good deal for himself where he is. Maybe a promotion would be a power demotion for him.*

In addition to bringing together "equal" people in unequal statuses, organizations create conflict by putting you in situations where you cannot do your job without coming into conflict with others, which forces you to develop power resources.

As if there was not enough conflict in organizations, we find that some management manuals recommend its creation as a technique. Books on management usually have a section devoted to *conflict as a motivational tool.* The advice is: *Stir things up, get people moving, watch productivity soar.* You will probably not be surprised by the customary division in such books between positive conflict (the kind that managers stir up) and negative conflict (the kind resulting from the nature of organizations). Management consultant Fred Jandt gives us an example of management-induced conflict:

> *One of my clients, a distributor of office equipment, discontinued a line of desktop calculators, replacing it with a line of desktop personal computers. All of a sudden, the people who used to sell calculators were no longer called 'sales representatives,' they were known as 'data consultants.'*
>
> *Their duties were essentially the same, as were their earnings, but their new title drew envy from other employees who continued to be called 'sales representatives.' The new title was seen as a badge of success and recognition, and the drives for success and recognition of the people who did not receive the new title were frustrated.*
>
> *The president of this company, whose idea it was to change the title . . . could have, if he chose, dubbed everyone on the payroll 'data consultant.'*
>
> *In practice, however, he would not do this—for he deliberately was using the title selectively as a motivational tool. . . .*
>
> *Meanwhile, the change of titles stimulated intense conflict in the company's training department. One division of the department trained sales personnel; another trained managers. The division that trained managers*

regarded the change of titles as more than merely cosmetic. This division viewed the change as a symbol that the new line of desktop computers represented a priority project. The division therefore wanted the responsibility for training the new 'data consultants,' who under their old titles would have been trained by the other division.

Please note that none of this conflict came about by accident. The president of the company orchestrated the changes intending to accomplish exactly what he did. He wanted conflict of the sort he got because he wanted the competition it stimulated.

Coalitions

The search for power leads the individual into coalitions. You will spot power-seeking behavior in individuals faster than you will see the coalitions underlying behavior. The statements "I don't know why she did it." "I don't see what's in it for her?" can be an illustration of the failure to see the coalition reasons for "her" behavior.

A coalition is an unofficial association of two or more persons or groups held together by favors and influence. You are probably familiar with national coalitions like the one joining the dairy industry, some members of Congress, some State Governors, and some city officials in an association that leads to and supports federal subsidies for dairy farmers. Organizational coalitions are less visible than that.

Every day, in most organizations, some flagrant behavior is being protected by coalitions. Sometimes it takes an unusual set of circumstances to force the organization to admit that such flagrant behavior exists.

When Pamela Martens, a stockbroker trainee at *Shearson/ American Express*, went into the office of her branch manager, Nicholas Cuneo, to ask a question, he opened his desk drawer, took out a gun, laid it on his desk in front of himself, and then asked her what she wanted. Later in the day Pamela complained about this to another manager, who down played Cuneo's behavior, by saying *"Oh, Nick just does that to intimidate the trainees."*

That was in 1985, and it was just the beginning of Pamela's troubles with Cuneo and his cohorts. She sent letters about the situation—in which she explained, with examples, that Cuneo was a bully who was supported by his peers and the male stockbrokers with whom she worked—to various senior executives at *Smith Barney*, which acquired Shearson in 1993. Then, after two years of unanswered such letter-sending, she hired an attorney. The two of them documented a 25-year record of power abuses by Cuneo. Suddenly, the *Smith Barney* brass paid attention. Cuneo was placed on leave of absence. Then he retired. Two days later, Pamela was fired on the grounds that she had not attended a compliance meeting.

Coalitions often stretch beyond the boundaries of any one organization, linking managers or technicians in one organization with those in another, as happened in the Challenger incident.

Between the annoying but relatively unimportant politics at Rick's restaurant workplace and the awful consequences of the *Challenger* launching, there are myriad outcomes of coalition behavior. Every organization will have power struggles and consequences because it is in the nature of organizations to create conditions for conflict that cannot be handled by the organization's official authority system. There are four major reasons why this is so: scarce resources, divisional interests, the intoxication of power, and interdependencies between jobs.

We have looked at examples of the fact that unofficial power can be used to achieve one's goals. Now we will look at examples of why and how this is hazardous to your survival in an organization.

Unofficial Power Is Used Covertly

Mary Foster's power network at *Potswana Power Company* was unknown except to her. Stakeholders in the network knew about their individual roles, that they were responding to a request from Mary because they "owed her," but they were unfamiliar with the structure and names of other stakeholders in Mary's network.

If you suffer because Mary gets in your way—perhaps a friend of a friend of Mary's was given the job you wanted on the city's planning commission—there is no way you can show that he got the job because Mary went to bat for him. The paperwork on the appointment will follow the policies and regulations pertaining to such an appointment with absolutely no reference to Mary Foster.

Challenging the Unofficial Power Systems Can Be Risky

Unofficial power systems are well-kept secrets. If you raise questions about them, you are inviting trouble not only from the people who are stakeholders in a Mary Foster network but also from the officials who are supposed to be keeping that sort of thing from going on.

These Systems Use Vagueness to Your Disadvantage

Because they are covert, the unofficial coalitions behind official decisions do not have spokespersons or any public methods of explaining why they produced the decision other than the official process of decision making. However, the real process of making a decision must be protected. This is accomplished (better to say: "pulled off") by employing vagueness in official statements.

People Near the Bottom Are Sometimes "Fall Guys"

Sometimes management points the accusing finger at the workers. Thomas Mueller and his wife, Rosa, can tell you about that. In 1995, Air Force Technical Sergeant Mueller was charged with criminally negligent homicide after an F-15 cartwheeled off the runway in a huge explosion at Germany's Spangdahlem air base, killing the pilot. Mueller had been one of the last mechanics to work on the plane.

Twelve months after the charges were brought, investigations by impartial authorities found that the Air Force was covering up for structural defects in the F-15, which had surfaced twice before, but were kept secret. Also uncovered was a systematic unprofessional and unethical use of documents on the part of the Air Forces' lawyers. But before these things were revealed to the public, Mueller took his own life. Although he knew he was not negligent, and said so in his suicide note, the Air Force authorities dealing with the case had left him in mental shambles to question everything about himself.

Sergeant Mueller lacked power; his superiors had spent years developing their power bases and coalitions. In a way, most of the activity of high-level managers and executives is at least partly done to increase their power base and/or improve their position in a coalition and increase the effectiveness of that coalition.

The Set-Up-To-Fail Syndrome

Perhaps your biggest problem with the official and unofficial power held by your boss over you is explained in the "Set-Up-To-Fail Syndrome." In the late 1990s, two faculty members at the *International Institute for Management Development* in Laussane, Switzerland, published an article on how bosses create their own poor performers. I discussed it in one of my newspaper columns as did many other columnists. The reaction was so overwhelmingly positive that the article's authors produced a book four years later, getting into much more detail than an article would allow.

The syndrome goes likes this. An employee makes a mistake or what appears to be a mistake; he misses a deadline, loses a client, or gives an uninspiring presentation at an important meeting. The boss begins to doubt the employee's competence or he may have had some doubts before, due to some vague thoughts, that are reinforced by this mistake.

The boss does what good bosses are supposed to do. He pays more attention to the employee, gives more than his usual guidance when explaining an assignment, unsubtly, though he tries earnestly to be subtle, making suggestions about how the assignment should be carried out, and checks up on progress more than he usually does on assignments he gives his subordinates.

For example, if my boss has confidence in me, when I seek feedback on my performance, he sees it as a sign of my trying to do even better, whereas if my boss perceives me as an under performer, when I seek feedback, he sees it as a sign of weakness.

What the boss does not do, because he doesn't know how to, is establish an understanding with the subordinate about why he has doubts and what will dispel the doubts and build trust in competence. All the subordinate sees is the extra guidance and increased monitoring, which, to him, means lack of trust and confidence. And it follows as the night the day, subordinates, from the bottom to the top of organizations, become problems when they sense lack of trust and confidence. If they try to discuss the problem, they make little progress because bosses don't know how to do that.

How does one say, *You made a mistake. Of course, we all make mistakes, but I've lost some confidence in you. So I'll be keeping an eye on you.*

When subordinates are cast as weaker performers, they will play that role no matter what their potential. People are, as I said, role performers, and roles are given in the stage play. The employee becomes incompetent.

You've heard of self-fulfilling prophecies. This syndrome can become one. The employee believes the boss' belief and becomes incompetent. The boss concludes he was right in the first place. Also, the organization praises the boss for giving the subordinate more "guidance" and "supervision."

Workplace Bullying

Workplace bullying is common. It doesn't necessarily mean physical terrorization. Here's a list of bullying practices compiled from various questionnaires filled out by workers and verbal interviews:

- Constantly changing work standards.
- Assigning impossible work targets.
- Public insults.
- Laughing at work efforts.
- Excessive criticism.

Though workplace bullying is gaining considerably more attention in the U.S., the French have publicized it far beyond what we have. In 1998, a book titled *Stop Psychological Violence* was outselling the top fiction best sellers within weeks of publication. In its first three years, it sold four-hundred thousand copies. The book provoked new laws placing a fine of $13,000 and a jail sentence of up to one year.

The Power to Control Us Is Often Us

In the previous chapter, "What are People . . . Really?," we discussed how our needs create a basis for our acceptance of bad leadership. It is also ourselves who keep us from challenging our organizations. In the final chapter, "Tactics," I will advise you to use experimentation in your battle of wits and wills with your organization. That is a problem for those of us who are dominated by the left side of our brain. The left side is the safe-keeping side. The right side is the experimental side.

The left side guides us based on analysis and evaluation. It loves words, is realistic and logical, is concerned with consequences of actions, is cautious, aware of dangers, avoids surprises, wrongness, and mistakes. The right side imagines, speculates, is impetuous, does not mind being confused or wrong, breaks rules and takes risks.

Organizational authority loves the left side of our brain and encourages us to be guided by it, while disparaging that cheeky right side.

Visionary Leaders. Careful What You Wish For

When the 1990s began, the classic corporate CEO cut costs and increased productivity. By the end of the decade, he was replaced by a visionary CEO who talked dramatically about missions rather than bottom-line. For example, you seldom hear anything about corporate profits, and do hear a lot about how *we aim to make tools to make peoples' lives better.* Michael Maccoby, a highly-respected student of leadership, describes the change this way:

> *Were you to review the cover of Fortune magazine over the years, the rise of the visionary CEO would be starkly evident. A composite of routine work life—the inner machinery of a factory, oil drums, a nameless worker, the VW logo usually appears on the cover throughout the magazine's first fifty years after its launch in the 1930s. But as the millennium approaches, more CEOs make it on the cover solo, the logo or actual product of a corporation giving way to the CEO's well-known persona.*

At first, visionary leaders were praised, even revered. Slowly, over the years of their reign, they were questioned, doubted, denounced. Not because shortcomings were found in the theory of visionary leaders, but because of the many inept, stupid, and corrupt things they did. Not all of them fell short, but few reached the goals they set, and the average visionary leader, whether in business, academia, the military or the church has let people down.

Unfortunately, Rome is not destroyed in a day, so people do not catch on to the phoniness of a visionary CEO's promise to turn Rome into something much bigger and greater. In the meantime, the visionary leader has control over vast resources to waste away on his pipedream.

It's said that to attempt the impossible inevitably leads to corruption. Visionary leaders are corruption-prone. And the deeper in they get, the more likely it is that you and your fellow workers will be at least scarred, perhaps worse by the fallout. Their power comes from our deep-seated hopes for miraculous leadership. You are not powerless in your attempt to oppose their direction, but, sometimes, almost.

Conclusions

Power is not necessarily good or bad, positive or negative, functional or dysfunctional, desirable or undesirable. It simply is. Find something that happens in an organization, and you have found an example of power.

In the following chapters, we look at the importance of strategy and tactics as you try to find a sound basis for "taking on organization." Remember, this is a book on survival, not on self-destruction. Most of us need organizations to achieve our basic purposes in life. This is a book about coping, not about heroic, larger-than-life feats.

Organizations provide enormous authority figures who both scare us and inspire us. Think of how well you did, or didn't do, with your parents. It's no simple thing to get along with authority figures on your own terms, to know how to outwit them without their knowing you're doing it. And that is what we're talking about. That's what I mean by "coping."

—Ten—

Strategy: Presentation of Self

Believe in institutions, but do not marry them. You are likely to work for some company or other, but keep a safe distance. There is no contempt as bitter as that felt by compromised minds for the independent ones that have joined them. Grin broadly at the water cooler, and go home to where you live.

—Roger Rosenblatt

If you know the enemy and know yourself, you need not fear the result of a hundred battles. If you know yourself but not the enemy, for every victory gained you will also suffer a defeat. If you know neither the enemy nor yourself, you will succumb in every battle.

—Sun Tzu

Charles Sheeler is remembered as the American artist who best captured the spirit and soul of industrialization. He admired the precision of machinery and the rationality of industrial plant design. His paintings were intended to displace the "Natural Sublime" with the "Industrial Sublime," a goal he considered accomplished when he presented American Landscape, 1930. The painting is a hard and flat, almost photographic rendition of silos, smokestacks, factory buildings, and grand loading machinery. There are railroad tracks and a coal-bearing train in the foreground. If you look very carefully you will find one human being in the picture—an insignificant, ant-sized person walking toward a train car.

Sheeler brought to canvas Henry Ford's words, "The man who builds a factory builds a temple. The man who works there, worships there."

Captains of industry and managers in organizations are more subtle today. They try to be less obvious about their feelings, using euphemisms and code words and hypocrisy. You saw in chapter one that the spirit of Henry Ford survives, though now worshipped in secret. In many ways you are better off today than you would have been had you worked for Ford, thanks largely to unions and the courts. Organizations have yielded better salaries and working conditions only because of economic and legal pressures.

Despite the gains, you are up against a mighty foe in organizations, for the following reasons:

- In the private sector, you do not have direct access to the persons giving orders to your immediate boss, unless you are at the level just below the president or CEO. In the public sector, you have no access to the levels from which your boss gets her marching orders. In both private and public sectors, your immediate supervisor can tell you that he's "only enforcing policies made upstairs." She can refer vaguely to "them" and "they," sharing little bits and pieces of information because she's not supposed to tell you the whole story, and she's already told you too much. He can shrug his shoulders when he tells you that you didn't get the promotion or pay raise or money for your project or whatever because even though he really went to bat for you, "they" had other ideas.
- When something goes wrong in an organization there is no specific person or thing that is clearly to blame. Assigning blame becomes a prize in the power struggle. The less power you have, the more you are likely

to be blamed. This is endemic to organizations, particularly American ones.

• Organizations are organized hypocrisies, as you now
understand from chapter one.

• You have been socialized to be pliant so that you are
easy for organizations to control with hypocrisy. You
have been taught to honor values that organizations
manipulate, and you have learned to obey organizational authority. As Ivan Illich describes it, we forget
most of what we learn in schools except what was
perhaps the major reason for our being there, which
was to teach us to obey organized authority. We don't
forget that. We don't forget how to sit still with hands
folded. We remember to ask permission, and that
teachers are women and administrators are men.

• Most of us hesitate to criticize organizational leadership because we fear retaliation from both leadership
and our peers. Studies of whistle blowers come to the
conclusion that the whistle blower usually ends up
ostracized by his peers, an "outsider within," to use
the sociologist Judith Loeber's description, which
makes him very vulnerable to leadership's punishment. No one cares what they do to him.

The first two of these reasons why organizations are mighty
foes were evident in a memorandum shown me by Walter Goldstein, office manager of a national real estate company. His
company had announced that "sales nationwide are soft, but we
are designing a reorganization that will guarantee recovery."
During the next month or so, Walter's budget for advertising
and support services was cut by 25%. To Walter this seemed
self-defeating because such cuts would surely diminish sales.
Advertising of houses for sale is one of the criteria by which sellers select real estate companies. Secretarial and legal support is
essential to closing sales quickly, another important competitive feature.

Walter tried calling national headquarters in Dallas to explain the dilemma and find out what was going on. He was blocked from direct access to the top guns, and was shunted off to a marketing analyst who said, "They're keeping the overall plan secret because we don't want the competition to know what we're doing. But this much I'll tell you on the "q.t." Things got so bad that they brought in some high-flying consultants. We're now in the first movement of their orchestration."

A few months later Walter received the memo he showed me:

TO: All Office Managers
FROM: Seymour M. Lippencott, Chief Executive Office

Some of you have commented on the reduced budgets of recent months. Certain area offices have seen less desig-nation of funds for advertising and support services. This is due to the fact that company-wide resources have been reallocated to put us on a better financial footing.
I am fully confident that each of you affected by this over-all mission realignment will call upon your inventiveness to meet the challenge of getting across the bridge from a troubled yesterday to a bountiful tomorrow. The future is ours if we have the courage and resourcefulness to carry out our responsibilities.

In addition to sending Walter to the nearest bar, this memo accomplished the following:

- It did not give an explanation of anything.
- It used the phrase "resources have been reallocated to put us on a better financial footing" to show that the problem had been solved, whatever it was.
- It also warned that if you are not resourceful enough and we slip off the bridge and are devoured by sharks, it's your fault!

You've Got To Have Strategy

Ethel Merman's "You've Got To Have Heart" is good advice, but you're better off with a sound strategy for yourself when you enter an organization. Don't leave your work future to fate. Remember, you are absolutely, positively on your own. By following your strategy and using tactics, you can develop allies and friends and become a member of some powerful coalitions; but when you enter an organization, you are usually on your own.

Notice in the previous sentence I said *you can*. I said that rather than *you will* because I want you to develop a strategy for yourself, and you might not want to become a person of power and significance in your organization. Your ambitions might be more modest. The purpose of this book is not to try and make everyone drive for great success. But if you have modest goals, you still need to protect yourself and your integrity. You still need a strategy and tactics.

Strategy is preparation for utilizing tactics. It provides your tactics with a framework that enables them to succeed and enables you to know when a tactic is succeeding. Many people try ad hoc tactics now and then. For example, they try to develop the right kinds of contacts because someone told them that networking is helpful. They try to get into positions that they think are secure. They lie a little. They might even marry the boss' daughter or son.

It's no great sin to lie and being an in-law to the boss has advantages if such tactics are consistent with your strategy for yourself. People who use tactics without a strategy are often seen as opportunists who have little regard for principles or consequences. You do want to take advantage of opportunities. Such action is required for success in anything. You do not want to be seen as an opportunist. People are programmed to dislike and work against opportunists. Even if you really are one, you don't want the show it. How you design your image, how, as Shakespeare said, you "proclaim yourself" must be decided and shaped before you utilize tactics.

Tactics, covered in the next chapter, have to do with others; strategy has to do with yourself. The reason Sun Tzu's words about knowing the enemy and yourself are quoted at the opening to this chapter is to help you understand that you need to be clear about your objectives (yourself) before employing tactics.

You start working on your strategy by wondering what you want to achieve, trying to understand why you want to achieve it, and gaining control over things by seeing clearly the illusions that dominate your organizational situation. While you want to know what the organization and your immediate working group have in mind for you, you must have your own agenda for yourself from the outset. Your own agenda will be severely tested— organizational illusions are powerful voodoo— so the stronger it is, the better off you are.

In the movie *Working Girl*, Melanie Griffith plays an ambitious high school graduate who has the talent for a corner office but is relegated to a secretarial desk by her lower middle class education and background. She takes public speaking and other classes after working hours, reads vociferously, and copies the behavior of successful executives. She learns that only when she pretends to be in an executive position with persons outside the organization where she works does she have the opportunity to gain recognition for her ideas, which previously were being stolen by her boss. From the moment she is able to place her skills and ideas in this masquerading role, she is seen as a brilliant deal maker. Even her love life takes a socio-economic lift—from a monosyllabic Staten Island working class guy to a suave Wall Street negotiator.

Griffith's close friend sees only pending disaster in the charade, and pleads with Griffith to give it up before she ruins her entire life. "I'm not screwing up my life," replies Griffith, "I'm trying to make it better. I'm tired of working my ass off and getting nowhere because I'm following rules that I didn't have anything to do with setting up."

This character has an irresistible attractiveness. We cheer for her to succeed because we agree that the system is constructed to banish her to jobs unworthy of her talent and ambition. She lies, misrepresents herself, borrows her boss's dresses without permission, takes advantage of people, and so on. At the end of the movie, this character tells a business magnate: "When you're at the top you can bend the rules all you want. When you're on the bottom you're not allowed to bend them. But you've got to bend them to get to where you are."

I will not attempt analysis of why we cheer for this character. I advise you to see the movie. Do your own analysis. Then try thinking of yourself, a strategy for yourself, along the same thoughts.

Thou Shalt Not Be Blindsided By The Elephant

Melanie Griffith's character was a nice girl who came to realize that if you go around thinking organizations are filled with nice people playing by the same rules they tell you to play by, you're going to be blindsided by the elephant.

Dwight Waldo, who spent his professional life studying how we think about organizations, likened our knowledge of them to an ancient Indian parable in which three blind men place their hands on different parts of an elephant, and therefore define "elephant" differently. Similarly, says Waldo, different observers touch different parts of organizations and come up with different characterizations.

Melanie Griffith's character came from a socio-economic class that accepted the view of the elephant commonly provided for her sort of people: Organizations are rational hierarchies of offices that are—as you move upwards—deserving of ascending respect and compensation. Work hard, be loyal, do what you are told, and the organization will find the right place in its pecking order for you. When her sophisticated boss stole her ideas, Griffith was blind sided by the real elephant, an organization in which power and privilege is used to gain more of the same while pretending to be just the opposite.

So the first commandment in your strategy is obvious: Always know where the elephant intends to sit and never trust what he tells you about his plans for sitting.

To Thine Own Self Be True

In Hamlet, Polonius sends his son, Laertes, into the world with advice about dressing well ("for clothes oft proclaim the man"), keeping his opinion to himself, not trusting people immediately, and, in general, about how to be practical in his dealing with others. His counsel is a model of what this book sets out to accomplish, realistic practical guidelines for a reasonably moral life. In his closing words on this occasion, Polonius presents the essence of a strategy for surviving with integrity: "This above all: to thine own self be true. And it must follow, as the night the day, thou canst not then be false to any man."

Being true to yourself is not a search for one self, one intractable highly-integrated self. In our discussion of "What are people . . . Really," we saw that each person contains many "selves," some of which seem contradictory to one another. You will be many people many times; only you will know how the variety weaves together. Your essential identity is what you are in the process of trying to achieve. You might at times appear to be helping someone achieve his goals. If your real purpose is not an achievement of your own, you are being false to yourself and to the other person. Your own purposes must always be what drive you. This is what Polonius meant: When you lapse into altruism you are not being true to yourself, so no one should trust you for a moment.

Self-love, then, is part of it. Pride is another. But you'll want to feign humility at times, so add deception to the list. Often there's a furrowing of the brow when I mention deception. The look seems to say, "You can't really mean that." Well, think about manners. When you practice good manners in the company of someone you'd rather have nothing to do with, aren't you trying to deceive that person? Should we outlaw good manners in circumstances where they are deceptive?

A message of this book is that your self is not something you find; it is something you create.

Another characteristic that you should have is a spirit of impudence. Though it should never be shown, you should maintain a cocky boldness and be shameless. Lady Montague noted that "a moderate merit with a large share of impudence is more probable to be advanced than the greatest qualifications without it."

Also important for your "own self" is to be firm about avoiding the standard organizational ideas about who you should be. Avoid above all the "spirit of cooperation," which managers extol because of life would be easier for them if everyone had it. Your interests are not always the same as the interests of your managers. More than forty years ago, William H. Whyte spotted what he called "the organization man" emerging in America. One of the characteristics of this man, Whyte wrote, is a delusion of "the social ethic." He believes that by throwing himself into the social virtues of cooperation and abiding by what the majority of people say is right, he will achieve a moral and happy existence. More specifically he believes that his opportunity to realize "the social ethic" is to be found in his organization. But, Whyte warned:

> *This is delusory. It is easy to fight obvious tyranny; it is not easy to fight benevolence, and few things are more calculated to rob the individual of his defenses than the idea that his interests and those of [The Organization] can be wholly compatible. . . . The good organization encourages individual expression, and many have done so. But there always remains some conflict between the individual and The Organization. The Organization will look to its own interests, but it will look to the individual's only as The Organization interprets them.*

You will have to fake the "spirit of cooperation" at times. Consider the following case in which deception was used maturely and aptly:

> *When Lt. Commander Michael Stetstrom returned to duty at Norfolk Naval Base after three years on special assignment in the Pentagon, he found Total Quality Leadership (TQL) brochures on his desk, TQL sayings posted on the walls, and parking lot spaces marked "Customer." He was required to attend TQL classes where he learned that TQL is "a totally new approach to organizations, in which workers are empowered to realize quality in the workplace, with quality being determined by customers." According to the books and articles he was given as mandatory reading, TQL "will completely change the culture of the Navy."*
>
> *Michael was very favorably impressed. He really liked this type of management thinking. He told his wife that it was the best thing he had come upon in the Navy since his student days at Annapolis.*
>
> *It took about two weeks for him to find out that TQL was window dressing. Although the top brass swore allegiance to it and everyone talked about it as "the new way," in his day-to-day work Michael found that traditional Navy ways dominated procedures, decisions, and behavior.*
>
> *In three weeks more time, Michael was expected to give a presentation in the TQL class on how he planned to apply TQL in the section he commanded. Michael did so, even putting many off-duty hours into his preparation. He did not believe what he said, but he said it with the appearance of conviction.*

It was the organizational hypocrisy about TQL that necessitated Michael's gamesmanship. There was nothing he could do about the hypocrisy because hypocrisies are self-sustaining so long as someone benefits from them. He could protect himself and his values by lying, by knowing he is lying—rather than fooling himself with euphemistic language—and by understanding why he was lying. There are no non-hypocritical organizations in which Michael can seek employment. He must adjust to the real world, using deception, while keeping his self-defined, self-determined, self-valued integrity. Imagine how ridiculous Michael's life would be if at times like that he insisted on being thoroughly honest.

Sometimes when I use this example, I am asked if I don't see that Michael is playing up to his superiors. My answer is: Of course. In real organizations, as opposed to our ideal notions of them, one is subject to the capriciousness of one's superiors. Working within rather than against this reality can be quite consistent with self-valued integrity. While it is not heroic, it is sensible.

Self-valued integrity is not virtuousness, which is to be avoided. What we traditionally refer to as virtues become vanities when we want to be known as possessing them. There is nothing wrong with a little of this virtue and a little of that one here and there. Any virtue strictly applied without relief is a social disaster. Of Pamela Harriman it was once written, "she often said we should tell people not what they want to hear, but what they need to know. Her own talent for doing both served her extraordinarily well."

Like Ambassador Harriman, your strategy should be based on the understanding that you will need to tell both the truth and the untruth throughout your career, while always praising truth. You will also need to project various images according to the situation. There will be times when you should be self-promoting, others when you should be modest. We will be more specific about this in the chapter on tactics. What is important now is that you incorporate this awareness into your own sense of self. Your purpose is to be a successful person, whatever the organizational level at which you intend to succeed. You manipulate appearances because it is necessary in the real world. But do avoid appearing as did one of Charles Dickens' characters "with affection beaming in one eye, and calculation shining out of the other."

Self-Improvement

The first pillar of your strategy is to be good for yourself and to know what that means as opposed to being good for others. The second pillar is to constantly seek self improvement. The purpose of this book is not to substitute strategy and tactics for self-improvement in the traditional sense of continuing education and skills-development. Success in an organization requires that you work continuously at your education and skills resources, and that you are seen as a hard-working, dependable person.

Continually improving your information- and technology-based skills is a good idea, but give more attention to improving your communication skills. Most experienced persons are not surprised by the well-known Carnegie-Mellon University study of its graduates over a thirty-year period. The point was to find out what elements account for success. Over that long period the former students said that 85 percent of an individual's success comes from communication skills; the remaining 15 percent of success was thought to be information- and technology-based.

Those numbers are consistent with studies on characteristics of persons who are perceived to be winners in the power game. When asked to describe the personal characteristics of organizational members who are skillful "politicians," managers from the supervisory to CEO levels give the following ordering from most important to least important characteristic: articulate, sensitive, socially adept, competent, popular, extroverted, self-confident, aggressive, ambitious, devious, organization person, highly intelligent, logical.

Although intelligence and logic don't seem to count for much when it comes to becoming an influential person, remember that people like to think that they are acting logically. You must always provide them with at least an illusion of logic when convincing them of something. As we will see when we discuss rhetoric, people are convinced by how well they accept you as a person and how important you make the subject seem to them personally. That accomplished, a veneer of logic does nicely.

You are going to get a lot of advice in this book on the significance of appearances and manipulation of situations. There are some things, however, that you cannot control with an appearance or an ability to manipulate a situation. Your basic education is one of those things. You must follow traditional ideas in that regard. While there are examples of persons who get away with falsely representing their qualifications, it is far too risky to be recommended.

Don't be misled by barroom wisdom about how a truly creative person can do anything despite his education. Bill Gates is sometimes held up as an example of how successful a college dropout can be. Well, yes, Bill Gates dropped out of Harvard after two years there. But you don't get into Harvard unless you're very well educated to begin with, and also very bright. Gates went back for some more course work at Harvard, and he hired as his second-in-command a Harvard graduate who also holds an MBA from Stanford.

While we're in the computer world, you should ignore those schools that promise you life with the rich and famous after a 12-month "education" in computer skills. Graduates of such schools usually become glorified file clerks. Unfortunately you also have to hold down your expectations from legitimate computer-skill training. While there is no doubt that any computer skills you pick up are going to be helpful, don't count on making a good living at the computer. Companies are farming out that kind of work to places like India and China, where programming and software analysis comes at a low labor cost. Think of it this way: If a job can be done in Calcutta, don't position yourself to have that kind of job, unless you like to travel and intend to make your fortune writing a book on how to live in Calcutta on $3.75 a day.

Another thing difficult to fake is your taste in hobbies and use of spare time. When you are asked in an interview "What do you do in your spare time?" or "What are your hobbies?" it is usually too late to become the person you would like to project at that moment. So why not think about how you would like to be able to answer those questions in advance, and prepare yourself accordingly.

In doing this, as in doing everything else regarding strategy, think long term. What "spare time usage" is both impressive and to your liking? The answer to that question often involves preparation, even training and education. You can't have "playing with a string quartet" as your hobby without serious previous investment of your time. Not everyone has the talent to play a stringed instrument, but there is no excuse for anyone having to list "reading and listening to music" as hobbies on her résumé.

Try to be really good at one thing, no matter what it is or how it fits into your life in general. This will tell you a lot about yourself and will give you confidence. You may want to concentrate on an aspect of your job, or a hobby, or something else. It doesn't matter what it is. We looked at the halo effect in chapter one. Now I'm saying: Get a halo. "One shining quality," says William Hazlitt, "lends a luster to another, or hides some glaring defect."

At any time in your life you will always have both strengths and weaknesses, no matter how hard you work at self improvement. Think of them as being the same insofar as career development is concerned. Strengths are weaknesses; weaknesses are strengths. Strengths account for as many failings as do weaknesses. Weaknesses account for as many successes as do strengths. If you have any doubt about this, read biographies of persons who have achieved greatness in government, business, religion, and the theater. Successful people do not overcome their weaknesses, they take advantage of them. And they are always concerned about the problems into which their strengths can lead them. Elizabeth Taylor could not maintain a marriage, so she built multi-romances into her highly successful persona. Napoleon's strength led him to defeat at Waterloo.

The Essentiality of Plan B

In a book you should read, *What Color Is Your Parachute?*, Richard Bolles says that you should never, ever put all your eggs in one career basket, the secret of surviving out there in the jungle, he says, *is having alternatives*.

Being All Things to All Men

To be at peace with an organization, one must learn how to carry on polite and even friendly discussions with people holding different views on what is going on and what it means. For example, when the people at the top send out an announcement of a new master plan, there are different ways that the announcement is judged depending on who is doing the judging. It can be seen as:

- A way to set objectives and rational steps to the objectives, or
- A way to elicit participation by the members of the organization, or
- A realignment of power.

The new master plan will be judged by the organization's members in terms of one of these three ways of seeing it. You need to converse pleasantly with fellow workers who might hold to any one of these three views. The best way to do this convincingly is to understand that there is no single truth when it comes to the meaning of organizational actions. The new master plan probably does mean all three of the interpretations listed above, and perhaps more.

Phrases like "I see your point" are enormously useful for doing this. But of greater help is your ability to mean it. None of these three views is nonsense. Each is reasonable and perceptive. But the people who hold to them can get ideologically fervent about their one of the three views, rejecting the other two as dangerous competitors.

Clothing

There are no general guidelines for clothing better than Shakespeare's lines:

> *Costly thy habit as thy purse can buy,*
> *But not expressed in fancy; rich not gaudy,*
> *For the apparel oft proclaims the man.*

Specifically, clothing should be:

- of first quality
- made from natural fibers
- along classic lines
- simple, understated, never "trendy"
- of one color or narrow stripe

More specifically, for women:

- blouses should be tailored
- wear suede or nubuck, never shiny leather
- have one quality leather bag, not five cheap ones
- never go into plastic for anything
- plain, sheer hose, no patterns
- jewelry for accent only, no bangles or beads
- closed, low-heeled pumps, well brushed or polished; no flats or extreme styles
- fresh, clean hair in style that requires minimum of grooming on job; long hair best worn up or back
- nails should be conservative
- make-up and perfume applied lightly

More specifically for men:

* small unobtrusive cuff links if needed
* conservative shoes, polished
* long socks
* no extreme style haricut
* careful attention to nails
* light or no aftershave lotion or cologne

Clothing should always fit well, and be forgotten once put on; wear it easily and never self consciously. Although you will buy first quality, only the clothing-wise eye will know that you are wearing, say, Ann Taylor or Brooks Brothers. For that person you will have left a very good impression. Most people are not clothing-wise; to them you'll make a good impression without them knowing why. As Anthony Trollope said, "the one who is best dressed is the one whose dress no one observes."

Quality clothing and accessories can often be found at reasonable prices. Find outlet malls that deal in quality goods such as Brooks Brothers, Talbots, Jones N.Y., Coach, J. Crew, Joseph Banks, etc. Watch for sales at department stores that deal in these types of goods.

The person you put into the clothing should be reasonably trim and athletic appearing. Find an exercise routine that you can stick with and follow it. To get two birds with one stone, combine your exercise time with what will be discussed below as your "strategic relationship time." Strategic relationships are those that you develop with persons in the organization who can be helpful to you in the future.

My final words on the importance of clothing are from Adlai Stevenson: *It's hard to lead a cavalry charge if you look funny on a horse.*

—Eleven—

Strategy: Ethics, Decorum, Rhetoric, and Getting Along

When we looked at what organizations really are, we saw that "ethics" has become a buzzword. Companies and government agencies are pretending to be (all of a sudden) highly concerned with ethics. Codes and regulations are being promulgated, consultants are being hired, and all but the angels arre being summoned to counsel on this grave matter. All the evidence, however, suggests that sleaze, corruption, and theft remain alive and well.

For the organization, you will provide the appropriate pretenses; for yourself you should know that ethical dilemmas are not choices between right and wrong, but rather between right and right.

You will be confronted almost daily with a need to select one desirable thing over another. You will also be the object of such difficult choices. There are many opportunities for you to lose in the decision not because the person making the decision feels negatively about you, but because you are viewed as the lesser of two "right" decisions. It gets tough when the outcome hurts someone. In a book titled *Defining Moments: When Managers Must Choose Between Right and Right*, a Harvard Business School professor presents this ethical problem as a dilemma confronting Peter Adario, a fictional marketing manager at a computer retailing firm that is losing money.

Most of Peter's sales force are single people who work long hours and weekends. The exception is Kathryn McNeil, 37, a single mother of a six-year-old son. Kathryn puts in only 60 hours a week because she must spend time with her son. She receives no financial help from her ex-husband.

The other workers resent Kathryn's special status. When her work falls slightly behind schedule, her supervisor, Lisa Walters, a 29-year-old rising star in the company, demands that Peter fire Kathryn.

Adario has an ethical problem. The company has espoused a "family friendly" culture. He himself has two children, so he understands the demands of children. Besides, Kathryn does very satisfactory work during the time she works. But there is the question of fairness to the others. And there is a question of survival for Peter. If he fails to deal with Kathryn in a way that is acceptable to Lisa, he could be fired. What should Peter do? The answer lies in the strategy he has developed for himself. There is nothing particularly honorable or dishonorable in firing or not firing Kathryn. Either choice has something to say for itself. People shred their souls in predicaments like this one. If Peter is clear and honest with himself about who he is and what he is about, the choice involves some pain, but is not traumatic.

Now, imagine that you are Kathryn. If you have not thought clearly about your situation prior to Lisa's demand that you be fired, you have done yourself a disservice. No matter how much encouragement Peter had given you for your approach to work and family, you would have seen trouble written on the wall the moment you noticed that everyone else was putting much more into the company than you were. You would not have been so naive as to believe that the others accepted your lower effort because of your family obligations, no matter what anyone said. You own ethical choice cannot become another person's obligation.

If you believed strongly enough in your ethical choice you would develop tactics for survival. Ethical choices do not settle anything really; they open up the need to defend them. We discus tactics in the next part of this book. For now, we just need to establish that ethics can require us to use tactics to protect the decisions we have made.

When Peter decides the decision he will make, he'll need to follow tactics to make it work. Some one is going to lose in this situation. Very few people accept losing graciously. The loser must be dealt with in realistic power terms. Explanations—even ones based on ethics—will not be persuasive.

For these reasons, you must incorporate in your strategy the understanding that ethics require tactics involving power, whether you are the person making the choice or the person affected.

Organizations as Theaters

As you pass through the entrance doors of your organization, think of where you are as a theater; that is, a building for dramatic performances. Each place you enter after that—an office, a meeting room, a lab, whatever—is a scene for a play. The people are actors playing roles assigned by the organization. They dress and speak to the part they play. For example, if you play the part of chief executive officer you will wear "suit-and-tie." If you play the part of mailroom supervisor, you will wear a tie, probably loosened at the neck, and no jacket. How you dress almost never has anything to do with doing the job. It is an accepted theater costume.

No one has ever been able to provide a rational explanation for why costuming varies within an organization. Explanations for this usually boil down to "it's expected." Which is a theatrical explanation; i.e., the audience expects certain clothing for certain roles. To wear the wrong clothing would give the wrong impression, which is to be avoided because the audience might question the entire presentation if the wrong impression is given.

The following conversation took place between a young attorney and a senior partner:

SENIOR PARTNER: *Dave, you're really doing well for us. I only wish I could convince you to be a suit and tie guy.*

YOUNG ATTORNEY: *I dress up when I'm going to court because the judge just might think I'm being disrespectful and take it out on my client. I also dress up when I have an appointment with a client. What difference can it make how I dress when I'm just working here in the office? I like casual clothes.*

SENIOR PARTNER: *I like to think that by dressing well here in the office, we tell one another that we take this work seriously. And what if a client just walked in without an appointment and wanted to see you. What kind of an impression would he get?*

It probably is true that some clients would lose confidence in an attorney who wore casual clothing in the office. The point remains that we are dealing with theater, not with rational functioning. Appearance cannot rationally reveal the capacity of the young attorney to serve a client, just as it cannot rationally tell the senior partner how seriously the young attorney takes his work. Only a theatrical explanation makes sense of what would, without the theatrical explanation, be nonsense.

After we dress for the part, we fit ourselves to the role by adopting manners and points of view that legitimize our playing it. People at the top talk about "this organization" or "this institution." Down in the lower ranks people talk about job security and living wages.

How seriously do people take themselves in the organizational roles they play? It varies. One person is fully taken in by her own act. Another person "sort of" believes her act. Another sees the act entirely as such and performs for the rewards only. Your strategy is to always go on the assumption that the person with whom you are dealing is fully taken in by her own act.

Remember also that the function of theater is to give coherence and meaning to what is going on. Following the script is crucial. It is acceptable to make jokes about the company's efficiency standards on the golf course, but not in the board room. When you're in a classroom, you can tell a professor that your organization's methods of evaluating worker performance are fatuous; but when you're in an official meeting, you are only allowed to critique the peripheries of that method.

One of the ways that organizations keep you at a disadvantage is by having control over the scripts. Almost always you are called to perform on a stage set by management. For example, the person who evaluates you might make jokes about the organization's evaluation system all year long, until it comes time to do evaluations. Because everyone pretends to take evaluation seriously, you must play along. Organizations need this pretense in order to be viewed as serious, judicious, and well managed.

Sometimes our devotion to the theater's decorum is absurd. In *Godfather II*, Michael Corleone, who has killed and ordered killings of hundreds of persons, expresses outrage over an attack on his family's living quarters in his compound. "Right in my bedroom! Where I read to my children!" That was violation of theatrical integrity. To sustain the Corleone sense of meaning and coherence in life, there has to be a separation of the family's stage from the others. In *The Godfather*, one of the Corleone sons shouts angrily to a son-in-law at the dinner table "We *never* talk business at the table!"

In our seats at the movies, we spot the incongruity. Barbarians are pretending to have civil norms of conduct. In our ongoing day to day activities, we are more likely to miss the absurdity. After Mike Tyson bit off a piece of his opponent's ear and spit it out on the ring, the world was aghast. Even though professional boxing has become a metaphor for sleaze, and the purpose of a fighter is to beat upon the body of his opponent, inflicting as much pain as he can, Tyson's action was in violation of that theater's decorum. For days newspapers and TV news programs overflowed with deprecatory sentences on the incident. The death of a fighter in the ring would not have received as much attention.

Heidi Gray tells us about the day she discovered theater in her organization and the implications of it for her:

> *During my first year with Cleveland Paint sales headquarters, things were really going very badly for the company. Sales were down, pay raises were non-existent, morale was low, good people were leaving. The company president announced that radical changes would be made, and that he wanted the participation of every worker in discussions on those changes. A series of meetings were scheduled within each of the company divisions.*
>
> *People in my division thought the meetings were a good idea. The company had made some blunders, as we saw things; the biggest of which was to put a big effort into a new product line that was overpriced for our traditional market.*
>
> *Our divisional meeting was impressive. The room where we met was a lot cleaner than it normally was. There was stereo music—also something new for that room. A platform had been set up for the President and our division head to stand on and talk from.*
>
> *The division head opened the meeting with an announcement that the president and he were about to share the playbook for the company's future with us. So we should not take any notes. And, of course, we were not to talk about it outside of this room.*
>
> *Then the president spoke. He talked about the challenges ahead for all of us, the need for teamwork and the rewards of success. He used the word 'we' a lot. He used slides to show pages from the playbook, which were presented in colorful tables, charts and diagrams, with bullet statements. The statements were not easy to understand, though they all had a ring to them. I'll never forget one of them: 'Business unit isolation has sub-optimized the power of our collective offering.'*

During the question-and-discussion period after the president's presentation, no one mentioned the new product blunder. All of the questions and comments were on small points, like when would the parking lot be enlarged. Someone did ask when there would be pay raises, but no one pushed the point when the president said "as soon as we get this company back on its feet."

That night I had drinks with someone who had been at the meeting. By the time we were on our second round, we had figured out how cleverly we had been seduced. 'It was all theater,' she said. 'Yes,' I replied, 'and look how we were sucked in by the words teamwork and playbook. Teams do what coaches tell them to do. Playbooks are there to be followed, not questioned.'

'But didn't it make you feel important,' she said sarcastically, 'to be let in on the top floor's top secrets.'

'Seriously,' I said, 'it really was brilliant. I wish those people were as good at running a paint business as they are at theater. None of us could attack their playbook without looking like a nay-saying person who's not a team player. We were assigned roles for that stage and that scene, and we had to stay in role.'

In the following days, I thought more about that meeting and began to see that it was not just that one instance in which I was being given a role in a scene. Everything was theater. Everything we did in the company was a scene with scripted parts for all of us to play.

At first I resented that. I developed a new appreciation for people who refuse to play by the scripts, though I knew I didn't have the courage to be a rebel. I still respect some rebellion, but I now feel that Shakespeare, or whoever it was, had it right when he said that the whole world's a stage. Everything is theater.

Perhaps no organization is as theatrically inclined as the military. Concern about appearances can dominate even at the expense of essentials like maintenance of equipment and munitions. Air Force Captain Cynthia Drummer tells us something about that:

> *I learned that how we look when VIP audiences are around is more important than what we do. For example, the 1ˢᵗ Fighter Wing has a munitions storage area five miles from the Wing's main area. It's tucked away in a woodsy place that no one ever sees, other than the people who work there. Certainly the people who maintain buildings and roads never see it. The walls and ceiling of the main storage building leak so bad when it rains that all available manpower is used to cover up and mop. Potholes in the roads are so big that only one road remains where it's safe to transport anything that could explode. And that road is going fast. There's no way that we could move stuff anywhere near as fast as our readiness plan says we can move it.*
>
> *Last year the Wing Commander said that one of his top priorities was to do something about the miserable condition of this storage area. To show us how serious he was, he set aside funds in his budget to do it. In the end those funds were diverted to dress up a road at the main area, which was in perfectly good shape for normal use. But it is the route used by distinguished visitors.*

Recognition of organization as theater is obvious in the famed Harvard Business School Case Method approach, and can be seen in various management tactics. Many companies and government agencies use training situations based on role playing to help employees learn to deal with stress, sexual harassment, and discipline. Tom Garrison, President of Brown, Moore and Flint, a Dallas-based food broker, takes advantage of his understanding of people playing roles in his recruitment strategies. He told *Ink Magazine* that he insists on a home visit as part of the overall selection process. "Coming at the end of the process, this meeting with the candidate's spouse isn't so much an interview as another window into the applicant's soul. I don't care what the house looks like, I just want to know that the husband or wife is supportive in this move." Bringing the spouse to the company offices can also be done but with much less effectiveness because spouses will more likely play their home role at home. And it is their home role that concerns Garrison.

Goals, Endings, and other Paradoxes

Every spring high school and college graduates and newly-married couples become aware of the meaning in one of Gertrude Stein's popular sayings: *When you get there, there isn't any there, there.*

We are counseled throughout our youth, and beyond for those who read self-help literature, to have goals. Wisely, we do so. But we learn that achieved goals are less satisfying than we hoped, and that there are no ends to things, only stepping stones. This is frustrating and confusing.

David Campbell, a vocational guidance psychologist, says that the media, *have misled us into thinking that the world is full of endings. The movie ends, the television show ends, the novel ends, the play ends. That is not the way the world is. In life there are no endings. . . . In the movie . . . the honeymooners may walk hand-in-hand down the lane to a climactic fade-out; but in real life, the honeymooners will awaken to an average day that may start with the scratchy realization that here they are in this expensive resort with no toothbrushes. . . .*

While you should have goals, you should also understand the following:

- There's an old saying about not wishing too hard for something because you might get it. Usually we do not think about the implications of our aspirations. So, we lament that we didn't realize that getting this position would mean that we'd have to work harder every day than we did when we were trying to get it. There's another old saying worth keeping in mind, "It's easier to appear worthy of a position one does not hold, than of the position one does hold."

- It is almost impossible to achieve anything in an organization without offending one or more persons. The day after your achievement, you may still be working with those persons. Think carefully about who loses, how people take losses, and how they can work against you in the future.

Decision-Making Is a Process

Organizations pretend to make decisions according to substantive rationality; in reality they follow procedural rationality. Substantive rationality takes all possibilities into account; this is impossible for almost all decisions because it requires exhaustive searches for alternative ways of doing something. There is hardly ever time for that in organizations.

Herbert Simon, a brilliant theorist in the field of organizational decision making, has coined a term, *satisficing*, to label what organizations really do: They adapt their searches to the amount of time available, and they set up procedures, or a process, for those searches. Setting up the process is a major battleground because it will both determine the outcome and be the justification for the outcome. Since everyone knows that this process will only be the representative of rationality, not rationality itself, there is a need to make sure everyone can live with it.

Did you ever notice what happens when someone in an organization is challenged about the outcome of a decision he, or his unit, made? He will usually recite the procedures and process that were established to make the decision, and stress how that process was followed. The defense usually rests on the argument that the procedures were followed, and the process completed.

Your goal is to learn in general the types of decision processes used in your organization so that you can, when you choose, manipulate decision processes in your favor. We will get into specifics on this when we deal with tactics. For now, understand that a process can be manipulated at any of three stages: the agenda for decision making, the identification of alternatives to be studied, and the criteria that will be applied for choosing among the alternatives.

Rhetoric

Rhetoric is the art of using language effectively and persuasively. In classical times it was a major component of philosophy, equal in importance to ethics and logic. The word is used pejoratively today, so you'll want to learn the tricks without telling anyone you're working on your rhetoric.

There are three parts to rhetoric: logos, ethos, pathos. If you want to be effective and persuasive, your language must have all three. Logos refers to logic, or just good sense. Does what you say make sense? Ethos refers to you as a speaker (or writer, of course). Are you seemingly trustworthy and are you the type of person to whom people want to respond positively? Pathos refers to significance. Does what you are arguing for, or proposing, have merit; does it matter?

When you want to be effective with people, you must remember that they are not computers. People cannot be moved by what you say or write if all you have is a very logical presentation. Organizations pretend to be logically driven. As we saw in chapter one, there is a host of organizational illusions about logic in decisions involving hiring, promotions, communications, planning, and so on. But ethos and pathos are ultimately more persuasive than logos.

Rhetorical skills can be learned in a college course on rhetoric, or one on persuasive speaking and persuasive writing, but for the most part only the logos skill is nurtured in college courses. Until you can get some books on rhetoric out of the library, here are some clues:

- Make first contact with pathos, not logos.
- Remember that pathos works when you address something that concerns the listener personally.
- Eye contact, but no staring. Be relaxed.
- Speak in quiet confident tones, not strident ones.
- Once you have pathos going for you, use logos but don't be too concerned and certainly don't be too detailed. People tend to accept emotionally and rationalize later with facts and arguments. Keep in mind the studies, mentioned above, showing that managers regard logic as a minor characteristic of persons they perceive to be good "politicians" in their organization.
- Ethos is developed over time. Work on it in your daily dealings with people.

You probably noticed that rhetoric is not about speaking grandly or perfectly. No need for you to work on British nobility speech patterns. But you do want to continually work at improving your voice quality and use of phrasing. Sing a lot. Singing develops natural and pleasing resonance and variation in your voice. Don't worry if you have a lousy singing voice. You'll still improve your speaking voice every time you squeak out a tune.

Susan Shulman, a communications consultant, advises her clients to practice each day: *I tell them to play back every voice mail they leave. It is a wonderful way to analyze your voice quality and use of phrasing. They have the opportunity to hear how they sound. They can determine how they project over the phone, how expressive they are, and the emotional impact of their message. They also get immediate feedback on how well they articulate.*

Getting Along

Your ability to get along is crucial. Rosabeth Moss Kanter, a fairly dependable advice giver, says that getting along is one of the biggest and most difficult challenges to people in the middle of organizations. Gaining access to resources—equipment, supplies, capital, support, etc.—requires a capacity to influence others because these resources are never fully accessible by formal position or authority alone.

Others are in need of the same resources. You must avoid appearing that you are competing for them. Don't try to take credit for winning if you do. Do what you can to be helpful to those with whom you competing.

It is always easier to get along with people if you like them. In the chapter, "What Are People . . . Really," I attempted to present realities so that you would interact with people as they are rather than as they would wish you to believe they are. I also tried to encourage you to like people as they are.

Knowing Social Reality

Professor John Kotter tells his students at Harvard Business School that knowing who's who and their personal, as well as their stated agendas, is the most important knowledge you can have in the workplace. Knowledge is power, but the type of knowledge that is the most powerful is not the kind one finds in books or in educational programs. The most powerful knowledge "is detailed information about the social reality in which your job is imbedded." This means "knowing the different perspectives of all the relevant groups: what they want, how they look at the world, and what their real interests are. It means knowing where the various perspectives are in conflict—where important differences lie. It means knowing what sources of power each group has to pursue its own interests, and to what extent they are willing to use that power."

As you rise in your organizational hierarchy, you will become increasingly in need of sufficient political clout to implement programs and advance ideas. Whose cooperation is necessary and under what conditions might they cooperate, or how do you neutralize them if their cooperation is highly unlikely? To answer these questions, you need information about the social reality.

Never assume that a person or a work group will cooperate because they are charged or assigned to cooperate. Persons and groups can just as easily find legitimate reasons or excuses to not cooperate with you as they can find reasons to cooperate with you. Usually they will pretend to be cooperating with you even when they are not, and it can be very difficult to prove that they are not doing what they are pretending to do. So don't depend on official policies, organization charts, or even higher-level mandates for cooperation. You must win the cooperation through astute manipulations. But you can't be a manipulator until you know what people want and what power they possess and how that power interrelates with the power of others in the organization.

Social reality consists of perceptions and myths. Something does not have to be literally true to be socially real. For some time many female recruits believed their Army drill sergeants had the power to rape them because the recruits perceived that to be the reality. No matter how much anyone tried to convince those recruits that the drill sergeants did not have that power, it took a major scandal and a massive education program to change the perceptions, if they have indeed been changed.

Your Subordinates

Don't forget your subordinates; they're a very important part of your social reality. They can make your life miserable if you proceed on the assumption that you are the authority figure in their midst, that you are the boss, and that is that. Chester Barnard, who is probably the most insightful organizational theorist American produced, said that authority is the willingness of your subordinates to obey your commands or requests. No one can sabotage you worse than your subordinates. What you need to know about them, if you want to control them, is:

- Who is well-liked by the others?
- Whose skills are the most respected? Whose skills are most crucial to completion of the unit's assigned work? What are the interdependencies of work—i.e., how is one person's work interconnected with others' work?
- Who are the opinion leaders?
- Who is well-connected to influential persons outside of your work unit?
- What are the complaints common to all of the subordinates?
- What is the major weakness of the unit's performance in the eyes of the subordinates?
- What is the major weakness of the unit's performance according to your boss and to others in the organization?

You will want to read the disingenuous management wizardry books so that you can master the language; never try any of that stuff with your subordinates, unless you are eager to lose their respect and gain their disgust. If your superior puts you in a spot where you must pretend to use it, be cunning enough to fool him without tormenting your subordinates.

Common Errors in Relating to Subordinates

A few years ago I studied a wide variety of written evaluations in which the subordinates wrote down their opinions of their bosses' direction during the first two months of work. More specifically, the workers were asked to state what was least effective or most lacking.

The two most frequently criticized managerial practices were "the laundry list" and the "sink or swim" approaches. In the former, the boss rattles off a wide range of his unit's responsibilities without indicating the subordinate's responsibilities, let alone what the priorities are. In the "sink or swim" approach, the boss says something like, "We'll give you some things to do and see how you do 'em."

Never Abuse Subordinates

There's a world-class living museum of American colonial history that ran into financial difficulties around the turn of the twenty-first century. The Board of Directors made the common mistake of defining the problem as fiscal and the solution as a combination of efficiencies and new money-making ideas. As part of the efficiency-drive, Edwin, already employed by the museum as an accountant, was assigned, in addition to his job as an accountant, to be director of the education division, which employed a group of highly-educated and dedicated people.

At his first meeting with the education division, Edwin told the group in somber terms that the days of wine and roses was over. "Time to roll up our sleeves and achieve," he said. "Every one of you will do two tours a day. That's the norm, and I know we've been lax about it. But these are new times."

Though the division's people had not been adhering to a two-tours-a-day routine, many of them actually did do that three or four days a week. The reasons why they had not adhered to the twice-a-day schedule were: Twice-a-day is a blackboard trick. Each trip takes three hours. Two times three equals six hours, a reasonable work day. But each trip is its own bundle of surrealism. Sometimes children get sick or lost. Sometimes an adult must find a toilet and be waited for. Sometimes a group of children rush off to the field where sheep graze.

It was bad enough as it was—Edwin's intent to conquer uncertainty with chalk and straight lines—but as it can be with people like Edwin, he deserted sanity to recover his lost control.

At another meeting with the education division, Edwin announced, not at all hesitantly, his "On Time" rules. "As everyone should know," he said, "sign-in time is eight-thirty. But if everyone shows up at eight-thirty, we can't get everyone signed in. Therefore, from today on anyone who shows up after eight-fifteen will be marked as late by me. I will be here at the entrance door with a stop-watch and pad, with all of your names on it. If I have you down three times as late, you are fired."

You can probably guess that many of the talented and dedicated people who worked under "Edwin's Rules" left that division. He's gone, too. Maybe on to better things. In the world of organizations, failure does not preclude success. That would happen in a rational world, perhaps, but by no means are organizations rational.

What's NOT in the Manual

You will probably be given a manual on personnel procedures. If you can read and understand it overnight, you've been given a bare-bones manual that does not cover many situations that will confront you. An adequate personnel manual is too long and complex for you to read and understand in a day, or week, or month, and yet you are expected to know it cover to cover. It includes relevant public law and company policies. The courts have ruled that managers cannot seek immunity from violation of public law protecting workers on the basis that they were unfamiliar with the law. Employers vary in the extent to which they hold their managers responsible for understanding the company's personnel policies. They also vary in how much they cover in their manuals.

George Fisher found out he was expected to handle physical fights among his subordinates in certain ways, though these ways were not printed in his company's personnel procedures manual. Two women on a line he ran who were usually friendly with one another started slugging it out one day. The only guidance in the manual for dealing with the situation instructed him to call the police, which he did, after separating the combatants.

The next day George's boss gave George a four-day suspension because he had not handled the fracas as the company expected it to be handled. George protested on the basis that there was nothing about company policy for such incidents other than the advice to call the police.

His boss pleasantly agreed that the company should have covered this matter in the manual, and in all fairness he would not have the four-day suspension placed in George's records; however, the suspension stood. Welcome to the world of organizational justice and mercy.

Footnote: I'll wager that the suspension was not entered into George's record because labor law requires the reasons for suspensions to be fully stated in the record, which would have given George the basis for a strong court case on the basis of unlawful use of the suspension powers.

George works for a fast-growing internet sales and distribution company. Such companies are expanding rapidly into new areas of service and production. Few of them are stopping to make sure their personnel policies cover these new areas. Managers like George should do what they can to keep themselves from being fall guys for bad business practices. Strategy, George, strategy.

Language

You have seen in previous chapters that managers do not really know what they are doing but must pretend that they do, that people in general are inconsistent and contradictory by nature, that many words, like "efficiency" and "evaluation" are symbols that can mean almost anything, and that organizations are playgrounds where "let's pretend" is the most popular game. It should, therefore, come as no surprise that the language used in organizations is often gobbledygook.

Consider the following chart put together by James R. Killingsworth. Almost any phrase can be combined with any other. What appear to be sensible statements are meaningless because they can mean almost anything depending on how you put the phrases together. Killingsworth and others argue that organizational policies are usually defended by making a self-serving compilation of whichever phraseology suits the defense of the policy. There's a name for this: *ORGSPEAK.*

Gentlemen . . . the realization of . . . leads us to . . . existing fiscal and . . . the program's . . . reexamine . . . administrative. . . goals . . . conditions.

Equally . . . the complexity . . . has played a vital . . .   areas of future . . . important . . . and diversity of . . . role in development. . . . the committee's . . . determining . . . areas of . . . concentration

At the same time, . . . the constant . . . directly affects the attitudes of . . . growth in the . . . the development . . .   key members . . . quality and . . . and advancement . . .   regarding their . . . scope of our . . . of . . . own work . . . activity

Still, let us not . . . the . . . requires the . . . a participatory   . . . forget that . . . infrastructure of . . . clarification and   system. . . . the organization . . . determination of

Thus, . . . the new shape . . . insures the . . . new proposals   . . of organizational . . . participation of . . . activity . . . key members in

A *Newsweek* poll in 1997 found ORGSPEAK alive and detested; the major complaint people have against their organization is the inability of their superiors to give them clear guidelines about what is expected. Almost 70% of the respondents said they were usually confused by communications from their superiors on what kind and level of work is expected. Interestingly, persons who were the objects of this criticism made the same criticism about their own superiors' communications.

ORGSPEAK obfuscates. A person obfuscates language with stilted terms for one of three reasons. He doesn't know any better. He wants to impress us. He's hiding something.

Your strategy is to learn how to ORGSPEAK, how to pretend that a conversation is going on while throwing these non-statements back and forth with another person. People who don't know any better or are trying to impress and you are the easiest to deal with; feed their insecure egos now and then. People who are hiding something are more important in your strategy. Always be on the search for what is being hidden.

Mentors

Mentors are important to you. They can provide you with invaluable help in your search for manipulative understanding of language, social reality, and "the right appearance." For you, there can be no more important person than the one who takes upon himself the commitment to steer you safely through the organization's backwaters.

There are never enough mentors to go around. You may have to work hard at finding one. "Finding one" means creating a situation in which the mentor voluntarily takes on that role. It has to be his idea. In a little while you'll be reading a section titled "Personal Relationships" which will provide suggestions on how to create this kind of situation.

Image-consultants like Susan Bixler and Lisa Scherrer provide their clients with specific areas in which to seek the advice of a mentor:

- Technical expertise
- Character, moral, and spiritual development
- Insight into how to get things done in your organization
- Understanding how things work and how to fix them
- Social finesse and grace
- Image and wardrobe improvement

Speaking skills
Community involvement
• Development of creativity in music, writing, culinary
  skills, or art
• Any business or personal talent you want to develop

Because glass ceilings remain in place, it is difficult for a
woman to find a female mentor. Only a small number of women
are climbing the ladder. Some observers argue that this—the
shortage of female mentors—is a major impediment to escape
from the pink collars. The laws and rhetoric for female advancement are in place. But the things that matter—the power structures—remain the same.

—Twelve—

Strategy: Avoidance of Entrapments

Let not a man guard his dignity, but let his dignity guard him.

—*Ralph Waldo Emerson*

The optimist proclaims that we live in the best of all possible worlds, and the pessimist fears this is true.

—*James Branch Cabell*

Like a chess master, you should prepare yourself to avoid walking into traps. Four major entrapments waiting for you in the workplace are the superficial values of thinking positively, being adjustable, preserving dignity, and being consistent. You must prepare yourself to value negative thinking, to adapt things to yourself rather than adjust yourself to things, and to understand that dignity is an opium and consistency a hobgoblin.

The Power of Negative Thinking

Long before Norman Vincent Peale got rich on it, Americans celebrated the power of positive thinking. And for good reason. Positive thinking influences one's self and others to believe in one's actions. On the other hand, negative thinking is not necessarily a drawback. Being honest with oneself about what is probably impossible can save a lot of time and energy and can avoid disaster.

Negative thinking is a problem if it compels you to wallow in it, or if you express it in the presence of an individual or group of individuals who are hostile to what they have termed "nay saying." You have to control and disguise your negative thinking so that it does not destroy you from within or draw anger from others. As we saw in the discussion on people, groups in particular, even more than individuals, can demand agreement of their members and ostracize a person who questions a group norm or intent. When we consider tactics, we will look at specifics about disguising negative thoughts; for now, what you need to incorporate in your strategy is the understanding that both positive and negative thinking have pros and cons for your success.

One of the major false messages of positive thinking in organizations is delivered in the myth of meritocracy, which holds that if a person is hardworking, intelligent, and cooperative, the organization will reward her with organizational success; if she does not succeed it is because she deserves to fail. As you have seen in the discussion on organizations and people, meritocracy is a delusion that is useful for maintaining authority in organizations, which explains its appeal; but you would be foolish to adopt it as one of your myths. Hard work, intelligence, and cooperation combined with realistic strategy and tactics will be rewarded. Those same qualities without strategy and tactics often go unrewarded.

And so it goes with the myths and hypocrisies that we have discussed. They serve the purposes of the organizations or the individuals with whom you work. Therefore, you will be encouraged, pressured to believe them. Or at least to not rock the boat by publicly questioning them. You have to learn to have and keep for yourself the power of negative thinking while not voicing your thoughts. The power of negative thinking lies in being able to turn hypocrisies, myths, self-deceptions, and conceits to your own advantage.

In her introduction of Lee Zhong Chang's *Thick Black Theory* to an English-speaking audience, Chin-Ning Chu offers the following relevant observations about negative thinking:

> *The idea that we need to change our negative attitudes to positive ones before we can succeed has been pounded into us. . . .*
>
> *If you do not consider yourself the most positive person you have ever known, don't worry. The secret is that most of the perky people lie about how positive they are . . . Those whose livelihood depends upon promoting the concept of positive thinking have been able to convince the rest of the world that if you are not absolutely positive about life at all times and under any circumstances, then you are an inferior being. . . .*
>
> *Success has no rules. Success comes in every shape and profile . . . [It] comes to some of the most negative people, as well as the most positive ones. Success comes to those who try hard and even to those who make no visible effort. What promoters of positive thinking theories fail to realize is that success does not discriminate.*

Concentrate on success, Chin-Ning Chu advises, not on becoming a positive person or any kind of person proposed by the social ethic or your organization.

Adaptation, Not Adjustment

Your strategy should not be to adjust to life in an organization; you should adapt it to yourself. Adjustment to organizational hypocrisies, for example, would involve no more than accepting them with the phrase "that's life," or "that's the real world." If you adjust yourself to phoniness, deceit, and greed, what of value can you become? If you adjust to lies, you'll probably soon find yourself believing them.

Adaptation to organizational hypocrisies involves manipulating them for your own success. Let the oyster be your role model. As the oyster takes the relative meaninglessness of what is given to it and creates a pearl, so do you want to take the sands of life and, without kidding yourself that this is anything other than sand, make some pearls for yourself.

It's all too easy to be seduced by praise for being adjustable. People will praise you for your adjustability because it is a convenience for them. But we all enjoy praise, so we fail to concentrate on the self-serving aspects of those who give it. As you select tactics for particular situations, you may want to give the appearance of readily adjusting, and receiving praise for it; but you must establish as your strategy to never be sucked in by such praise. Always know yourself and your own goals. Your art should be more opportunistic than altruistic.

Though adjustment and adaptation have some similar appearances, there is a world of difference in what they mean to you. When you adjust you balance your own needs with the needs of others. When you adapt, you satisfy your needs partly through a subterfuge of adjustment—that is, you appear to be adjusting—while you find tactics that enable you to turn the situation to your own advantage. In the study of successful men referred to in chapter two, the researcher found a common strategy followed by the most successful subjects in his study: they learned over time to mask their aggressiveness as competitiveness because the latter is praised, while the former is at best questionable behavior in our society. On the other hand, many of the subjects in the study who went from being aggressive youngsters to passive adults failed in their careers, marriages, and at parenthood.

Idealism is an extreme form of adjustability, in which we fall into a euphoria of believing everything is "swell." It has been said that: *The idealist is incorrigible; if he is thrown out of his heaven he makes an ideal of his hell.*

The Dignity Entrapment

Dignity in the workplace is like a masquerade ball where we know who the person behind the mask is, but pretend we don't to let him "save face." We resort to such mutually required charades because Americans cling to the myth that a man's work is a man's dignity, and we genuflect to that myth when we go on and on about "the work ethic."

There's a certain common sense involved in "the dignity thing." Most of us have to work to make money, so why not have some mythology about work being dignified. The Japanese go so far as to say that work is the most important thing a man does.

As with the other myths and symbols, you must pretend to honor dignity, while not being entrapped by it. It may be to your advantage to play along with someone who tells you: "I believe in providing my people with dignity at work." But always remember that it doesn't take any resources to provide "dignity." Like words, it's cheap. As for yourself, don't be sidetracked by it. If you have to play humble to get what you want, value what you want more than the charade of dignity. Don't be bought off from what you want.

Consistency Is Sometimes Foolish

Mahatma Gandhi was challenged once with the following question: *If, as you say, you follow non-violence as a matter of principle, would you follow it if your adversary were Hitler rather than the honorable British?*

There is a consistency that is wise, answered Gandhi, *and a consistency that is foolish. A man who, in order to be consistent, would go bare-bodied in the hot sun of India or the sunless mid-winter of Norway would be considered a fool and would lose his life in the bargain.*

Follow Gandhi's wisdom. You could do far worse. Beware the hoax that men of honor are men of consistency, or avoid seeking that kind of honor. You want to be committed to goals you have set for yourself, but that doesn't mean you have to always react the same way to what appear to be the same circumstances. The fact is that circumstances are never the same, and, as Winston Churchill said, *the only way a man can remain consistent amid changing circumstances is to change with them while preserving the same dominating purpose.*

Resist Collaboration, Cooperation and Trust . . . Unless

In addition to the seductions of positive thinking, adjustment, dignity, and consistency, organizations dangle collaboration, cooperation, and trust as admirable virtues. They are not necessarily bad for you; nor are they necessarily good for you.

Those books at the airport goad their readers to declare war on people who resist collaboration, cooperation, and trust. Such resistance should be overcome by the manager not only because it is anti-organization, but also because those resistors benefit when you help them repent their ways. People are happier when they are going along than when they are dragging their heels. Chapters on "How to Build Cooperation and Trust Despite Resistance!" are found in management manuals, with the exalting message that "the result is good for the organization and for all within it."

Discovering that what is good for the organization is good for all its employees is the most astounding achievement of this literature. It rivals a comment made by a president of General Motors: *What's good for General Motors is good for America!*

H.B. Karp, a workers' consultant, wonders if employees might lose something valuable as they lower their resistance to management proposals. He doubts that helping an individual overcome his resistance is always good for the individual. After all, says Karp, resistance is a personal asset:

Resistance Protects You from Being Hurt

It is your resistance that stops you from rushing head-long into actions or projects that have a potential for causing you harm.

Resistance Guards Your Effectiveness

Honoring your resistance not to take on a task or an objective that clearly exceeds the limits of your competence is every bit as essential to your effectiveness and success as is being willing to take on those challenges and responsibilities that stretch your limits.

Resistance Heightens Your Awareness of Who You Are

Resistance contributes to your development by heightening your awareness of your personal boundaries.

Resistance Keeps You from Being Overstimulated

Resisting others' information or viewpoints can be as effective as listening to them. For example, it is very important to listen to why something won't work before you make a final decision. Once you have made your decision, however, listening to one more round of why it won't work is not only a bore but also an energy drain.

Cooperate When It Is to Your Advantage and on Your Terms

The success of your tactics will largely depend on how skillfully you manage your willingness to cooperate. You will get nowhere in an organization without the cooperation of other people. At the beginning of chapter one you were told "You are absolutely, positively on your own." The message now is: You get nowhere on your own, you must learn when and where and on what terms to cooperate with others. Don't trust anyone else to decide when and how you should cooperate.

Cooperation is an exchange between you and another person from which each of you subjectively believes you are gaining something. It is not an economic exchange, although there can be elements of an economic exchange in it. It is a psychological exchange. Much of what you gain in your organization will be based on such exchanges. Your strategy, while based on an understanding of this phenomenon, is also based on your intention to be tactful about what you get from the exchanges.

Exchanges sometimes provide concrete gains to one party and what we will call "vanity and feelings" gains to the other. You want to maximize being on the concrete side of the gains. Let others accumulate "vanity and feelings" gains. If Betty asks Ann to help her do her job, and it is not in Ann's "job description" to give Betty that help, Betty is asking for something concrete. If Ann responds positively, her gain could be increased prestige, or good feelings about helping, or avoidance of bad feelings that could result from not helping.

In general you want to be on the concrete side of exchanges. Obviously no one can or should entirely resist the seductions of vanity and feelings. But be forewarned that when you accept that kind of payoff in an exchange, you have communicated that to the other person. People are eager to see exchanges completed (both parties rewarded) because they do not want to feel in debt. Beware falling into the trap of allowing the other person to feel an exchange is completed when it is not in your interest to do so.

Others may also misunderstand you and think that not only is the exchange completed, but your satisfaction is so great that you owe them a little. Sometimes we fall into this trap when we try to graciously honor another's request. I have made many mistakes in this regard, as I did at a "company-type" party many years ago.

Fred Lenczowski, the dean of a school where I was a faculty member, asked me to participate in party games at a Saturday picnic. *We need more people for your department team*, he said. *I know you don't like that kind of thing, but we're desperate.* I agreed and tried to make it look interesting as I ran around that

Saturday morning playing silly games. I figured that since I was there, I should help the others enjoy themselves.

A few days later at lunch with Fred and some others, I learned that I had made a serious mistake. Fred said: *The picnic was a great success. Even Jim had a wonderful time. He thought he hated picnic games, but he learned how much fun they can be.*

Fred saw the exchange as completed. He didn't owe me anything for responding to his "we're desperate" plea. Indeed, I suspected that Fred thought I now owed him something for learning at his prompting how much I enjoy company picnic games.

This entrapment—"look what a good time you're having doing what I asked"—is very common in organizations. Managers stuffed with human relations lore want you to be happy because, they are told at their weekend personal development seminars, that "good managers make work enjoyable for their subordinates."

Norms of Exchange

You need to learn the norms of exchange in your organization. Norms of exchange are expectations of responses for favors done. Social psychologist Roger Brown tells a story about tipping.

> *At Christmas time in 1982, I had a chance to talk (in a hospital waiting room) with a gentleman whose occupation was doorman at an expensive Park Avenue apartment house, and his Christmas tips were on his mind. . . . He had a very definite idea about what constituted a fair tip. To each tenant he gave the same benefits and from each tenant he expected an equivalent benefit, not objectively defined, but subjectively. He expected a tip proportionate to tenant income—as roughly assessed by him from apartment occupied, automobile owned, and so*

forth—with a kind of corollary that five dollars was the smallest amount acceptable.

You want to work the norms of exchange so that when you respond to a favor done, you do so both appropriately (not too much, not too little, as dictated by organizational norms) and in a way that facilitates the relationship you want with that particular person in the future. We will deal more with this in the chapter on tactics.

Tit For Tat

At any particular time on any day you may be in situations that are unanalyzed in terms of strategic relationships. You come in contact with someone whose relationship to your strategy for success is unknown. Or, someone whose relationship to you is strategically known, but that person does something that is not understandable in terms of what you have developed so far in your analysis of yourself in the organization. So, what do you do then?

Game theorists who deal with this kind of situation advise you to play Tit For Tat, respond in kind. According to their research, which involves analyzing historical situations and literally playing the games, making Tit For Tat your game will enable you to win more times than with any other game, no matter what game is being played by the other person. We are dealing here with odds, not with a prediction on a single instance.

Sandra Dunn is trying to get a printer along with her usual load of pocketbook and briefcase onto an elevator at work. Ginger Blake—who works on another floor—not only helps her getting on and off the elevator, but also offers to carry the printer to Sandra's office. Sandra accepts the offer because she figures the odds are that even if Ginger is doing this to establish a relationship upon which to build something else, what Ginger wants to build will be compatible with her own interests.

Sandra made the right choice. Often people do favors because it makes them feel good to do so, and even if they have ulterior motives (or develop them after the fact), Ginger was right to assume that those motives would be compatible with, perhaps even enhancing to, her own interests. Some of our best networking results from others making the first contact with us.

Power Exchanges

It is said that power is like love, you have to give it to get it. Political scientists advise us to use power like entrepreneurs use capital: Invest, take risks, in order to grow. John P. Kotter illustrates this for his Harvard Business School students by telling them about Mark Schechtman:

> *During a three-year period Mark increased his power considerably by first seeking and obtaining a transfer into an area that he knew was critical to the company's five-year growth plans. He was put in charge of a construction project, where he used all the power he had to finish the project one day ahead of schedule. This cost him a significant investment of power, but led directly to a large increase in his professional reputation, the development of a strong mentor relationship with a vice president, and a promotion in the same area. He gained more formal authority, more responsibilities, more tangible assets, and the control of some new information channels.*

Note that Mark took a risk, but went into an area already designated by his company as critical to its growth plans. Ghandi said that *a leader is a person who understands where people are going and stands in front of them.*

Personal Power Knowledge

Most of us are unaware of our power. As we discussed in chapter three, power usually originates in activities, not in individuals. So, what kinds of power are there in your activities, and all the activities around you. For example:

- Who looks good or bad if you do your work well or poorly?
- What happens to whom if you do not do some basic task?
- On whom is your work dependent?
- Who controls the resources (manpower, equipment, etc.) necessary for work to be done?
- Who is in charge of scheduling things? How critical are schedules?

These relationships change, of course, and you should be in a position to know how they do and how you can influence the changes. If you are thinking of applying for another position in your organization, you should do so only after carefully analyzing how these power relationships would change for you if you did.

A seasoned warrior in organizational conflicts gives us a good example of knowing your power:

> *Let us say that you are a bookkeeper, responsible for recording in a journal which checks have been okayed by certain officers of the company. You control how accurately and how quickly entries are made. You also are the best source of information about entries in the journal.*
>
> *Obvious enough? Okay. But you may also control some resources that are not quite so obvious to you. For example, you spend all day looking at checks and invoices. If you're astute, you probably know as much about how your company uses its cash as anyone else in*

the organization. You may also be the first person to find irregularities in how the money is spent.

Suppose that you notice that a inordinately large number of checks are being written to a particular supplier of paper. Although the checks are accompanied by what appear to be legitimate invoices, you cannot imagine corporate headquarters going through that many cartons of paper in a single week. Your suspicions are confirmed when you inspect previous year's journals and find that this year the company is spending 10 times as much for paper as it did in previous years. You then pull out the suspicious purchase orders and see that they all have been requisitioned by the same person.

You now have a source of power. How can you use it? You could report what you found to the vice president for finance, to your supervisor, or you could share your knowledge with the person doing the suspicious requisitioning.

What you do depends on what tactic is best at the time. The point here in this discussion of strategy is that you should learn to think this way: What power do I have and to what uses can it be put? In addition, think of alliances with people like the bookkeeper. In the discussion on tactics, you will be advised to get yourself into positions of control over such numbers and accounting systems. The next best thing is to make allies with those who have that control.

Your power assets are for you alone to know. There's an old saying attributed to one of those legendary Chinese warlords: *Power is not only what you have but what others think you have.* In the 1960s Jesse Unruh emerged as a major power figure in California politics because he was known to have large financial resources to help candidates in elections. I once asked him if he had raised as much money as rumor had it. His reply: *The largest amount rumored is the one I want you to believe.*

Strategic Personal Relationships

Work on your strategic personal network within the organization from your first day on the job. Some places for doing this are:

Sports and workouts
Serving on community committees
Membership in a local lodge or brotherhood
Church fellowship
Alumni associations

Your purpose in establishing a personal relationship is not to enjoy friendship. Your purpose is to develop a relationship that can be useful to you in the future. You do this by establishing enough of a relationship to find out and meet the expectations and needs of the other person. *When you have done this for a while,* says John P. Kotter, *the other party naturally begins to trust you, to listen more carefully to your ideas and advice, and generally to want to reciprocate by meeting your needs."*

Do not hesitate to establish personal relationships with the high and mighty people in your organization. Find out as much as you can about them, then consider how you can make social contact with a few of them in a natural seemingly-effortless way. This calls for extreme subtlety. David Biehn shows us how to do it:

Fresh out of college Dave joined the San Diego headquarters of a large international airline as an administrative assistant in the food and beverage division. He researched the personal lives of the company's top management by finding magazine articles that had been written on some of them. He also telephoned likely churches to find out if any of these managers were in the congregation. He also did this with health clubs, hobbyists' associations, and local lodges. In each instance he claimed to be a reporter gathering background information. He would say *My notes are unclear. I think he said he's a member of your congre-*

gation (lodge, etc.), and to be truthful with you I forgot and I'm embarrassed to ask him again. Can you help me out?

Some of the information was of no use. There were some churches David did not want to attend, he did not play squash, and there were some lodges, such as the Masonic, which did not interest him. While it was his intention to make friends in high places, he wished to do so on a basis that he himself would enjoy. He did not want to be phony. That never works in the long run, and it did not suit his sense of character.

His first useful piece of information was about an executive, Newton Randall, who was very active with the Lions Club. David had a deaf cousin whom the Lions had helped, so he had a respect for the organization and thought he could feel good about participating in Lions activities. So he joined. The Lions are a very decentralized organization. Individual committees are isolated and self-run. David volunteered for the committee on speech and hearing because he felt a commitment there and also because he knew that Mr. Randall was on the sight committee. His strategy was long-range. He did not want to do anything obvious.

A useful piece of information was that another executive, George Langley, worked out at the YMCA. David had always worked out with weights and aerobic equipment two or three times a week. So he joined the "Y" but stayed away on the days that Mr. Langley was there for a few months. He wanted to have been using the "Y" on a regular basis for at least two months before he designed his "bumping into" Mr. Langley there.

This was a long-term strategy for David. He had no immediate purpose. He was thinking in terms of years. It took six months before he was placed on a planning committee for the Lions with Mr. Randall. He made his first contact at the "Y" with Mr. Langley three months after he joined. There was no real conversation between them for another month although David worked out once a week at the same time as Mr. Langley.

As the relationships grew, David never discussed the company unless the executive brought it up. Eventually Mr. Langley opened the door for talking about the company on a regular basis.

The strategy of engaging in outside-work activities that benefits one at work is usually only practiced at higher levels of organizations. Executives will join certain clubs and groups to make contacts. You are wise to follow that strategy from the beginning of your employment.

There will be some opportunities for you to make friends in high places immediately when you join the organization, as was the case for Dan Kropf.

When Lt. Col. Daniel Kropf was assigned to the Air Combat Command as chief of the manpower requirements division, he looked around for natural allies. The best possibility was Col. Ralph Torres, Commander of Manpower Supply. Torres and he graduated in the same West Point class, so it was a natural gesture for Dan to suggest lunch and build a relationship. A few months later, he found the relationship very useful. He was having difficulties getting the manpower assignments he needed to make. His supplier, the chief of manpower supply, was a procrastinator who believed that it was better to make no decision than one which might be criticized down the road. Dan mentioned his problem to Ralph, who was the procrastinator's boss, and the problem was solved.

Networking

Professors at research universities have developed what are probably the most effective networks in American organizations. These networks are based on fields—business administration, sociology, accounting, psychology, computer engineering, etc. A professor's reputation in his field is his power base. The better the reputation (*Phineas Wharton is one of the country's leading experts on corporate finance.*), the better the rewards. Research universities rely on a professor's reputation in his field for all hiring and promotion decisions. What people within the university who are not themselves prestigious members of the field involved think of the professor is irrelevant. A professor networks by publishing and reading papers at conferences that catch the attention of the field's influential elite.

Networking can be professional or social or both. Do not, however, think that a social relationship is a network. You will undoubtedly have many social relationships just for the fun of it. If that is as far as it goes, it is not a network.

You consciously cultivate your networks for practical job-oriented purposes. Sometimes they are also enjoyable, but beware having fun in a network that was intended for practical ends. You want to project a calculated image of yourself in your networks. Have fun in other groups.

Your first step in networking is to join every professional or career association that appears to have anything to do with your current or desired career line. Everyone who works in government should begin with membership in the American Society of Public Administration and get active in the local chapter. Even if you are not working in government, consider joining this association if there is a strong local chapter where you live. Whether you are in the private or public sector, being in some of the local government loops is useful. If the local chapter is vibrant, its membership will include the top and middle-level government (federal, state, and city) officials working in your area.

If you find useful contacts in the local chapter, volunteer to work on activities such as planning conferences, increasing membership, and membership communications. You may find, as many have, that there are situations in which you'll get a bigger payoff for doing a good job for the association than there is for doing a good job in your full-time-job organization. Many people gain advantages within their organization by being a known entity in a local professional association. Many also find new and better jobs with a different organization because of this recognition.

Similarly, the American Management Association, Kiwanis Clubs, local chambers of commerce, and many more associations provide valuable sources of networking.

—Thirteen—

Strategy: Legal Matters Dealing with Management and Meaning

Where you find the laws most numerous, there you will find also the greatest injustice.

—Arcesilaus

There could come a time when you need to exercise your legal rights on the job, or when you want to threaten using them. Do not wait until that time, which is a time for tactics, to get yourself informed on legal rights. Knowing them ahead of "tactics time" enables you to develop your tactics carefully over a period of time. If you wait until you've been handed a pink slip to investigate this legal area and your company's policies regarding those rights, you've waited too long.

This is not the place to even attempt a summary of workplace law. In general you should know that you can go to court or file charges with the Equal Employment Opportunity Commission. Your company or agency might have its own internal grievance procedures. Many companies, such as Alcoa, Brown & Root, Fairchild Aircraft, Levi Strauss, and The McGraw-Hill Companies, have "alternate dispute resolution (ADR)" programs, which usually involve using third-party mediation.

Never think, no matter who advises you otherwise, that organizations welcome "frank criticism," "challenging behavior," or "individuals speaking up for themselves." If you challenge a decision through any of the legal or in-house procedures, expect to be persona non grata to the higher-ups of that organization. Also understand that those higher-ups can affect your search for a position in another organization.

James Henry, President of CPR Institute for Dispute Resolution, a nonprofit coalition of 500 companies involved with ADR, says that even if you prevail, you might end up with a Pyrrhic victory when someone retaliates with a whisper: *I wouldn't hire that troublemaker.*

The prevailing wisdom is that you should retain an employment lawyer to advise you on which out-of- or in-house procedure you should follow, and how to do it. The state in which you work might provide free and highly capable counsel. There are a lot of differences in the way states protect employees. Where you live can be significant to your job rights. Patrick Cihon, Professor of Law and Public Policy at Syracuse University, evaluated state laws on employment and around 500 court decisions to compose a list of the best—and worst—states to be an employee, based on how state laws provide for job protection and legal precedents.

Alabama, Georgia, and Mississippi are at the bottom of Cihon's rankings. Among other things, each of those states allows employers to fire workers who refuse to commit crimes. Yes, you read it right. If you work in any of those states, you can get your employer arrested for trying to get you to commit a crime, but you can't get your job back or successfully sue that employer for lost wages, even if you prove that you were fired simply because you refused to commit the crime.

Alabama, says Cihon, *also has no state fair-employment laws, meaning that businesses employing fewer than 15 persons may legally fire an employee because they are African American, a woman, a Baptist, whatever.*

The best states for protection of workers in Cihon's survey are California, Minnesota, New Jersey, Massachusetts, Rhode Island, and Wisconsin, where "state law bolstered by court rulings" prevents employees from being fired capriciously. These states also allow employees to take time for family emergencies; California even gives parents unpaid time off to meet with their children's teachers.

Try to include an expert on labor law in your network. This will provide you with a continuing source of strategic knowledge. It also does not hurt for you to be seen as a person who has such an acquaintance or friend.

Validation—Know About This Technical Word!

"Projective" tests are often used in organizations, for hiring, promoting, and so forth. A projective test is one that is supposed to indicate which of a group of candidates will best perform the job in question. This type of test has a legal Achilles' Heel called "validation," a word used by courts to challenge the claim that a test can actually differentiate between how candidates will perform on a job.

In the majority of organizational positions, there is no way to design a test that can validly project which of several candidates will do the best job. Most positions are too complicated, and it is just about impossible to know what types of qualifications lead to success in that position. Even the concept of success is highly subjective.

The courts have taken a lively interest in this Achilles' Heel, going as high as the U.S. Supreme Court. Large numbers of persons who have been denied positions based on scoring lower than others on a projective test have successfully sued employers in court based on the courts' rulings that the test lacked validity.

In any organization there are many positions for which no one could develop a valid projective test. Some companies and agencies thought they had when they used persons on the job as benchmarks. First they took the characteristics of persons successfully carrying out the work; then, they used these characteristics as job qualifications. This approach had a short life in the courts. Judges were not won over by arguments that this approach made sense, particularly when it was used to defend tests that used the arm strength of a bus driver to ascertain the qualifications of a woman to drive a bus.

Organizations are scared by these legal intrusions into what had been their own comfortable niches. You want to know about this because:

- In an interview you can take advantage of the knowledge that there probably is not a legally-acceptable method of selecting the most qualified candidate.
- If others know you are aware of this and other legally sensitive decisions in your organization, they are more likely to treat you with kid gloves.
- When you want to see "your" person get a particular position, you'll have some useful ideas on how to manipulate the situation.

Keeping Up With What's Hip in "How to Manage"

As we saw in chapter one, managers like to read and hear about the latest fad in "how to manage." You should know the latest so that you can talk the talk. There are two sources you'll want to continuously tap: Leading business magazines and top management in your organization.

Audrey James, a middle-level manager in an electrical appliances manufacturing company, provides an example of keeping up with the literature and using it to your advantage when you know the thoughts of your top managers:

> *Two years ago I started skimming the most prestigious journals and magazines that cover recent management trends. Once a week I spend an evening in the library looking through Fortune, Forbes, The Harvard Business Review, the Wall Street Journal, Inc., and some other sources. I could tell you about a number of times that this reading has paid off nicely for me.*
>
> *Just a month ago I made a great impression on a vice president in the company who's a key decision maker on my budget proposals. I learned a long time ago that this*

guy doesn't want to hear about increasing salaries, but likes to image himself as someone who really cares about the workers. It's a real bore to have to listen to this guy go on and on about how he's nothing and people like me and the people below me are everything. Especially when he's scooping it out in his very plush office. But it's what I have to deal with.

An article had appeared in Forbes on psychological research that supposedly reveals that happiness is in one of the genes. According to these findings, salary increases bring a spurt of happiness, but it dies shortly after. A conclusion to the article was that all the stuff coming out about income inequality is wrong-headed. You're not going to increase people's happiness by redistributing the wealth.

I got that into a conversation I was having with the vice president. He said he'd heard about the findings. He was very interested in discussing them.

That's a good subject for people like me to keep up on because there are a lot of two-faced vice presidents around who are more than ready to succumb to bullshit like that happiness-gene thing. They need constant stroking in that regard.

Audrey knew how to manipulate the vice president because she was attentive to what he said. When managers talk about their management approaches most of us tune them out, especially when they use the term "management philosophy." Don't do that. They are providing you with vital information in your struggle for survival. Pay close attention and search for ways to win their trust by showing you know what they are talking about.

You can experiment with ideas to gain insights about your managers' thinking. For example, many managers believe that the people below them do not understand what the managers are trying to do for them. A familiar lament is: My people simply do not have any appreciation for how hard I am fighting for them.

In some cases the manager is right, in some cases he's not doing much fighting, but likes to think he does. It doesn't matter which is the case in your situation; you should find ways to give him emotional support in his beliefs.

The Cause, The Cause . . . But What Is The Problem?

Organizations like to assume that any particular problem has a particular cause. The notion of cause-and-effect is an outmoded way of thinking in the sciences, but organizations wouldn't know what to do if they tried to follow current scientific thinking, which attribute happenings to an enormous variety of causes, some of which we don't even know. Imagine an executive confronted with red ink disease who said: *None of us can have any true sense of what's causing our problem.*

Be sympathetic with management's need to believe simplistically about cause-and-effect. Pretend to be whole-hearted as you help search for the cause. If you are following the advice to keep up with management literature, you will be able to refer to it when discussing possible causes. If your organization has not yet gone through the latest fad in re-engineering, suggest it as something to consider because "maybe the cause lies in obsolete processes." If your organization does not have anything that you have read about in the past year, suggest it. Keep in mind something that Willa Cather said: *Give the people a new word and they think they have a new fact.*

Winning and Losing are Strands in the Fabric

Charles Dickens said, *For everything you gain you lose a little; for everything you lose, you gain a little.* Every day of your life will include winnings and losses, so either one is no big deal.

What's important is how you react. For example, when you win you want to be sure that no one is going away angry who could hurt you in the future. When you lose you want to review your tactics and the analysis underlying them, and you want to see if you might gain from an alliance with the winner. There is no possibility for you to always be at your best. *Only the mediocre,* said Jean Giraudoux, *are always at their best.*

Many people have difficulty matching their gains and losses with their priorities. When something goes wrong, you should assess it according to the importance is has in your overall strategy. If, for example, you try an experiment and it doesn't work out as you hoped it would, you should first ask yourself how important the gain would have been in your overall strategy. Then analyze the failure with an appropriate sense of significance.

Remember that in an organization it is not what happens that matters; what matters is how people interpret what happens. Your relationships with people are more important than the ups and downs of daily successes and failures. If people like you or if people are apprehensive about your power, they will be prone to interpret failures as successes. Even when they sense a failure they will want to rationalize it in your favor. Seize advantage of these ways that people tend to be. Give them reasons to interpret happenings to your advantage.

Selection of Jobs Based on Self Knowledge

It would be helpful if you could take a test to determine where in the organization you would best fit. There are tests that can be of some help in this. Many psychotherapists and corporations use variations on Carl Jung's personality types to provide insight into differences between people. If you know you prefer working with people and working with facts rather than feelings, you have valuable insight regarding the type of job you would probably like. Similarly, there are other tests that give you some idea of how comfortable you are dealing with power. You should take advantage of such tests, always looking for more ways to understand yourself, but there is still lacking one overall test that can provide clear guidance for job selection. Until one comes along, here are some things for you to think about:

- As you saw in the discussion on power, interdependencies create power relationships that don't show up on charts and aren't covered by rules and regulations. Some jobs are magnets for such power relationships, so you'll need to perfect your political skills to succeed in them. If you are uncomfortable in power-charged situations, you can try to steer yourself away from them.

You can analyze power implications of a job by asking the question: How many people over whom I have no formal authority must cooperate with me to complete my job?

- If you want to be an innovator you should understand that the idea is only a small part of the accomplishment. Implementing new ideas requires consummate political skills. New projects require resources, which must come from units and individuals. They will resist giving up these resources. Being a planner is not what I'm talking about. For the most part, planners assemble reports for files. You can do that, and make a decent living at it, without becoming politically savvy.
- If you are looking for situations that have potential as power bases, try to find a job where the organization believes it has a critically important relationship with its environment. For example, in a company that considers its major task to be development of new markets, the marketing division is opportune. If

developing new products is considered to be the
major task, then the products division is opportune.

Another good place for power-building is a unit that has a
critical position in the flow of decisions and work. When other
persons cannot accomplish their work without your cooperation,
you are in an excellent position to amass power.

Improving Your Power Position

Following is a list of ways to improve your power position.

Uniqueness and Relevancy: Ask yourself how easy it would
be for anyone else (or, gulp, a computer) to do your job. If "1" is
for "very easy," and "10" is for "it's impossible", you work
towards being a "10." Of course, the organization must feel a
need for what you do. To the extent that your job is both relevant and unique, your power base is increased.

*Office Location Close to Main Traffic Flows and Power Hold-
ers*: Fans of the power game agree that it's better to have a tiny
desk with no office in an area where the action is, than to have a
splendidly plush and spacious suite in a remote part of the
building where only you and your staff work. The expression
"being in the right place at the right time" sometimes has to do
with being the first person the CEO sees when he needs a personal favor from someone. It can also mean being in the presence of a conversation that leads to the ad hoc formation of a
team to take on a new task. Or, being available for helping out
on an important job. Maybe it's only helping carry things out to
the limousines. But remember the *New Yorker* cartoon pictur-
ing a dog behind an executive-type desk, saying to a man seated
at the side of the desk, *I started out just fetching.*

Being in the flow of things also facilitates your access to
impromptu meetings, at which some of the most important communications and decisions take place. Rick De Herder, senior
vice president for sales and support at Mattel Inc., says that he
does much of his brainstorming at 7:45 a.m., as he dresses in

the locker room after working out in the company gym. He and others inevitably ask one another questions about major projects.

Jim Demary, a marketing and communications manager at Massachusetts Mutual Life Insurance, will tell you that he never quite believed the old female complaint about being kept out of the loop by being kept out of informal male gatherings until he found himself shut off from places like the female bathrooms at Massachusetts Mutual. Demary's boss was female, and the company was dominated by women.

Jan Margolis says she made a vocation of "running into" senior executives of her company when she worked as a human resources director for a leading drug company. One of her ploys involved befriending secretaries who booked flights on the company jet. When she wanted to have an impromptu meeting with a certain executive, she tried to get on his flight. *Conversation during the flights came naturally*, she says. *With the seats arranged living-room style, I could easily strike up discussions. I would start a conversation based on what was in that morning's Wall Street Journal, the stock prices suddenly jumping, or a new product launch. The executives would then ask something like, 'What brings you to Chicago?' or they would mention a project that I was working on, or ask for my input.*

If you've done a study of the people you're trying to influence, you'll be able to spot those whose comments at the water cooler are serious as opposed to those who don't take seriously anything they say away from their desks. As one middle-level manager puts it, "I've worked with some people who you could get their hallway opinion on something and count on it. There are other people who let you assume from a hallway discussion that your idea is golden. But then in a formal setting you hear otherwise."

You should also be responsive to people who resent your turning a social conversation into an impromptu meeting. Follow these rules:

- Have very brief (five seconds, or so) hooks memo-
  rized. A hook is a trick used in music and writing to
  get attention. Jan Margolis used *The Wall Street
  Journal* as a source of hooks. You should do the
  same—that is, have ready as hooks news about something relevant to your company or agency—and you
  should also have various aspects of the projects you
  are working on or some you would like to propose
  reduced to hooks.
- Watch for body language as well as what is said. If
  you detect aggravation, retreat from the hook and
  comment on the weather, or something like that.
- Even if you don't detect aggravation, never go to a
  second hook if there was no bite on the first.

Be Seen and Heard: Wherever you do your work, make it visible. Try to find work that will be seen, and you with it. Cheer to yourself when others withdraw from getting involved in activities requiring extra work and stand-up talking to the executives. Jump at the chance to spend a weekend preparing materials for such presentations. And give it your all. Think of it as auditioning for a part that might be cast a month from now. You want to be the one referred to in the statement "I think that fellow who gave the presentation on our inventory status last month might be just right for this new job."

Work at Personal Name Recognition: If your name appears in the paper (favorably, of course) find subtle ways to get copies around the building.

Increase Ambiguity in Your Job Description: Have you ever noticed how clear-cut a janitor's job is, and how obscure the CEO's job is? How easily you could say what a combat marine does, and how difficult it would be to explain what his general does? A measure of the power in a position could very well lie in the job description. So, work at making what you do less under-standable. If there is a set of code words available to you, use them. Semanticist S.I. Hayakawa often made the point that people can establish a mystique about their job by using esoteric language when they talk shop. Computer types have perfected this almost as well as Harvard MBAs. They know well the wisdom of Philip Dick's insight: *The basic tool for the manipulation of reality is the manipulation of words.*

When the parameters and content of your job are ambiguous, and you control the interpretation of your job, your position power is enhanced. Consider, for example, the matter of luck discussed in chapter one on what organizations really are. If no one knows for sure the mix of your actions and luck in outcomes because they are unclear about what you do, you have far more control over interpretation of failure than if others are perfectly clear about how much your actions affect outcomes.

President Bill Clinton will go down in history as a genius at controlling the meaning of words and his position. During the first two years of his presidency he presented himself as, for example, the president who would bring a national health care plan to the country. That and other things failed. His popularity with the people shrunk. Then he began defining what he was doing in vague terms. When something happened that was apparently popular with the people, he moved in with words to claim credit. When something happened that the people appeared to dislike, he moved in with words to say he disliked it, too.

Even when his own actions were under attack, he knew how to avoid personal criticism. For example, when there was negative fever all around about the allegations that campaign financing had gotten so out of hand that foreign governments were buying their way into American policy making. President Clinton, who by all accounts would be on the cover of future textbooks on shady campaign financing, grabbed the torch and said he would lead the fight against loose campaign financing.

That deserves attention in and of itself, but the real lesson for you to ponder is this: Even though the American people knew all of this about President Clinton, his popularity, as measured in the polls, soared to new heights after he adopted this strategy about keeping his job description, and his role in what was going on, unclear; until, of course, credit, or avoidance of blame, for something was to be seized upon.

In previous chapters, you read about how organizations use gobbledygook to their advantage. Study how your organization does this—study how Clinton used language, also—so that you can develop your own skills at "controlling with words."

Controlling Discretionary Funds

Organizations usually have two types of funds: Committed and discretionary. Committed funds are tucked away in an operating departmental budget. Discretionary funds are often kept loosely at the high levels of the organizations, to be used for undefined new programs and activities. Typically, they are very limited. Every dollar spent from them represents a power symbol much greater than the amount involved. To get any money from this source is regarded as a significant accomplishment.

Try to tie your position in some way to the discretionary funds in your organization. Even a nominal position, without a vote, on the committee authorized to allocate these funds can be important to you. You can extract something from those who receive some of these treasured funds, even if your role is minimal in the decision process. You can provide an illusion of being much more involved than you are, but you must be involved enough to give the illusion credibility.

It is usually better to be involved in the allocation rather than in the receiving of discretionary funds. When you are on the receiving side you are using up too much of your power reserves for the amount of money involved. Be on the other side of the exchange.

Diffuse Those Who Control You

The easiest way to explain this is with an example. Frederick Rowan was a university president who felt too constrained by his board of trustees. At a meeting he called with a group of us whom he trusted, he brought this up as a problem and asked for suggestions. One of my colleagues recommended that Dr. Rowan should appoint a full-time staff person as an aide to the trustees. Although it would look as though the appointment recognized the importance of the board, in fact it would create a control over all information going to the trustees. Thus would the president be in a position to put his own spin on everything they read.

Another colleague suggested that the president give a major policy address in which he would introduce a number of new directions for the university and state his continuing commitment to traditional directions. None of the new directions, save one, would be really new. They would be new packaging of programs already in place. The one truly new commitment would be that of increasing alumni participation in presidential decisions and policies. To do this he would increase the number of trustees from 11 to 23.

This increase in numbers made it easier for the president to control the board rather than vice-versa because the politics of going to 23 was bound to work in his favor. There would be a conflict on the board over who (what kind of persons) would be the new members. This conflict would divide the board into groups which would probably remain in conflict for a long time after the new members took their seats. The president could study the process and formulate a political strategy accordingly.

Uncertainty—Tango With the Hobgoblin

One word that emerges from all the analyses of organizations is uncertainty. Except for the legendary government file clerk with civil service protection of his job, everyone in an organization wrestles with the hobgoblin of uncertainty. We have seen in chapter one that CEOs are socialized to speak confidently while not having a clue about the possible outcomes of what they decide today. Middle managers are uncertain about whether they even understand what the CEO wants, let alone whether or not they can do it. Workers worry from one reorganization to another about their jobs.

Clare Booth Luce was a woman who dared tango with hobgoblins. Her biographer says that she charmed publishing maven Condé Nast into an interview for the job as photo-caption writer at *Vogue*, then simply showed up at the magazine to work, fooling each of her two bosses into thinking that she'd been hired by the other.

If you wrestle with the hobgoblin of uncertainty you'll lose. If you tango with it, the hobgoblin gets in step with you, even through the daring moves. The trick is to find out where it is and take control. In an organization where the greatest uncertainty is hiring and keeping software engineers, get yourself into the personnel office charged with that task. In an organization where the greatest uncertainty is the market, become a market analyst.

Most organizations have a number of uncertainty hobgoblins, so you can have a choice. There are two reasons why you want to be in those spots: (1) This is where you can build a significant power base. (2) It is difficult for anyone to accuse you of failure. After all, this is a troubled area where no one really knows the sure path home. You have enormous space in which to maneuver with tactics that you'll learn in the next chapter. You also have a great deal of control over whether what happens is labeled "success" or "failure."

Characteristics of Climbers

Studies of successful organizational climbers suggest that they:

- Gravitate to positions where the critical action is, the kind of action everyone has their eyes on, the things that make or break a company or government agency.

- Conversely, avoid routine work.
- Step forward to take responsibility for important activities, especially when it appears that a gamble must be taken.
- Increase the dependence of others on them, and decrease their dependence on others.
- Appear to be thoroughly dedicated to the organization.
- Gain a reputation for being tough when necessary, yet are generally well-liked.

Conclusion

Remember how often you have postponed minding your interest and let slip those opportunities the gods have given you. It is now high time to consider what sort of world you are part of, and what kind of governor of it you are. You have a set period assigned you to act in this world. Do so, or it will quickly run off with you.

–Marcus Aurelius

—Fourteen—

Tactics: Dealing with Coworkers and Managers

> To secure ourselves against defeat lies in our own hands, but the opportunity of defeating the enemy is provided by the enemy himself.
>
> —Sun Tzu

> While it may be a sin to believe evil of others, seldom is it a mistake.
>
> —H.L. Mencken

> If your Mother tells you something, check it out.
> —Old Saying of Newspaper Reporters

Your strategy is a focus on yourself, who you want to be, how you want to present yourself, and what you want to achieve. Your tactics focus on others. The first step in learning how to deal with others is to see them as people playing roles.

Picture yourself in the office of a CEO for a large international company, on the top floor of a New York skyscraper. He arrived just minutes ago in his private helicopter, which he boarded after getting out of his private jet, which had brought him from a meeting in London with three of Europe's biggest investors.

The office furniture is sturdy oak with soft leather, trimmed with touches of the finest craftsmanship. There are not many paintings, but each is clearly a classic. The windows give you an unending view of the city.

The CEO wears a tailored dark suit, beige soft-collared shirt, a colorful comfortable tie. His face is tan, handsome; his body athletic. He speaks calmly and confidently.

Now remember that everything is theater. This is just another guy playing this role of being a sophisticated big shot CEO. He is no different than the guy who piloted the helicopter, or the guy who cleans this office. Every one of these three persons is a mixture of security and insecurity, realized and dashed hopes, truthfulness and untruthfulness, sincerity and insincerity, fears and dreams. The person playing the CEO is a human being like yourself and everyone else. In organizational theater CEOs are expected to give the appearance of power and confidence.

So the question is not how to deal with a CEO; the question is how to deal with a person playing a CEO. Similarly, you want to know how to deal with a person playing a secretary to a CEO, or a person playing a salesman, an accountant, a supervisor, and so on.

Two questions should always be in your mind. How would you act if you were playing the role of the CEO, and how do you think the person playing the CEO would act if he were playing your role? If you think about answers to these two questions on a continuing basis, as you come into contact with CEOs, secretaries, salesmen, accountants, and supervisors, you will gain insights that will serve you well. These insights come from your having separated the people from the roles they are playing.

You will usually gain something by playing upon the contrasts between the nature of people and the roles assigned by organizations. Show empathy for the person playing the role and you tap into a potentially powerful relationship. Keep in mind that most organizations physically remind its members where they are on the totem pole. Clothing, working space, and routine movements in the building are constant reminders of status.

If the person playing the janitor realizes that you see him as a person who is better than the role, he appreciates it. If the person playing the CEO realizes that you see the tremendous effort he must put into his daily performances, he appreciates it. This must be done with sensitivity. Never suggest that you think that being a janitor is demeaning, nor that being a CEO is beyond the acting talents of the player.

When you are in the CEO's office forget nothing from chapter two: "What Are People . . . Really?" Promotions to larger offices on higher floors in a building do not change the essentials of being a person. Better paychecks and clothing do not change the realities of our imperfections. No matter what role we assume we still have selective memories, tell lies when it is convenient to do so, maintain a capacity for cruelty, and strive to avoid ridicule.

Likewise, forget nothing from chapter one: "What Is An Organization . . . Really?" Organizations put people into roles that often demand irrational behavior. Organizations customarily reward performances that are contradictory to the stated goals of the organization. Organizations recurrently require lying, deceit and treachery. Even if people were more than 80% good before they entered an organization they would soon be re-engineered to a leaner percentage.

Each person in your organization deals with you in less than complete candor because she is a human being and because the organization often requires and rewards dishonesty. You can never be sure when a person is being dishonest with you, therefore your tactics must take that possibility into account without assuming it. Memorize the following: Never assume that anyone is being completely honest with you. Always pretend to trust everyone. Never dislike a person because he lies to you. Understand people; don't even think about reforming them.

In this chapter tactics are presented both for defense and offense. All readers, I presume, will want to protect themselves and so will be interested in tactics for defense. Some readers will want to go for the top of the hill, to know everything they can about offensive tactics. Now and then readers interested only in defense will find it necessary to go on the offensive because some one or some thing has become an enemy to the status quo these readers seek. Therefore, all readers should learn all tactics.

Although the tactics are presented individually, you'll be most successful when you are combining them. For example, when you manipulate statistics to reach the conclusions you prefer, you'll want to also prepare people to want those conclusions.

Not all readers will be comfortable with all tactics. You will learn as you go along those for which you are best suited. But keep an open mind and be willing to try some of those tactics you think may not be appropriate for you. If you have not consciously utilized tactics in the past you may not really know what's best for you until you try them.

Learning Self-Presentation

In the previous chapter, we discussed organizations as theaters. Many aspects of theater are clear to you as you walk on stage. You don't bring your dog to an interview. You stand, not sit, in an elevator. You don't ask the security guard for his revolver. You don't appear anywhere outside a toilet stall in your underwear.

Etiquette manuals, which are guides to playing your role properly in any scene, have warned against such indiscretions since they were first conceived. A manual published in 1836 cautions about situations in which you do not know the players and their roles:

If there is anyone in the company whom you do not know, be careful how you let off any epigrams or pleasant little sarcasms. You might be very witty upon halters to a man whose father had been hanged. The first requisite for successful conversation is to know your company well.

One learns and follows manners to survive and be successful. They are self-serving. And they have nothing to do with goodness or morality.

The purpose of polite behavior is never virtuous. Deception, surrender, and concealment, these are not virtues. The goal of the mannerly is comfort, per se.

Learning how to behave in your organization is the same as learning how to behave in society. There are general rules for all situations and there are specific rules for specific situations.

Be Reasonable, and Be Careful

We have seen that organizations and people are imperfect. Don't sound the trumpets when you make the same observations in your organization. Don't compare your mistake-prone organization to an illusion of perfection. Don't despair at finding people falling short of an illusory ideal. Be unsurprised by hypocrisy, inefficiency, waste and political maneuverings. Expect little candor. Remember that all this, no matter how elegant the decor or soaring the rhetoric, is just people.

The Caine Mutiny, a successful Broadway Play and movie, has a good lesson. Midway through World War II, a few newly-commissioned officers, fresh from the campuses of Princeton and Yale, find the old-timer Captain of their vessel lacking in intelligence and leadership. More clever than he, it is easy for them to psychologically drive him to act so foolishly that they must mutiny. There is a court martial trial to ascertain guilt. The clever young officers' lawyer enables the Captain to ridicule himself on the stand. The mutineers are exonerated. But the real message of author Herman Wouk is yet to come.

At the celebration party the lawyer enters. There is the expected hurrah and toasting. But the lawyer refuses to drink with them. He came, he says, to tell them his true thoughts. Getting them off was his duty as their defender. What he, and they before him, did to the Captain was morally reprehensible. Here is a man, he says, an imperfect man to be sure, who had for years done a reasonably good job at something few people want to do. He helped keep the nation militarily safe while these bright, young men played their games on ivy campuses. All those years took a toll, as they would have on anyone. What happened on the ship and in the courtroom was perhaps legally correct, but it was an assault on decency and gratefulness.

Keep this in mind, first, as you discover and suffer mediocrity. Second, assume that someone is always gaining from things being as they are. These are the most sensitive persons with whom you must deal if you decide to affect those things. Shirley Rice, a detective in a medium-sized Southwestern city, tells about one of her experiences with what she calls *finding the method in the madness*.

> *All of a sudden one day the chief announced that there would be no more overtime. It was getting too expensive. The scuttlebutt, which turned out to be true, was that money that had been budgeted for overtime had been spent on a training program. Some of us had been trained to carry out some procedures for the FBI. The deal was that the FBI would pay the department as we carried out those procedures, so the overtime budget would be replenished. But the FBI never got the budget it expected, so there was no FBI money to pay.*
>
> *What we could not understand was why the Chief didn't complain. The overtime we were putting in was at the specific request of the Mayor, who had just won an election based on a campaign of having more law enforcement in the streets. He had made the overtime budget a*

big deal, telling everyone that this is how he carried through on promises.

So we figured the Chief had a great case to take to the Mayor. We knew from his closest associate that he had not and had no intention of going to the Mayor with it.

Then it dawned on me. I remembered that it was the Mayor's idea for us to be trained to do that FBI work. The Chief was not going to embarrass, and maybe anger, the Mayor. I don't know if that was right or wrong. I do understand it.

Try to understand what's going on around you in terms of real people who want to protect their jobs. Be careful. Don't stand still, but move cunningly.

Experimentation

Trying things out, experimenting, is a fundamental tactic you should use on a continuing basis. We have seen that people hide behind illusions, that these illusions are often taken very seriously, and that you should pretend to respect the illusions as truth. But we have also seen that a person's behavior is based more on her perception of awards and punishments than on her stated attitudes or beliefs. A person might defend his illusions to his death, though he may never act on them.

Therefore, you will try some things out, to see how a person reacts rather than basing your prediction of her reaction on her stated attitudes and beliefs. It is in this way that you gather the best knowledge about how people react. In general you will always refuse to base your expectations of another person's behavior on anything other than your own behavior.

There are two ways to get into experimentation: Start with something that is relatively unimportant to you or start with very tentative probes into something that is important to you. Fred Wingate says that he honed his skills by probing tentatively with office procedures:

My first real job as an accountant was with a high-powered firm. I knew that I would have difficulty with rigid office working hours because I exercise vigorously for one to two hours almost every day. I didn't mention that during my interview because I thought it would hurt my chances. My exercise routine in the middle of the day doesn't fit the stereotype of an accountant. I figured that the interviewers couldn't handle that. So I left it out.

I put my exercise on hold for the first two weeks on the job. I found out how to work after normal office hours. Then I gradually included exercising in my schedule. On the day I exercised I stayed at work later. No one said anything. Eventually I was exercising and working after hours as a normal routine. I get kidded about my exercising. Now and then there's a meeting that interferes with the time I'd like to exercise, but no one really seems to mind.

From that experience, I learned that there are two kinds of rules, those that must be followed and those that are there to keep control over the screwups. Once you establish yourself as a competent person your boss will let you go around the second type of rules. But you've still got to test the waters. There are some bosses who don't seem to know the difference between rules that must be followed and those that are there for to control the screwups. When I encountered bosses who don't know the difference I went to war with them, but on an experimental basis. I always assumed that they were ready to back down if I pushed a little. So I pushed a little at first, and often that was enough.

One of the things I learned in the trenches was that those bosses who are petty about rules like to avoid confrontations and are scared to death of their own bosses. I would usually try confrontation first, because going over the head of a boss was something I avoided as much as possible.

My best opener was to state in a calm and friendly voice that I just couldn't accept his position (on whatever was at issue). Often the boss would say something about how he was sorry to hear that so maybe we should talk some more about it and try to work something out. If he got tough about it and said something like 'that's the way it is,' I matched his tone and stridency. I'd move away from focusing on myself as I did when I said I couldn't accept his decision and focus on him by saying something like 'Well, so now I know your viewpoint on this.' I'd try to let him know that I was on the verge of paying a visit to his boss. Sometimes that worked. When it didn't I'd have to really think about how important what I wanted was. Going over the boss' head is something I did only when something was really important to me. There were times when I just let it go, let him win that one.

Lynn Taylor, an accounts executive with a company that makes automobile parts, had the following comments after reading Fred's statement:

I think that second type of boss, the one who thinks all rules are the same, is sometimes just afraid of what might happen if she were to let you bend one. My approach is to assume that is the case, then combine bending a rule with an obvious success. I simply go ahead and do it, figuring that the worst thing that can happen is that I'll get a mild scolding because nobody's going to bite you hard for succeeding.

What I'm really after though, and what I often get, is praise for bending the rule, or praise for the accomplishment with no comment about the rule. If I get that then I have a precedent going for me and I can bend that rule whenever I want because my boss' fear is gone.

I experiment in order to get people committed after the fact. Most people will say 'no' to most proposals for bend-

ing the rules. What else can they say? Even after I get some precedents going I never go up to my superior and say 'Hey, I'm going to bend that rule I've bent a few times before in order to get another great success. OK?' The only possible reply to that is: 'Now, Lynn, I'm sure that you can figure out a way to accomplish this without bending a rule.

I believe that you've got to practice experimentation, especially when you're new to that sort of thing. It opens up a whole new world to you. You see people as they don't otherwise appear. It's awesome, really. I had a tremendous positive experience with it my second year as an accounts exec that I hope you include in your book.

We had bookkeeping procedures for our muffler accounts that required monthly reports. We were on an electronic system. Often that caused inaccuracies in the monthly report because, for example, at the very moment that we'd be putting down that Jones' Body Shop owed us two thousand dollars, Jones would be electronically paying the bill. I brought this up at a department meeting, but no one picked up on it.

One month I didn't file the report and filed a statement explaining that I considered it improper accounting to file such a report. Of course, I used the terms 'in this company's best financial interests' a lot.

I was praised by my bosses and by others for doing it. The praise was so strong that it took me by surprise. It came from some of the same people who at a department meeting were deaf to my pointing out the problem. I learned from that: There is something sacred about action.

I've continued to learn about this hidden dimension of behavior in organizations. For example, I now realize that I lucked out with that experiment. Suppose that at that time the company was being analyzed for a bank loan. The accounting system could have been working to its advantage because my report would show a certain amount of dollars that were also showing up in the company's bank balance. This false picture of solvency would work in the company's favor. So, you should warn people to look around for things like that before experimenting.

Bill Ligman, a management information systems director with a motel chain, says that Lynn Taylor and Fred Wingate are smart operators, and he adds another consideration:

I was an idealistic activist during the civil rights movement in the 1960s. What I saw was blacks being denied simple ordinary decent treatment by whites. What I heard on the networks and read in the papers was that this was a civil rights versus states rights issue. I learned then that the way people talk about an issue can have maybe a theoretical link to what's really going on, but isn't anywhere near the real problem.

When I began my organizational life I kept that lesson in mind and never believed that the way people in the organization talked about an issue was really the issue itself. People talk in codes. Most of the time, especially in my early experience, I didn't have a clue to what the real issues were, so I'd experiment, try this, try that, just to see if the reactions were consistent with what I wanted to happen.

Sometimes I'd get a reaction I liked and still didn't know what the real issues were. But what did I care. Organizations are kind of like insane asylums—you never know what someone is going to do, and he doesn't either. Even at the top—hell, especially at the top—people are experimenting, but they've got to pretend to know what they're doing so they don't admit that.

Nerve Intact, Propose Project Premortem

Let's suppose you've tried some experiments that have worked in your favor. Ready to take on one of the big organizational myths? The myth is this: Almost all new organizational projects are successes.

Anyone you corner at the water fountain will agree with you if you say, "Our projects fail at a spectacular rate," if you guarantee privacy of conversation. With that as a basis for general understanding and support, find a way and place to propose a new method for analyzing new projects called *premortem*, a method to reveal why a project will fail. Managers involved with the new project will be so confident of the project's infallibility that they will gladly take on the challenge, even welcome it. They are deep into their own illusions.

New projects usually go through a typical critiquing session, in which project team members are asked what might go wrong. The premortem starts with the assumption that the project died and asks "what went wrong?" The participants, task is to provide reasonable reasons for the failure.

You will hopefully remember from earlier in this book how groupthink can paralyze a decision group's ability to be critical of the group's thoughts. Premortem forces the group members to focus on plausible reasons why the project dies.

A premortem should reveal some avoidable errors and some unavoidable ones. Except for some project supporters who couldn't care less about problems with the project, all they are after is credit for conceiving the project, you should enhance your image for having suggested the premortem.

But Beware the Invitation to Risk-Taking

Experimenting in your own interests for your own reasons under your control is one thing. Accepting the invitation to be a risk-taker in a general, abstract way is another, and is to be avoided.

Supervisors and company mission statements are full of terms like: "We encourage initiative around here." "We want risk-takers not stand-patters." Of course they do, so long as initiation and risk-taking have pleasant results. If you take a risk, and it results in something negative that can reflect on your supervisor or his, watch out. All of a sudden the words become: "Well, I certainly didn't mean to suggest that you do anything like that!"

Seldom will you find a supervisor who stands up for you when blame goes around. So, don't assume you've got one. Stay with the odds. If you take a risk, do so because there's something you want to get done; don't do so because you think risk-takers are rewarded. Try to make sure you've got some allies in important places who will support you if things go wrong. In other words, take a risk when it is part of your game.

Some Things to Avoid

In the first chapter, we discussed some key examples of organizational hypocrisies and myths. They were:

- Productivity is essential
- We care about our workers as people.
- There are techniques that enable organizations to place the most qualified individuals in the right positions.
- We can evaluate the value of programs, projects, departments and individual workers in terms of the organization's goals.
- The most valuable programs, projects, departments and individuals are rewarded.
- Training plus continuing direction leads to rational worker behavior.
- Organizations pursue efficient ways of doing things.

There is a proclivity in organizations to pretend zealous pursuit of these goals and ideals. Programs, projects and, above all, committees, are established to do this. For example, a committee to study and make recommendations on improving productivity is announced with fanfare and overstated promise.

Avoid participation in any of these committees or programs. Never accept a leadership role. As you know, the goals are very lip-service in nature, and it is impossible to know if and when they are accomplished. Don't put yourself in a potential sacrificial position even if short-term glory appears attainable. In the long run, all of these projects fade into failure.

Also in the first chapter, we discussed the hazards of getting yourself involved in projects designed to improve one of the empty buzzwords of organizations, like productivity, efficiency, and morale. Be twice on alert for these even grander projects, such as this one by Macy's, whose warning calls are trumpeted in words like *boldest stroke, daring innovation*, and *your once in a lifetime opportunity*. Go willingly into those quick sands only if you figure your days at this company are numbered anyway, or if you have accumulated enough power to either make it work or you or have a scapegoat at hand and it doesn't bother you to use one.

Tactics of Self-Presentation

The appearance of competence is more important to your success in an organization than competence itself. In the movie *Broadcast News* Albert Brooks and William Hurt play characters working on a TV news program. Brooks is highly competent. He understands the news and writes first-rate news summaries. But he sweats when on camera. Hurt doesn't understand the news and cannot write. He concentrates on appearing cool, in control, and pretending to feel the right emotion at the right time. Hurt is promoted to a coveted anchor position that Brooks would die to get. Brooks remains a writer-in-the-background.

There is a booming consultancy business today called "Strategic Self-Presentation." If you put yourself in their hands, you are taught how to present yourself in what is called the high status position. High status people are:

- calm
- speak in complete sentences
- maintain eye contact
- have no jerky body movement
- generally positive, but seldom more than moderately enthusiastic
- speak confidently about themselves

Remember that this is theater. Play a role for the audience. William James once observed that we have as many social selves as there are distinct groups of persons about whose opinion we care.

Remember also that the "art" of management decision-making on personnel matters is often based on the attempt to unnerve you, to get you to talk about yourself in ways that are not in your interest. In giving advice to interviewers, an expert on personnel decision once wrote:

> Doing a good job in interviews is tricky because of one unalterable fact about those presumably polite interchanges: you want to get under the applicant's skin, and he doesn't want you to.
>
> Because you're in a position of power, you can take your pick of techniques that encourage the truth to surface.

She advises the interviewer to use time; it's a key ally, and the interviewer controls it. She relates the techniques used by one major company:

The interview lasts two to five hours and contains carefully timed peaks and valleys. Prior to it the candidate has taken personality and math tests. The interview begins with a quick review of the tests, then a longer period during which the candidate speaks of their experience beginning with high school. She quotes the president of a corporation to express what is going on here regarding the psychology of interviewing:

When you're talking about yourself, that's an upper. Then we take the candidates on a downhill portion of the roller coaster. We'll express concern with certain aspects of the quiz's findings. The applicants must defend themselves. After a little bit of that, we say we want to tell them a little more about the job. That sends the applicants' spirits soaring again, because they figure they might get an offer. After a few ups and downs you'll see their role playing come down. They'll say, 'Let me tell you the truth about something.'

Dave Wiegand, President of *Advanced Network Design*, sees that as the point of surrender. *Once they hit that point, you can ask incredible questions about their job history and they'll just tell you.*

Wiegand represents a trend in interviewing: break down the interviewees' preparation for the interview and trick him into revealing behavioral traits that are important to the company doing the hiring, or promoting, or transferring of the candidate. One technique is to put the candidate into situations for which she could not have prepared. For example, says Wiegand, one of the behavioral traits we value highly is

healthy self-talk, the mental dialogue we have with ourselves. To uncover that characteristic, we might ask the applicants what they would say to a fellow salesperson who was getting a lot of rejections and having difficulty making appointments. By twisting the situation around and suggesting that they're helping others, you are discovering what they say to themselves. What we want to hear is a buck-up-and-keep-going speech to the imaginary colleague; the inclination toward that response, rather than emphatic pessimism, is a key predictor of a salesperson's success.

There is one other very popular technique used to select winners from a list of candidates for selection, promotion, or transfer. This technique searches for your superior qualifications that are too subjective to be measured in a test or quiz. Sometimes the candidate is asked outright: Why would you be particularly good for our company? Even when the question is not asked outright it is implicit in the entire interview. Prior to the interview the selection process has usually targeted persons who meet all criteria that can be precisely defined. Attributes that can be precisely defined—such as specific skills and education—can be measured without an interview. The purpose of the interview is to see which of the candidates on the short list are perceived by the interviewers as being the best "fit" with the company or agency.

Self-promotion is far more likely to win in that contest than is modesty and submissiveness. It is also the best way to beat the techniques designed to break you down. This may sound wrong to you because of the negative popular culture myth about self-promotion. But research and theory indicate that playing a submissive role in the interview, whether for the initial job or for a promotion within, works against you, whereas controlling and self-promoting behavior succeeds.

There are other interview techniques, such as having two or more persons involved who try to confuse you, and all of them are best approached with your intention to control the situation and engage in self-promotion. Some people are good at pretending to be submissive; for them the pretense can be a clever tactic. But in general, remember what Muhammad Ali said: Humble people don't get very far.

You would never know how important appearance is if you believed the propaganda handed out by personnel departments or by executives when they're speaking publicly. According to the company line, the people they look for are skilled as needed, dependable, teachable, etc. Nothing is said about appearance. They can't tell it like it is, the way they could before hiring on appearance became illegal. In 1953, we find the following comments on hiring at and above the level of middle manager:

Placement expert Ann Hoff observes that employers now seem to be looking for an ideal Hollywood type. One company rejected a candidate because he had teeth that were too square and others have been disqualified because their ears stuck out. Racial and religious requirements also are frankly stipulated by employers.

Assume that such standards are alive and well, though not admitted because of the tidal wave of legislation that began in the sixties to protect you against them.

First appearances are particularly critical. There's an interesting psychological test in which you are given descriptions of two people. You are told that the first person is arrogant, selfish, unreliable, hard-working, attractive, and loyal. The second person is described as loyal, attractive, hard-working, unreliable, selfish, and arrogant. Then you are asked to select one of these people for a job, a promotion, or something like that. Almost everyone always picks the second person. In personnel circles this is called "the halo effect." Early perceptions ("loyal, attractive, hard-working") overpower later perceptions ("unreliable, selfish, arrogant").

A seasoned campaigner in the *Fortune 500* has offered this *first appearances advice for job interviews:*

> *Check with the receptionist on the pronunciation of the interviewer's name if you're unsure. While you wait, keep an opening remark on the tip of your tongue. Make an entrance! Walk into the room animated, energetic, head up, chest high. Being pleasant to be with is written by implication into every*

job description. You never get a second chance to make a first impression.

Talking about your weaknesses is an opportunity to show your strengths. 'I have a tendency toward perfectionism,' is something most employers welcome. 'I tend to be a bit of a workaholic' is another. Employers love workaholics.

Be wary when you talk about your weaknesses. There is a rule of thumb being used by many organizations: When it is difficult to choose between candidates' strong points, look at the weak points and do not hire or promote those lowest on the weak points. There is a growing feeling in the field of interview evaluations that the smallest number will always bring down the highest numbers.

Some writers say that success may come most readily to organizational chameleons who readily adapt their appearances to reflect norms and beliefs that are valued by the chameleons' audiences. So long as being a chameleon is tactic rather than strategy, the success thus gained is of value. Otherwise there is nothing intrinsically rewarding in it. To paraphrase an old saying: nothing recedes like success that exists only in others' eyes.

—Fifteen—

Tactics: Managers Come in Different Shapes and Sizes

> *I tell you, sir, the only safeguard of order and discipline in an organization is a standardized manager with interchangeable parts. That would solve the entire problem of management.*
>
> —Jean Giraudoux

A fundamental guideline in organizational survival is *Learn how to manage your manager.* There are different kinds of managers, so you have to adjust your tactics accordingly. The managerial types to be discussed here are found at all organizational levels. Examples of the types and how to deal with them will always be at a specific level in the organization; but this is not meant to suggest that the type under discussion is found only at that specific level. Therefore, in the discussion on Control Freaks, an example is given of a district manager, although examples of Control Freaks could be drawn from any level or part of any organization.

Consensus Builders

Consensus builders strive to gain a general agreement among their supervisors before making a decision or implementing anything. They, along with Team Leaders, are the ideal in current management literature. You may have seen a book at the airport on *How to Build Consensus in Your Organization*, or *Eight Steps to Effective Team Leadership*. If you work for a large organization, there might have been a weekend workshop in the woods on one of those topics.

You will find some pleasant aspects in the consensus builder's domain. It's far better to be there than in the grasp of a bully. But keep your guard up, nonetheless. As we saw when we discussed group behavior in chapter seven, the "consensus" group can be oppressive—limiting, if not outright forbidding, disagreements.

If your consensus building manager has the support of your group, you must pretend to be going along with, and even valuing, the process and the decisions. But you should always keep in mind that what is happening may not be in your best interest. When it is not, the best tactic is to develop and play upon doubt. This is easiest done during the decision-making process when you can suggest problems that might emerge if the decision were to go in a certain direction. The problems should be threats to the group or to the individuals. If you do this skillfully you will at least achieve a delay in the process. During the change, circumstances can change, and you will have more time to cultivate doubt.

If your consensus-building manager does not have the support of your group, that is, if he is trying to manage through consensus, but your group is not cooperating, you have more room for manipulation because it is all the easier to create doubt. You can also keep things moving in your preferred directions because the manager will be highly susceptible to your influence. By helping him in his consensus building efforts, you gain power.

Control Freaks

Management is about control. Managers are supposed to control the behavior of "the managed" in ways desired by the organization. That's logical enough as an abstract thought. But as we saw in the first chapter, real organizations either don't know what they want by way of behavior, or want a lot of things that contradict one another. For example, the organization wants you to be productive and also wants you to follow organizational rules; often, following the rules leads to unproductive behavior.

Managers face a dilemma. They are supposed to do something when no one knows what that something is. No one knows what behavior the organization really wants. When the organization speaks to that point it issues contradictory directives. Some managers deal with this crazy situation by becoming control freaks; they try to control everything. Control itself becomes the purpose of their management. This management style not only makes the life of "the managed" painful, it also leads to power clashes between managers who sense that other managers are invading their control. Many power battles are all about who gets to control who and what.

Do not argue with the control freak on the merits of control. His dependency on it drowns his ability to reason about it. You want to prevent this dependency from harming you and to manipulate it to your own advantage. Here is how you do it.

Every control freak has his own benchmarks. For one "being on time for work" is the key whereas another might insist on wanting to know where you are at all times. Usually he has a combination of specific types of behavior that tells him you are under control. Find out what your control freak's checklist is, and play to it by either actually behaving according to his control needs or providing for him the illusion that you do. You should decide which it will be by considering difficulties and advantages.

For example, if it is not difficult for you to always be available to your control freak, then do so and take advantage of your doing so by making it very clear to him that you are. You might go out of your way to make sure he has the numbers at which you can be reached, or volunteer to call in now and then. As you do that, emphasize to him that you consider it important for him to be able to reach you at all times. Remember that control freaks are often subjected to criticism, sometimes bordering on ridicule. Your appearance of sharing his need for control should endear you to him.

But what if you have a problem with "being available?" Create an illusion of availability, as Bill Satron does:

Howard Hazard is a district manager for *Carpetpure Rug Cleaning Co.* with responsibilities for twenty rug-cleaning teams in the greater Chicago area. He tells his team captains he wants to know where they are at any given moment. One of the captains, Bill Satron, has a very effective and efficient team which Bill rewards by giving them unofficial time off. Sometimes he lets them go earlier than the official "quit work" time; sometimes he lets them have a longer lunch break; sometimes he allows one worker to miss a day for a family emergency. The only reasonable way for Howard to check on his teams is by calling the location where they are scheduled to be. Not on a cell phone because Howard discovered long ago that people can pretend to be anywhere when they're on cell phones. Usually a team does four to six locations a day.

Bill manipulates the situation by calling Howard throughout the day with questions about techniques he knows Howard takes pride in being expert about, or with other questions and comments. He gambles that Howard will not call him when he makes his calls to check on the teams. He also works at having a friendly, trusting relationship with Howard. On one Friday when he was planning to let his men go home early, he called Howard to say *We're done with all our work for today and the men have been really effective all week, I thought I'd let them go now. But I told them I'd have to clear it with you. What do you think?* As you would probably guess, Bill has a cover story ready should Howard call him some time and not find him.

Illusions work when they address felt needs of the persons you wish to mislead. Just as an innate desire to "get rich, quick" makes one an easy touch for con men, the passion for control leaves one vulnerable to manipulation. While discussing every type of control would be more than can be done in this book, we will consider one more to help you get the point:

Donna Torret thought she'd never survive in the sales division of *Baxter Cereals*. On one hand her boss told her there is no slack on the monthly reports; they must be in on time and they must be complete. On the other hand, she had already found out that all the data she needed for her reports did not arrive on her desk until after the monthly reports were due. She tried explaining her problem to her boss, but quickly realized that her boss was not listening.

So, Donna got the idea of getting estimates for data she needed by averaging previous years' reports. To draw her boss in on the manipulation, she would discuss with the boss one of the thirty or more data fudgings she did every month. A day before the report was due, she would say to her boss: *I'm all set to go if you think it'd be okay to do an estimate on* (whatever). Her boss always approved.

Donna realized that her boss was not concerned about the accuracy of the report. Control freaks focus on appearances rather than substance. Furthermore, while she never said she was fudging thirty or more data entries each month, by getting permission from her boss to fudge one, she was implicating him in what she was doing. Therefore, if the boss found out what she was doing (which is not likely because the boss is not focused on accuracy), he would be only superficially upset, and he would have to be careful about how he handled it because over a period of time he had approved some of the fudgings.

A final consideration regarding control freaks: Your power is not necessarily more limited under them than it is under management that appears more relaxed and flexible. As you'll see in the section below on "Phony Empowerers," managers who profess to be leaving things to your judgment may be masters of tricky, and, for you, dangerous ambiguity. When they are artful, they can keep you twisting in the wind puzzling over why they are rejecting your work with a vague mention of "standards." It goes like this:

> *Bertha, I know how hard you've worked on this, but it just misses the mark. Try to do it over and keep in mind the agency's standards and general guidelines, but don't be shackled by them. As I keep telling you, I want you to think on your own.*

If you ask for specificity, these masters will respond in vague generalities or throw up their hands and say: *You know what I mean, don't you.* (In case you missed it, that is a period, not a question mark, at the end of the quote.) But do not despair; we'll see some ways to get the advantage over these types when we take on the "phony empowerers" later.

The Busy Busy Busy Manager

The role of manager demands that the player always appear busy. High-level managers play this game religiously. One New York-based executive describes his peers' "busy-busy" behavior as follows:

> *Many executives stroll to work in a leisurely fashion, stopping to look in shop windows and pausing to glance at pretty girls; then, as soon as they pass through the revolving doors of their office buildings, gather themselves up in a kind of Groucho Marx crouch, as if they wanted to run but felt constrained to hold themselves down to a fast, breathless walk. By the time they reach their offices, they are moving at top speed, already giving dictation while they're struggling out of their overcoats. Men who could easily allow themselves a good hour to get to the airport for a flight will happily waste time until they have to leave in a dramatic rush, shouting out last-minute instructions as they run down the hall pursued to the elevator by people with telephone messages and letters to be signed.*

In reality, some managers really do have more work than time to do it in. Often this results from inability to delegate. And much of a manager's workload results from his having made bad decisions in the past. Then there are managers who simply want to always look busy. There's an old joke: Managers write unnecessarily lengthy reports to look busy; and the reports prove that they were busy.

Your tactics should be guided by the intention to show respect for the manager's time, no matter what is really going on. Never suggest that you think one of your superiors has the time to deal with anything you are proposing. Always preface your requests with acknowledgment of how busy she is: *I hate to bother you with this. I know you don't have time for it, but . . .*

Another tactic is to use your recognition of the manager's impossible workload as an excuse to do something you want to do without clearing it with her. *I just went ahead and sent the report to Accounting. I didn't want to bother you with all those details. If you want me to, of course I'll send it to you for clearance first.*

Some managers like to display power by keeping you waiting or standing by. You'll get a call from his secretary asking you to hold off going to lunch until he gets off a conference call (it's always something that indicates his importance) and can get to you about something. You cancel any lunch plans you had and sit around waiting. There's not much you can do about this other than doing the waiting; however, do take advantage of the insight it gives you. People who have the need to show their power have some basic insecurities that leave them vulnerable to your manipulations. Whether their problem is lack of confidence or ego trips they get from displays of power, you can play upon it to your advantage.

Seldom-Seen Susans

Throughout organizations, and often at the higher levels, there are persons who are seldom around and/or unproductive when they are around. They get away with it for reasons we discussed in the chapter on power. Here we consider how you can deal with such a type when she is your supervisor or coworker.

Despite their power, Seldom-Seen Susans are sensitive and highly protective. They are usually ruthless when it comes to maintaining their jobs. For one reason or another they have talked themselves into believing that they have a right to their jobs, salary, etc. So, never set off their trip wires. Appear to share with them their notion that what they have is something like a god-given right.

When Seldom-Seen Susan is your boss you should:

- Find someone at her level or higher who can be relied upon as a supporter. Seldom-Seens have lots of enemies in the organization, and people who simply do not like them. So, if you look around, you'll find an ally. Use this person as "a knowledgeable other", a person who knows what's going on. Sometimes you'll do this verbally, sometimes you'll provide some documentation. Ask for advice; draw this person into your problem. But always remember that you established this relationship to help you with your problem. Don't become a pawn in power struggles between this person and your boss. Be careful, select carefully, proceed cautiously.

- Help your Seldom-Seen cover her oversights and mistakes. Take on some of her tasks. Do them well and let her take all the credit in public. If you're playing your cards wisely, the right people in the organization will know what's really going on, and they will appreciate it. Always remember that her power base is well known and a source of irritation to others in the organization. Take on the role of a person who is dedicated to task accomplishment despite the shortcomings of your boss. You'll find people gaining respect for you. Your reputation overall will be enhanced. But remember to never be seen by your boss as a threat to her safe haven.

- If you're offered a transfer, think at least twice before accepting it, particularly if it's a reward for your suffering. Consider what's to be gained by staying where you are—not as a martyr, but as a person dedicated to your work. Consider that with the transfer you might be viewed as a person who has been paid in full for your suffering. The offer of the transfer might be an indicator to you that your tactics are working, that people are seeing you as someone who makes things happen effectively despite who your boss is. If that is so, it could be just the beginning of a growth in others' respect for you. Maybe you want to milk this a little more.

If Seldom-Seen is a coworker, you should first find out why she continues to hold the job. She might have considerable informal power or her supervisor might want to avoid confrontation.

When Seldom-Seen coworkers have power, you should resign yourself to their presence. Do not complain about her to your supervisor—he knows about her, but cannot do anything about it—or to anyone else. Everyone already knows, so you gain nothing by complaining. If others avoid being teamed with Seldom-Seen, consider teaming with her when you can accomplish the task on your own. And don't brag about how you are doing all the work. Everyone will already know that. Your position, if asked, is that you are primarily interested in the work and do not mind doing it mostly on your own. This will impress people.

When Seldom-Seen coworkers do not have power but benefit from having a non-confrontational supervisor, you will probably anger your other coworkers by teaming with her and carrying the load by yourself. In these situations, your coworkers are usually furious about the supervisor's inaction, so you do not want to become a focus for that anger. Your best tactic is to do nothing if your coworkers are doing nothing about it, but to join with them if they develop a plan for getting rid of Seldom-Seen.

Possibly, doing nothing could become hazardous because Seldom-Seen is a problem for you personally. Then you must go to your supervisor and pleasantly demand something be done. Your style should be very friendly, but your message must be confrontational; i.e., you must make it clear that at this meeting you are demanding a solution, that this is not just a conversation. He will most likely reach an agreement with you that negates the possible harm you sense from Seldom-Seen. Or, he might be pushed to confront Seldom-Seen.

Martyrs

Every organization has its workaholics who call a lot of attention to the amount of time they give to the company. Sometimes they moan, sometimes they brag about it. What is certain is that you're going to hear about it, a lot. While they seldom criticize you directly for not working the hours they do, they insidiously compare your working schedule to theirs, all the time.

Workaholics are insecure people, even when their jobs are not threatened. Sometimes there's trouble at home, although workaholics invariably tell you they wish they had "more time to spend with the wife and kids." In case you miss that message, there are usually family pictures on his desk.

The major cause of the workaholic's insecurity is usually that he senses he has been promoted to a position he is not fully qualified to fill. He begins overworking as a defense mechanism. If he maintains the position, he then associates overworking with the way he keeps the job. It is, of course, always possible that a job requires overworking, that there is no other way to get all the work done. But this is seldom the explanation for the workaholic. People who are overworking because the work demands it usually find ways to relieve themselves of some of the work. They often delegate.

If your boss plays martyr, he probably needs considerable stroking from his subordinates. The signals you send him should leave little room for doubt about your approval. Don't send any kind of signals of disapproval because this manager is low on self-esteem. Don't be misled by any appearances to the contrary. He may be skillful at pretending to be tough and able to take criticism; he might even brag about it. The tip-off to you that he is insecure and has low self-esteem is that he is a work-aholic. Keep him within a friendly distance, so that he desires your approval, but is never certain he has it entirely. Do special things for him now and then—remembering a birthday or something like that.

These types of persons are poor time managers, so you may suffer from their lack of priority organization. When they give you work that must be done yesterday, or ask you to work over-time, do it in good spirit; but if it causes you inconvenience, do not hesitate to mention that. If you are at a lower level in the organization, be sure to inquire about overtime pay if it is not offered; if you are in a higher level you, of course, do not mention things like overtime pay. Emphasize that you are willing to work overtime occasionally. Unless you have a specific tactical reason for doing otherwise, communicate that you are not a martyr, that you do not expect to work overtime as part of your job. Emphasize that you will do so from time to time because you want to be a team player.

Of course, your language will never reveal a criticism of this person as a workaholic. When you don't want to work overtime you won't say "I'm not a dumb workaholic like you." Rather, you'll say something like this:

> FRED: *Sorry about this, George, but I'll need the March figures from you before Monday, so it looks like both of us will have to come in Saturday. You know, I really try to keep the rest of you from working these crazy hours that I do. But this is an exception.*
>
> GEORGE: *No problem, Fred. These things happen. I wouldn't be able to come in here every Saturday like you do. But I expect to have to now and then.*

George should not say: *No problem, Fred. I'll be here.* If he did, he would be setting up an expectation that he does not want to fulfill; that is, that he is available anytime.

The workaholic might try to send you on a guilt trip. So let's look at that phenomenon—being invited to take a guilt trip—in general.

Guilt Trippers

The techniques of making people feel guilty have gone underground. It is no longer socially correct to scold or berate, and there are even legal sanctions for some forms of scolding at work. Thus, we see the emergence of a new social language to send people on guilt trips with benign and kindly phrases: "I know you can do better." "I'm disappointed." "You poor dear, you were probably hoping it would come out much better than that."

Force the guilt-trippers out into the open. Find out what they are after. If, for example, yours is a control freak, treat her accordingly. Or, he might be a martyr, to be so treated.

Coaches

Modern management theory loves the image of "the coach." Managers are pictured as "coaches rather than policemen."

While a coach may appear more attractive than a policeman, you are better off sometimes with a policeman than a coach. A policeman may be threatening, but he is restricted in his relationships with you. He is allowed to act only within a narrow legal scope, and you have recourse within the legal system should he overstep his boundaries. A coach owns you, and the ways in which he is allowed to interact with you are virtually endless. Coaches want you to play better so that the team and he win. While you may find, here and there, a coach who is truly interested in your personal development, don't assume that the coach you're looking at right now is one of those.

If you are doing decently at your organizational assignments, you have nothing to fear from the manager-as-policeman, and you have something to gain. He will come down hard on those around you who are not doing what they should at their jobs.

The manager-as-coach is supposed to be able to motivate those people the manager-as-policeman will punish. So, when managers purport to be coaches, they are forced by that role to "work with" some incorrigible people.

When you hear "coach" used, ask yourself if he means that you're on a rowing crew or a soccer team. The role of individuals is quite different in those games. In rowing, synchronization is the key to everything. In soccer, individual efforts play a significant part.

Another undesirable characteristic of coaches: they are masters at making you feel guilty. It's a major tool in their bag of motivational tricks. *You have it in you to play harder and better." "I'm only asking you to do well for yourself." "Years from now you'll look back on this day. Play today so that when you look back you'll feel proud.*

Coaches have always been praised for getting the best from the players. So they are attractive as models for managers. Managers like to think of themselves as coaches and can get really carried away with that self-image. So what do you do when someone at work plays coach and gives you the old pep talk about "only wanting to help you do better." Do you say: "Get off my back. I don't need any guilt trips. I'm doing well enough for myself." No, for two reasons. First, it would only make you sound defensive, unwilling to accept sincerely-offered assistance. Second, the manager probably believes he means what he is saying; so, you'll get him angry with that response.

What you want to say and do depends on which of three types of situations you're in:

Situation One: The person giving the pep talk satisfies herself with the pep talk; i.e., she doesn't really expect you to do anything different. For whatever reason, she just needed to utter the phrases.

Situation Two: The person expects to see something different, but is not really clear about what it is she wants to see.

Situation Three: The person knows exactly the changes she wants to see happen.

When in Situation One, show appreciation for the performance. If appropriate, even thank the person. Then forget about it.

When in Situation Two, bring about some changes that would appear reasonably positive to any observer, and that are easy for you to accomplish, then point to them as the other person's creation. This could be an opportunity for you to do something you've wanted to do for some time.

When in Situation Three, you have various possibilities:

- If you're in a "numbers game" situation—e.g., "increase your output by x in two months"—look to see if a creative use of statistics will enable you to make it appear you have achieved the goal.
- If you're in a "numbers game" situation and cannot manipulate the statistics in your favor, try to co-opt the person into working with you on a plan to achieve the goal. "I'd really like to have your guidance, at least initially, on how to go about achieving this," or something like that.
- If neither of the above works, warn the person about undesirable side effects that might result from your attempts to achieve the new goal. If the person is not receptive, you might want to work your loop in the organization. Tell someone in another department who might be affected by the alleged undesirable side effects.
- If you're not in a "numbers game" situation, press for precision in expectations. Too many managers use this situation and then later say that you just didn't under-

stand what they had in mind. They know that they want change because they are being badgered by their superiors to improve things. The only way that what you do will satisfy them is if it satisfies their superiors. If you sense this is what the situation is, be insistent on getting precise marching orders. You can facilitate this by stating hypothetical possibilities, then adding "is that what you have in mind?"

Imprecision as a Managerial Weapon

Some managers are masters in the art of imprecision, and are encouraged to be so in some of the books and articles on "modern management."

The advice goes something like this: Provide your bosses and your subordinates with the feeling that your unit has a sense of direction without publicly committing yourself to a specific set of objectives. Use opaque and ambiguous phrases like:

- Our company aims to be number one in its industry.
- Our objective is growth with profit.
- We seek the maximum return on investment.
- Management's goal is to meet its responsibilities to stockholders, employees, and the public.

Statements like these provide almost no guidance to anyone. Yet they are quite readily accepted as objectives by large numbers of intelligent people.

This is very sound advice, even though it may surprise you to find out that this type of manipulation is part of professional management's repertoire. Here's how knowing about it can provide you with an advantage. If your superior is using imprecision because she does not want to be committed publicly, you should use one of the following tactics after assessing her intent and seriousness: (1) Respond with imprecision that serves your interests. She can hardly correct your imprecision without getting more precise about her own statements. (2) Suggest some very precise ways of responding that benefit you. She may well accept that. (3) Tell her you don't understand what she's saying.

Teamwork

"Teamwork" is a buzzword. It captures the imaginations of some managers and you will find yourself from time to time the victim of their enthusiasm. Although you know that this, like all the other managerial fads, will pass, there will be a short period of time when you must play along with management's temporary conversion.

Some managers who like to think of themselves as enlightened will tell you they want to try out some teamwork projects and will ask you what you think of teamwork. Don't consider this to be a serious question. The manager may be only self-affirming her enlightenment as a manager who talks things over with the troops. She wants you to say you like teamwork, so say you do. If she wanted you to say you don't like teamwork, she would have said she'd been *told* she should try some teamwork.

Going on the assumption that her enthusiasm will be short-lived, your goal is to emerge from the "trying" with an image of a person who supported her all the way, who wanted her to look good. So be prepared to take leadership in the team project she proposes and to do most of the work. Mark Rider, a district inventory manager for a nationwide chain of office supplies' stores, show us how to do it:

> *We had this new vice-president who I think was looking around for ways to make his mark. He came up with a dumb idea about copying Japanese lean manufacturing techniques. He wanted us to have minimum inventories. I could see that he didn't want to hear anything about how inapplicable that idea was in our business, so I went*

along with him, even when he asked at a meeting of district inventory managers if we thought we could work as a team on this exciting new project. We'd already heard from him how he was going to bring 'cutting-edge modern management science' to our work, and how to him that meant 'empowerment, teamwork, and quality.' So we nodded in the right places and looked impressed both with him and ourselves.

I was placed on a team that would lay out a plan for minimum inventories in paper products. Being real big on delegation and empowerment, he told us he would leave it all in our capable hands. He wanted a report in six months. The rest was up to us. Little things like how do busy district managers with offices spread all over the country get together were no challenge for a bunch of creative people that he knew we all were.

He left us the rest of the afternoon to meet in our teams and design approaches. I suppose he went off to a management improvement workshop with Tom Peters or someone like that.

I knew the five other people on my team. All of them would be looking for a way to avoid letting this get in the way of their real work. So they jumped at my offer to be secretary for the group. I offered to take notes and suggested that we brainstorm the VP's ideas. Once they saw that all they had to do was talk while I took notes with a promise to organize and distribute those notes, they relaxed and did a lot of talking.

Over the next six months, it was easy to maintain control over the team. At the end of the first month I arranged a meeting with the VP. Over lunch I told him I was pulling together ideas from the team and wanted some of his input to guide us along. I ended the lunch meeting on a note that established continuing contact with him on this matter. I made it clear that all he would be asked to do was to give me advice.

Our final report never saw life outside a filing cabinet, but it looked good. And the VP was my useful ally for the time he stayed on. He left after about a year to become CEO of an office equipment manufacturer. Every so often, when I'm in his city, we have lunch.

Mark Rider knows how to take advantage of a potentially time-wasting activity. As things go, he might find his next job to be a step up in another company, on the recommendation of the VP he helped. Such a fruitful ending does not have to happen for Mark's tactics to be winners. Even if that VP had been fired in disgrace, Mark's actions would be viewed as indicative of a loyal employee and a team player.

Interdepartmental Cooperation

Just as teamwork is a buzzword, interdepartmental cooperation is a buzz phrase. It is elusive for the organization because its rewards are often abstract, whereas reward for departmental achievements are normally concrete. Raise your unit's production, and you are likely to get a reward. Participate in interdepartmental planning sessions and there is no concrete reward.

Your superior—whether he be the president to your vice-presidency, or the production supervisor to your foremanship—has "interdepartmental cooperation" as an essential raison d'etre for his role in the organization. He will keep coming back to it in one way or another.

Like teamwork, it appears to make sense. Why would anyone be against it? All presentations of it as a goal are argued as win-win situations. Everyone gains when we have cooperation.

But departments are natural-made enemies. In production organizations, universities, government agencies, service companies, churches, and schools, organizations encourage departments to fight over budget allocations and personnel levels.

Department heads resent the time they waste on efforts at "interdepartmental cooperation." They know there are no rewards for individuals they involve in it, so they dislike being forced to assign man-hours to it. Most attempts at "interdepartmental cooperation" go no further than establishment of committees to discuss the potential benefits. A department head of a manufacturing company once said to me, *It's just all bullshit.*

You should do two things regarding your role in "interdepartmental cooperation" efforts. Avoid a role in them without alienating your boss, if he's a fan of the effort.

Phony Empowerers

If your boss tells you she wants to give you power over your own job so that you do it according to your own standards and no one else's, and then turns around and moans about what you have done, she's a "phony empowerer." Words like "empowerment," "worker participation," and "workers know best" become popular from time to time. Be wary. A revealing study of empowerment was done of an architectural design firm in a large metropolitan area on the west coast. The firm's ownership and top-management announced that they were sold on the empowerment concept; so, when a project was given to a designer, he was told to do it to meet the needs of the client in the best way he could. No more direction was ostensibly given.

Nonetheless, designers found some of their products rejected in the final approval stage, which was kept in the hands of ownership and top management. Reasons given for rejection were ambiguous. References were made to elusive criteria.

The study revealed that while those at the top said they were empowering, they had their own unexpressed model of what their firm should produce.

When your "empowerer" has hidden criteria, you should find out what they are and either meet them or give the appearance of meeting them. "Empowerers" who don't have criteria, but refuse to accept the consequences of empowerment, are more difficult to deal with because what they want may merely be the power to have the final word or may change from day to day.

Innovation

Having a good idea is not sufficient for its implementation. A good idea becomes an organizational policy or practice only if it is salable. Rosabeth Moss Kanter suggests that the most salable ideas are:

> *Trialable (can be demonstrated on a pilot basis); Reversible (allowing the organization to go back to pre-project status if it doesn't work); Divisible (can be done in steps or phases); Consistent with sunk costs (builds on prior resource commitments); Concrete (tangible, discrete); and with Publicity Value (visible potential if it works).*

When these features are not present, projects should be either *marginal (appear off-to-the-sidelines so they can slip in unnoticed) or should have support from one or more very powerful people in the organization.*

Another tactic is to stress the disposability of your project. *If you don't like it, it can be scratched at any point.* The facts are that once someone approves a project, their reputation is built into it, so they have a commitment to keeping it alive. You can string them along for a long period of time by suggesting that a breakthrough is right around the corner.

But, you might protest, if the project ultimately fails, doesn't that seriously damage my reputation. Not necessarily. First of all, there are in any organization many projects ongoing for a long time that are not successes because (a) no one knows how to ascertain if something is failing or succeeding, or (b) people are used to its being around and rationalize its existence. By the time a project has been around awhile, it becomes of value to those involved in it. Second, even if a project is scrapped, you can walk away respected if you play your cards right. If you are, in general, respected and liked, people around you will find any number of reasons for the project's failure without blaming you.

—*Sixteen*—

Tactics: Manipulating Numbers, Office Space, and Whistle-Blowing

Statistics: The only science that enables different experts using the same figures to draw different conclusions.

—Evan Esar

Someone said that if you torture numbers long enough they will confess to anything. As you saw in our discussion on what organizations really are, numbers have a mystical authority even though they are supremely protean. Everyone knows that companies use accounting systems that make their bottom lines look best, that universities and individual university researchers statisticulate, that just about everything is presented in whatever number system makes the presenter look good.

Your ability to manipulate numbers is essential to your survival. You must put yourself into positions where you can do this, and you must know the specific tactics involved.

The following techniques will put you on the road to understanding how to use statistics, but to really have a full command of what is possible, you'll need to study statistical and accounting basics, along with computer software techniques. Highly-intelligent students often begged me to be spared an encounter with a mathematical technique such as regression analysis. If we were to give a prize for "How Best to Ensure Lack of Success," it would be difficult to choose between those students and students who avoid improving their verbal skills. You should seize every opportunity to improve your ability to work with numbers. You also want to get yourself into positions where you, not someone else, has control over the numbers relating to your personal and your work section's reputation.

Here and there one finds a presentation of numbers that is completely objective. But normally everything has a spin on it. Statistics is an art as well as a science because even though you are working with mathematics that must be correct, you have choices between ways of calculating things. In those choices lies your success or failure. Many things can be presented as either succeeding or failing, with both conclusions being statistically correct.

Even organizations as dedicated to scientific objectivity as hospitals select statistical ways of presenting things that make them look good. Although deaths from preventable errors in hospitals are probably twice the number of deaths from automobile accidents, the major medical associations say that hospitals report a far lower number. The hospital that is slow to identify its problems often comes to be regarded as a good hospital because its statistics look good.

There is fury in the scientific community about statisticulation. In 1995, a group of scientists from a wide number of fields gathered in a conference to discuss the rampant manipulation of statistics just about anyplace you look. The following proposition was discussed: *At risk is public trust in such scientific tools as statistical analysis, controlled laboratory and clinical experiments, the rational analysis of political oratory, and the study of history, anthropology and every other field dependent on disciplined, rational thought.*

Just about all the number crunching going on in your organization is being done to promote someone's interests. Why should it be otherwise? Why should a person who has three or more legitimate ways to state "the facts" not state them in the way most helpful to himself? So get some control over the spins affecting your job and career. Here's how it's done.

Samples With Built-In Biases

Sally Fountain is a marketing analyst for a manufacturer of men's shirts and ties. She has been told to do a marketing survey to test the demand for a new tie design by George Blankenship, who is the company's top designer. George and Sally have cooperated many times informally in various coalitions. Recently they joined with the head of the shipping division to get a decision they wanted the budget division to make on automation in the shipping division.

George tells Sally that he really wants this design to have a chance, which is sufficient for Sally to know that he wants her to design a survey that will give his design the maximum opportunity. She asks George who he sees as the buyer for this tie. He tells her that the typical buyer will be a 35-year-old businessman in a large corporation.

Sally now knows that she needs to have results—replies to her survey—that suggest that the respondents prefer the design tie to some alternatives. She tests George's judgment by having the tie shown to the buyers he targeted. This is done in men's upscale clothing stores. Salesmen with whom Sally's division have worked in the past are selected on the basis of whether or not they like the tie when they first see it. Those who like it become part of the survey. Those who don't like it are dropped from the survey.

Sally now has ninety salesmen participating in the survey. She asks Francis Gomez, a pricer in the company, to estimate what the company might charge for this tie during a slack season. She also lets Francis know that she "likes" this tie. Francis puts it at anywhere from $100 to $150.

Sally asks the ninety salesmen to show the tie in comparison with a few other ties made by rival manufacturers that sell
at around $100. She does not say anything about the season
being slack or peak. She pays each of the salesmen $750.

Are you surprised to find out that the results showed that
this tie would have a good market?

Colleges and universities are masters at the built-in bias
game. As you prepare to select a postgraduate program have
you ever been impressed by that figure the school presents as
the average annual salary of its graduates? Well, think about
how that "average" was statisticulated.

- Those who replied were more likely to exaggerate
  than to understate their salaries. (That's just human
  nature, especially when you're talking about yourself
  to your old school group.)
- The questionnaires could be sent only to alumni who
  had addresses listed with the alumni office or who
  were listed in Who's Who type publications. It is
  highly probable that this group of alumni have considerably higher salaries than alumni who drop out
  of contact with the school and are not listed in any
  directory of notables.

Then there's that statistic about how college graduates earn
so much more money than high school graduates. In the late
1990's, the figure most commonly used was 60%. If you're thinking of getting a bachelor's degree from an ordinary college, that
60% is a balloon of hot air. It is disfigured by two things: (1) It
includes persons who hold graduate degrees and are earning
75% more than the average high school graduate. (2) It includes
persons from prestige schools who make 88% more than the
high school graduate.

This, of course, does not keep your local Southeastern
Hobunk State from trumpeting the 60% figure, suggesting that
you will gain accordingly by getting one of its degrees.

The built-in bias tactic can be used on a smaller scale, as well. Meetings and conferences are commonly "stacked" to assure the conclusion. Executives are transparently playing that game when they say "Everyone I've talked to likes the idea!"

Numbers à la carte

Colleges and universities are good case studies for statisticulation because we think they are above that tawdry stuff practiced by money-grubbing businesses and politically sleazy government bureaucracies. So let's go back on campus to learn about how you can have almost anything any way you like by choosing the most convenient accounting system.

Erik Larson revisited his alma mater, *The University Of Pennsylvania*, in 1996, to find out why tuition had increased twice as fast as the overall cost of living. He discovered and wrote about some creative bookkeeping practices, one of which he writes about below:

> *Measuring Penn's overall health turns out to be a tricky matter. The numbers it reports to the IRS are very different from those it discloses in its annual reports to the university community. Its latest federal tax return shows Penn finishing fiscal 1995 with an apparent surplus of revenue over expenses totaling $182.8 million, which is more than its undergraduates paid in tuition. But its annual report for the same period, compiled under a different set of accounting rules, shows a surplus of $63.4 million—which then, through the miracle of university accounting, disappears to yield a deficit.*

Which Average Would You Like?

There are many situations in which you do not have control over the numbers to be crunched. For example, the salaries of people in your organization are given, but when it comes to talking about average salary, you have your choice of three averages. The nice thing about this is you can pick the one that best serves your purpose at the moment. The even nicer thing is that all three are perfectly legitimate statistical conclusions. Sheila Dawn told me how she learned about this.

> *My first decent job was with a bank. I was one of fifteen loan officers. The head of that section, Rita Sikely, told me that she believed in getting the best salaries around for her people. The average salary in her section, she said, was $27,000. My beginning salary was $21,450.*
>
> *I was active in the local American Management Association chapter, so I was at a conference in a nearby town when Rita appeared on a panel discussing productivity improvement in banks. At that time I'd been with the bank a month or so. Each panelist told about how she or he had improved productivity in her organization. I distinctly hear Rita say that the average salary in her section was $23,000.*
>
> *That night I was thinking about the discrepancy in the averages and then it came to me that averages come in the form of means, medians and modes. If seven of us in the section had salaries below $23,000, one had a salary of $23,000, and the other seven had salaries above $23,000, then the median was $23,000. And it is statistically proper to call a median 'the average.' The mean is derived by adding up all fifteen section salaries and dividing that total by fifteen. If some salaries were well into the $30,000 level, then you could also have a legitimate average (the mean) of $27,000.*

It was convenient for Rita to use the higher figure to get my attention, and the lower figure when she wanted to impress her peers with how good a job she does even with a low average salary to work with. At first I was angry, and then I decided I owed her one for teaching me a lesson. Now I use 'the average' that suits me best.

How to Be All Things to All Men

You will also want to be able to show different things to different audiences. During his second presidential term, Bill Clinton showed his mastery of this skill. For example, in the summer of 1997, he struck a budget deal with Congress that could be defended in contradictory ways, as the President did during a news conference on August 6. If you were one of those who worried about budget cuts jeopardizing social programs, President Clinton had this soothing response: *This plan includes the largest increase in college aid since the GI bill 50 years ago, the largest increase in children's health since Medicaid was enacted over 30 years ago.*

If you were one of those who worried that there were not enough budget cuts in social programs, the President went into another pocket and came up with this: *Let me remind you, when you adjust for inflation, all these departments with discretionary budgets are going to have to cut spending 10 percent during this budget, and in addition sizable entitlement savings will be made in Medicare.*

Notice that Mr. Clinton avoided the issue of whether social programs should be increased or decreased, and avoided directly stating whether this budget increased or decreased spending on social programs. Notice also that he was able to do this without directly lying because he had a vast array of figures to work with.

There will be many times when you find yourself confronting contradictory demands. One vice-president is yelling for cost reductions, another for production increases, another for development of new products. Perhaps you want to give each one a picture of how your unit is doing that appears to meet each of their demands. Or perhaps you have a new project to launch and want to sell each of them on it. Generate a lot of numbers in a lot of categories. Statisticulate. Then pull out appropriate numbers for each vice-president, spin with appealing words, and package slickly.

Half-Truths and Skewing

Have you ever been told that we live longer today than our forefathers did? You probably take that as a fact. But did you ever check the ages when famous people died and been surprised by how much older they were than what you'd been told about life spans? For example, the average age at death of American males in the 18th century was 47. But Jefferson and all of those famous people we know about lived well beyond that age.

Here's the explanation: Using the mean as the average, and including every death, the average was 47. However, a very large percentage of children died at an early age. If you lived to be a teenager your life span expectancy went up to around sixty years or more.

When you have a large number of incidents (deaths, births, steering columns that break, loaves of bread that are inedible, people unemployed, cable wires that break, or whatever) look to see if there is a skewing in the data, something that is not a normal progression. (For example, we expect the vast majority of children to live today, so if you look at the data of the 18th century, all those children's deaths look like a skewing of the data.) If there is, then you have an advantage in presenting the data. You can present it as average life spans are presented, or you can point out the skewing.

This is often done with unemployment figures at the beginning of summer. Those analysts who want to present the economy as getting worse point out that unemployment has gone up.

Those who want to present the economy as not getting worse point out that school students seeking and not finding employment always increases the unemployment rate at the beginning of summer.

Perhaps the most common use of half-truthing is conjured with charts. Let's say that William has a project running for a year now. It could involve production, training, or just about anything else. His staff does an evaluation study, which shows on a graph how there has been steady improvement (in whatever project is supposed to improve) since the project started. Unfortunately, the staff included in the study a time span of twelve months prior to the beginning of the project, and the same level of improvement is shown on the chart for that pre-project time period. No problem. The graph presented in William's final report begins with the month the project began.

To the Vivid Belongs the Attention

It is crucial for William to present his evaluation person-to-person and on a graph because he wants to control attention. Both the person-to-person and the graph are vivid communications. Language itself, no matter how logical or empirically sound, is usually a losing competitor to graphics and person-to-person as an attention-grabber. Once attention is grabbed, commitment often follows close behind if personal interests are evoked. Lynn, a high-level executive, sees that graph vividly portraying PROGRESS, hears William say it is, and psychologically buys it. She becomes committed to believing it. If someone thinks of pointing out that the graph doesn't capture the "before project" period, he will probably think twice before mentioning it if he is aware of Lynn's commitment. Imagine a group of managers sitting around a sturdy oak oval table watching William's presentation. Jim spots the self-serving half-truth. He also notices Lynn and a couple of other heavy hitters nodding appreciatively. Jim will probably not say anything.

Don't Tread on My Commitment

If Jim does speak up, it will be no problem for William. He can say something like *Well, the data for pre-project period is questionable.* (Data, particularly the data gathered in an organization are always questionable.) Or he can say a number of other things that Lynn and those others will accept, because they are committed. All he has to do is provide a plausible response to Jim.

Also, Lynn and some of the others have probably bought into the project in one way or another prior to William's presentation. Perhaps Lynn actually approved it, or one of the others approved some resources for it. Someone, probably a number of persons, want this project to succeed for their own personal reasons.

Selective Subgroup Comparisons

You may find yourself in the position of doing a survey in your organization, wanting a positive finding but unsure about whether it will be forthcoming. Your best bet is to use a large number of possible verbal, not numerical, responses. A verbal response is a check in a box labeled "Good" or "Poor", or another word. A numerical response is a check in a box that has a number label; the word "Good" might have the number "3" assigned to it, which you check. You do not want to do numerical responses unless you are very confident that the number will be high. (Or low, if it is in your interest to rate a program as a failure.)

You want to use a large number of possible responses to increase your choices when you make your selection of what to report and to increase the likelihood that a respondent will check a favorable rating box. Give respondents a choice between excellent, very good, good, poor, and very poor, rather than good or poor. The former will significantly raise your chances of getting a large percentage of checks in the good box. Given any large number of people, there will be a tendency to grade toward the center of the possibilities you provide.

You may also want to use a "Don't Know" or "Uncertain" box because it can provide you with advantageous selection possibilities. Suppose that you are surveying interest in flextime in your organization and you want the results to be as negative as you can make them. Your boxes should read "Pro," and "Con," "Uncertain." Obviously you would not want to provide a lot of information on what flextime would mean in practice.

Let's say that the responses are 34% Pro, 26% Con, and 40% Uncertain. You can report that only 34% of the respondents were favorable. If you had been in favor of flextime you could, of course, report that only 26% of the respondents were opposed to the idea. If you want your organization to put this on hold, stress the high number of people who are uncertain.

The bigger your reputation for "scientific" numbers crunching, the better your chances are for being taken seriously when you opt for one subgroup of numbers over another. If you're Chairman of the Federal Reserve Board, your words are magically credible. When Chairman Alan Greenspan declared in July of 1997 that the productivity of the U.S. worker was accelerating at an awesome rate, most people probably accepted the declaration as an objective conclusion based on a rigorous methodology.

Louis Uchitelle, writing for *The New York Times*, looked beyond the statement and found Greenspan statisticulating so as to come to conclusions compatible with The White House's version of the economy:

> *The overall statistic that has been used in the past covers all three private sectors: financial, corporate, and non-corporate.*
>
> *Greenspan's new favorite measure covers only the corporate sector, leaving out the two others. While the overall productivity statistic shows just under 1 percent annual growth in the 1990s, the corporate sector has averaged*

1.5 percent, surging to more than 2.5 percent in the last 24 months. What Mr. Greenspan is doing is taking apart the national trend and finding a piece of it that fit his story.

Making a Little Bit Go a Long Way

Legend has it that this tactic was invented and perfected by the military. So we'll let Army First Lieutenant Linda Tunney tell you about it:

When I took over as maintenance officer for the tanks at a camp in Germany, I was surprised to see that according to the last readiness report only two of the twenty tanks had failed to pass combat readiness inspection. I figured I was following a tough act. I was the first woman to be given that command. I sure didn't want to blow it.

During the first month, we seemed to be having an awful lot of snafus with the tanks. I was signing beaucoup repair requests and parts orders. When I did a hands on, I was told that this one didn't even start, that one has a crazy gear problem, this one over here has a jammed cannon, that one to the left has a faulty air filtering system. And on and on it went like that.

I struggled to get things better for five months and then what I really dreaded came due: the semi-annual combat readiness report. Sometime over a period of 48 hours, I was charged to see how many of my tanks were ready to go out and do battle. It was obvious to me that I was going to have a lot fewer on my report than my predecessor had. I could see it already: they'd all say that it proves you can't give a woman command of weaponry. I was despondent and desperate. So I did what every young officer does in a new situation when frustration roars. I had beer with my top sergeant.

No problem, he told me, here's what we do: At 0800 tomorrow, we test all the tanks we know will pass. I figure there's six of them. After that we take each of the other tanks one at a time, fit it with whatever it needs from the other tanks, test it, pass it. By the time we're done—it usually takes us thirty hours or so—we'll only have two or three tanks that we couldn't fix good enough to pass the test. No sweat. No lying. We test every tank and we give a report on its readiness. You're gonna look fine, ma'am.

So-Called Cost Benefit Analysis

You will find many decision-makers who like to have the comfort of "cost-benefit analysis" before they sign on. This is an analysis that supposedly shows the relationship of what something will cost to what that something will provide. For example, I show you that the cost of a new computer for my secretary will enable her to do twice as much work. I then show the cost of her salary and benefits over the period of the expected life of the computer.

Cost-benefit analysis is always subjective. There is always room for differences of opinion on which costs to include (do you or do you not include costs of training the secretary to use the new computer?). Figuring the benefits is open to even more debate because there is a question on how far into the future you will look; there are also questions about which things to consider benefits, and you get into some plain guesswork when it comes to putting dollar figures on many of the benefits it is decided to include.

Therefore, on decisions that are important to you, get yourself at least into the process, if you can't gain control of the cost-benefit analysis. An even better tactic is to learn the types of cost-benefit analysis commonly used in your organization. Then find out the pros and cons on each in the literature. (Academics in this field thrive on putting out articles and books in which they claim to be demonstrating objective advantages and disadvantages of the method under discussion.) You will then be prepared to tailor an argument for the type of analysis most biased toward your preferences.

Knowing the various methods of cost-benefit analysis may put you in the position of being asked to participate in analyses of projects that are of no interest to you. In that case, find out who wants the analysis to come out which way. Then pick the person you most want to cultivate as an ally. The rest is obvious.

Where's the Methodology?

Just as your knowledge of statistical methods helps you get things to add up the way you would like them to, being savvy about methodology helps you pulverize the opposition. The rule of thumb is this: If the conclusion to a study is contradictory to your interests, challenge the method that led to the conclusion.

This is usually a successful tactic because (a) there's a good chance that the conclusions are flagrantly faulty, and (b) even when conclusions are reasonable, they are vulnerable.

And don't be afraid to go after institutions that have an aura of research respectability. Back in 1979 *University of Colorado* researchers concluded that living near power lines causes elevated rates of childhood leukemia. After the study was reported in the media, parents of children with cancer sued power companies, and values of property near power lines went downhill. Twenty years later, a *National Cancer Institute* panel reported on an exhaustive study which found no evidence of that link. The panel also exposed the *University of Colorado* study as poorly designed and somewhat capriciously carried out.

Keep foremost in your mind that just as the CEO is a person playing that role, researchers are people playing those roles. As people they have needs. They have to keep their jobs. They have to come up with conclusions even when the available data and research methods support no conclusions. They might have an ego need to be recognized for having "discovered" something. Don't be misled by any rhetoric that goes with the role. Be distrustful! People are, after all, people. The percentage of saints in the average population is not in the double digits.

However, do beware making the mistake that Jim might have made in the example above about William's half-truthing with a graph. Don't get in the face of a committed person who does not want correction. If Jim wants to lower Lynn's enthusiasm for William's graph, he must mount a cunning tactical maneuver. Attacking William at the presentation may be correct in terms of pure statistics; it is also politically obtuse. In most cases, Jim will decide that the efforts of an appropriate set of tactics is not warranted. Unless he or his unit lose considerably if William's half-truth succeeds, or unless he can use exposure of the half-truth for reasons other than simply exposing William, the odds are very high that Jim, or anyone else in this position, will let it go. And that is a very wise choice.

Confidence, Yes; Accuracy, No

If you were exposed to any research methodology in high school or college, you learned that conclusions should be based on carefully-gathered data and that your data should be as accurate as possible. In an organization, accuracy can be detrimental to your presentation. Confidence is what you want, and confidence decreases as accuracy increases. This is one of those counterintuitive things that drives rationality-worshipers crazy. The more accurately we understand something, the less confident we are in what we think we know about it. The less accurately we understand it, the more confident we are about that understanding.

Social scientists have been studying this phenomenon for over forty years, analyzing case histories, interviewing people, and conducting experiments. It always comes out the same: confidence and accuracy are inversely correlated.

So, keep accuracy fuzzy—while pretending to be scientifically passionate by presenting everything in sophisticated quantitative formats—if you want to gain your audience's confidence in your conclusions. Put far more effort into putting a spin on the data which feeds your audience's self-interest than into accuracy.

If Caught, Plead the Big Picture

Now and then people get caught fudging figures. In a few of those cases, something is made of it. For example, there was a scandal in 1997 regarding reports coming out of the FBI laboratory. The Inspector General said that the following were common practice at the lab:

- Supervisors improperly altered or omitted examiners' reports, at times shading them to favor prosecutors' cases.
- Examiners went beyond their expertise, presenting scientifically flawed and inaccurate testimony in high-profile cases.

The FBI responded with "the big picture" argument. What the IG noted, said FBI Deputy Director William Esposito, is *only a small part of the total volume of work done by the lab.*

This tactic is most successful when you first plead the big picture and then add, as did Esposito, your deep concern, because *even one problem is too many.* Experienced users of this tactic spread their hands for the big picture statement, then stare intently into the TV camera and slam a hand on the podium, or air if a podium is not available, when they make the one-is-too-many statement.

However, I advise you to not invent numbers. Statisticulation is not invention, it is manipulation.

For the past fifteen years or more investigators have used a mathematical technique, Benford's Law, that is very useful in detecting when numbers are invented. I will spare you the details, which you can easily look up on the Internet, and give you an example.

A professor gave the following assignment to his students: Flip a coin 200 times. Record each outcome. Or, don't flip the coin and make up 200 recordings. Turn in your recordings at the next class meeting. Roughly ninety percent of falsified recordings were spotted as falsified by the professor, using Benford's Law.

Combine Tactics

Tactics work best when in combinations. Statisticulation succeeds to the extent that:

- You personally have power, popularity and legitimacy.
- You get support from others who will gain by the numbers' picture you present.

Along with your search for control over number crunching and reporting you should be on the alert for which persons and groups are likely to favor which types of reports. As H.L. Mencken once observed: *The truth that survives is simply the lie that is pleasantest to believe.*

How Far Dare You Go

You may receive signals from your superiors that they want you to statisticulate but don't want to hear about it. In the late 1980s, Daniel E. Gill, CEO at *Bausch & Lomb*, had a line that became famous among the division managers: *Make the numbers, but don't do anything stupid. What this means is: I hold you responsible for presenting numbers to me that make me look like I'm fulfilling the promises I made to the Board of Directors. If you get caught cheating on the numbers, you hang alone because that's stupid.*

It's not a bad assumption to figure that any supervisor wants you to make the numbers without doing anything stupid. You're in charge of knowing what's "stupid." Know what's illegal and stay away from it.

Memos

Now and then you will want to write a memo to protect yourself, by getting something done for the record, but think twice before you write any memo that directly or indirectly criticizes anything or anyone. And if you do write it, give serious consideration to shredding it.

If you send a memo to me decrying something going on that interferes with your work, I see you as a weak person crying for help. I wonder why you don't have enough clout to deal with your problem yourself. If I believe that there is nothing anyone could do about the matter other than myself, I resent your going on the written record. I expect you to come to me and talk about anything that could make me look bad.

If you send a memo to me that points out a problem that has nothing to do with your work, I suspect your motives, and I wonder if you are someone who likes to stir things up for the sake of creating conflict.

Now and then, write a memo that is highly constructive, with some alternate recommendations for action. Before you send it, review it with all relevant parties; i.e., anyone who could conceivably be seen in a negative light because of what you say. If there is anyone who is upset by your proposed memo, you should probably not send it. When you go after someone or after the way that he does his job, you should do so subtly and never in writing.

And, of course, never ever trust your company's espousals regarding wanting to hear about troubles in writing. Whistle-blowing and criticism of the organization, in general, is to be entered upon with caution. If you must engage in it, try to do so as a member of a coalition.

Whistle-Blowing

Whistle-blowing and other forms of organizational criticism are dangerous because a powerful enemy might be provoked and because from childhood "tattlers" are scorned even by persons unaffected by the criticism. In adulthood the labels change— from tattler to non-team player—but the contempt remains. In his study of why government professionals so often "go along" with policies and practices that they consider dangerous to the public, Walter Balk notes that *the costs of being regarded as non-team players by colleagues are extraordinarily high in [their] professional and private life.*

Retaliation against whistle-blowing is common. In an article on how companies and government agencies get even, *The Wall Street Journal* provided a number of examples, three of which were:

Agnes Connolly was fired because she forced her employer to make public two toxic chemical accidents.

Dave Jones was fired because he made public the fact that his employer used unqualified suppliers in the construction of a nuclear power plant.

After publicizing that their superiors were involved in work misconduct and corruption, two IRS officials were demoted.

If a scorecard were kept, whistle-blowers would be losing by a whopping margin. Whistle-blowers usually take on people higher up and more powerful in the organization than they are, and they often take on an organizational culture. Ernest Fitzgerald learned this and suffered because of it. He was a cost analyst with the Department of Defense who rose quickly in the ranks and received top performance ratings for his ideas on cost reduction.

When he took on top management in the Pentagon, showing how defense industry cost overruns were inappropriately tolerated by Defense Department administrators, he was warned. When he agreed to testify about this before Congress, he was demoted and given meaningless work. He took a position with the federal Joint Economic Commission, a positive outcome of his whistle-blowing activities, but when he tried to get a private consultancy business going, the defense industry marked him as an untouchable. Eventually, he went back to the Pentagon in a very non-sensitive position where he was carefully controlled.

The culture of the military-industry complex is both powerful and tolerant of things like cost overruns. Though the gains are ill-gotten, there are so many people in so many high places benefiting from these gains that it is often foolhardy to blow whistles in their midst. There are two conditions for sensible whistle-blowing.

Condition One: You understand the power complexities in your organization, and you yourself have gathered power resources at your disposal which you know how to use wisely. You also have allies who are themselves holders and skillful users of power. In addition, there are high-level persons who will benefit by the impeachment of the persons accused.

Condition Two: If you don't, you will lose respect for yourself. All of this book is about having your own independent sense of self-integrity and knowing how to succeed with it. If your self-integrity is seriously threatened, and there is no alternative, you might have to charge the hilltop.

Conclusion

These chapters on tactics are only a primer to provide you with some guidance on how to apply the other chapters. Hopefully, you yourself over time will develop an array of tactics for yourself that make the suggestions in this book look mediocre in comparison. It's up to you.

A Working Application

If you want to try out some of the ways of applying the guidelines in this book, I suggest the following. Pick four or five of the people presented in chapters one through nine. Then think about points made in the strategy and tactics chapters (ten through sixteen) and how the people you picked might have dealt successfully with the problems that confronted them.

Another thing you could do to would be to think of the people with whom you work, including, of course, your manager. Think aboout the kinds of problems you have with them and how you might deal with these people successfully in the future.

Another approach would be to think about the points where you disagree with me and explore the reasons for your disagreemnt. This could improve your ability to cope because you would choose tactics more suitable to either your personality or your sense of morality, or both.

What's important is that you think in terms of dealing with organizations in ways that enable you to survive and get ahead. My goal is that you think about organizations as they are and that you adopt a strategy for yourself that helps you pick the right tactics while, to lift from Shakespeare again, *to thine own self being true.*

As I said in the introduction: *this is not a catechism; it is a guide.*

Bibliography

Morin, W., "You Are Absolutely, Positively on Your Own,"
Fortune, Dec. 9, 1996.

Wolman, W. and Colamosca, A., *The Judas Economy* (New
York: Addison Wesley, 1997).

Tichy, N. and Devanna, M., *The Transformational Leader* (New
York: John Wiley & Sons, 1990).

Adams, G., "Blindsided by the Elephant," *Public
Administration Review* 54 (Jan.-Feb., 1994) pp. 77-83.

Bettman, J. and Watts, B., "Attributions in the Board Room,"
Administrative Science Quarterly, Vol. 28, No. 2 (June 1983)
pp. 165-183.

Mintzberg, H., "Musings on Management," *Harvard Business
Review*, July/Aug. 1996, pp. 63-64.

Champy, J. *Reengineering Management* (New York: Harper
Business, 1995).

Simon, H., "The Proverbs of Administration," in Shafritz, J. and
Ott, J., *Classics of Organization Theory* (Belmont: Wadsworth
Publishing, 4th ed., 1996) p. 112.

Millhauser, *Martin Dressler: The Tale of an American Dreamer*
(New York: Crown, 1996).

Shalit, R. "The Business of Faith," *New Republic* 18, April 4,
1994, p. 32.

Brunsson, N. and Olsen, J., *The Reforming Organization*
(Copenhagen: Copenhagen Business School Press, 1997).

Maccoby, M., *Narcissistic Leaders: Who Succeeds and Who Fails*
(Boston: Harvard Business School Press, 2007).

Crossen, C. *Tainted Truth: The Manipulation of Fact in
America* (New York: Simon & Shuster, 1994).

Balk, W. *Managerial Reform and Professional Empowerment in the Public Service* (Westport: Quorum, 1996).

Faiola, A., "Raking Up On Rain Forests," *The Washington Post,* Jan. 2, 1997, p. D12.

Bolman, L. and Deal, T., *Reframing Organizations* (San Francisco: Jossey-Bass, 2nd ed., 1997).

Lipmen-Blumen, J., *The Allure of Toxic Leaders* (Oxford: Oxford University Press, 2005).

Frankfurt, H., *On Bullshit* (Princeton: Princeton University Press, 2005).

Kornet, A., "The Truth About Lying," *Psychology Today,* May/June 1997, pp. 53-54.

Frankel, G., "Where There's Smoke, There's Ire," *The Washington Post,* Dec. 26, 1996, p. B1-2.

Darley, J. and Batson, C., "From Jeruselem to Jericho," *Journal of Personality and Social Psychology,* vol. 27, 1973, pp. 100-108,

DeMan, H., *The Psychology of Socialism* (New York: Henry Holt, 1927).

Roy, D., "Banana Time: Job Satisfaction and Informal Interaction," in Shafritz, J. and Ott, J., *Classics of Organization Theory* (Belmont: Wadsworth Publishing, 4th ed., 1996) pp. 112-113.

Kidder, T., *The Soul of a New Machine* (Boston: Little, Brown, 1981).

"How Different May One Be?" *Child Study,* Vol. 28, Spring 1951, p. 1.

Vaillant, G., *Adaptation to Life* (Boston: Little Brown, 1977).

Milgram, S., "Behavioral Study of Obediance," in Organ, D., ed. *The Applied Psychology of Work Behavior* (Dallas: Business Publications 1978) pp. 384-398.

McConnell, M., *Challenger: A Major Malfunction* (New York: Doubleday, 1987).

Jung, C. *Modern Man in Search of a Soul* (Orlando: Harcourt, Brace, Jovanovich, 1933).

Roethlisberger, F., "The Hawthorne Experiments," in *American Sociological Review*, Vol. 44, No. 5 (Oct., 1979), pp. 861-867.

Janis, I., *Victims of Groupthink* (New York: Houghton Mifflin, 1972).

McGregor, D., *The Human Side of Enterprise* (New York: McGraw-Hill, 1960).

Sun Tzu, *The Art of War* (New York: Delacorte, 1983.

Korda, Michael, *Power: How to Get It, How to Use It* (New York: Random House, 1975).

Scheff, T., "Control over Policy by Attendants in a Mental Hospital," *Journal of Health and Human Behavior*, 2 (1961), pp. 93-105.

Smith, H., *The Power Game* (New York: Random House, 1988).

Kanter, R., *Men and Women of the Corporation* (New York: Basic Books, 1993).

Manzoni, J. and Barsoux, J., "The Set-Up-To-Fail Syndrome," *Harvard Business Review*, 2002).

Pfeffer, J., *Managing With Power: Politics and Influence in Organizations* (Boston: Harvard Business School Press, 1993).

Cyert, R. and March, J., *A Behavioral Theory of the Firm* (Upper Saddle River, N.J.: Prentice Hall, 1963).

Whyte, W., *The Organization Man* (New York: Simon and Shuster, 1956).

Goffman, E., *The Presentation of Self in Everyday Life* (New York: Doubleday, 1959).

Bolles, R., *What Color Is Your Parachute* (Berkeley: Ten Speed Press, 2008).

Allen, R.W., *et al*, "Organizational Politics," *California Management Review*, Dec. 1979, p. 78.

Badarocco, J., *Defining Moments,* (Boston: Harvard Business School Press, 1997).

Bixler, S. and Scherrer, L., *5 Steps to Professional Presence* (Avon, MA: Adams, 2001).

Maier, C., *Bonjour Laziness: Jumping off the Corporate Ladder* (New York: Pantheon, 2005).

Chu, Chin-Ning, *Thick Face, Black Heart* (Beaverton, OR: AMC, 1992).

Bixler, S. and Scherrer, L, *Take Action* (New York:Fawcett Columbine, 1996).

Killingsworth, J., "Idle talk in modern organizations," *Administration and Society,* Vol. 16 pp. 346-384.

Kanter, R. and Stein, B., Editors, *Life in Organizations* (New York: Basic Books, 1979).

Karp, H., *Personal Power* (New York: AMACOM, 1985).

Brown, R., *Social Psychology* (New York: The Free Press, 1979).

Axelrod, R., *The Evolution of Cooperation* (New York: Basic Books, 1984).

Kotter, J., *Power in Management* (New York: AMACOM, 1979).

Kotter, J., *Power and Influence* (New York: The Free Press, 1985).

Kopytoff, V., "The Necessary Art of the Impromptu Meeting," *The New York Times*, Aug. 24, 1997, p. C3.

A Gentleman, *The Laws of Etiquette* (Philadelphia: Carey, Lee and Blanchard, 1836).

Spragins, E., "Hiring Without the Guesswork," *Inc.*, Feb. 1992, p. 5-7.

Stryker, P. "How Executives Get Jobs," *Fortune*, Aug. 1953, p. 182.

Newman, J. and Alexander, R., *Climbing the Corporate Matterhorn* (New York: John Wiley, 1985).

Klein, G. "Performing a Project Premortem," Sept. 1, 2007, pp. 24-27.

Carbonara, P. "Fire Me. I Dare You!" *Inc.* March 1997, p. 60.

Munk, N. and Oliver, S., "Think Fast!" *Forbes*, March 24, 1997, p. 146-9.

Whicker, M., *Toxic Leaders* (Westport, Connecticut: Quorum Books, 1996).

Farson, R., *Management of the Absurd* (New York: Simon & Shuster, 1996).

Jandt, F., *Win-Win Negotiating* (New York: John Wiley and Sons, 1985).

Malhotra, D. and Bazerman, M., "Investigative Negotiation," *Harvard Business Review*, Sept. 2007, pp. 73-78.

Skinner, B., *Beyond Freedom and Dignity* (New York: Bantam/Vantage, 1971).

Jaques, Elliott, "In Praise of Hierarchy," *Harvard Business Review*, Jan., 1990.

Mintzberg, H., "The Manager's Job: Folklore and Fact," *Harvard Business Review*: *On Human Relations* (New York: Harper & Row, 1979).

Pfeffer, J., "Understanding the Role of Power in Decision Making," in Shafritz, J. and Ott, J., *Classics of Organization Theory* (New York: Wadsworth, 1996) pp.359-374.

Yapko, M., "The Art of Avoiding Depression," *Psychology Today*, May/June 1997, p. 37.

Kanter, R., *The Change Masters* (New York: Simon & Shuster, 1983).

Flower, R., "Quantifying Cost and Quality," *Academe*, July/Aug., 1998.

Korda, op. cit.

Salvador, M. and Markham, et al, "The rhetoric of self-directive management and the operation of organizational power," *Communications Reports*, Winter 1995.

Walton, R., et al, "Organizational Context and Interdepartmental Conflict," *Administrative Science Quarterly*, 14, 4, Dec. 1969, pp. 522-542.

Index

A

accuracy, and confidence, 278–279

action, respect for, 233–239

adaptation
  to "change," 30
  human nature and, 77–81, 97–98
  as tactic, 193–194

Adario, Peter, 170–172

ADR. *See* "alternate dispute resolution (ADR)"

Advanced Network Design, 240

aggressiveness, 89–90, 194

Alabama law, 210

Allen, Fred, 108

Allen, Robert, 112

alliances, 203. *See also* coalitions

"alternate dispute resolution (ADR)", 209–210

altruism, 73–74

American Management Association, 208

American Motors, 61

American Society for Personnel Administration, 50–51

American Society of Public Administration, 206–208

appearances. *See also* self-presentation
  control freaks and, 248
  dedication and, 224
  screening techniques and, 50
  theater analogy and, 172–178

Arcesilaus, 209

Aristotle, 101

Astra, 60

AT&T, 112

attribution errors, 24–26, 48–49

authority
  humor and, 98

individual ethics and, 94–95

power and, 115–116, 131

subordinates and, 184

B

Babkins, Maury , 142–143

Bain and Company, 43–44

Balchen, Bernt, 75

Balk, Walter, 282

Barnard, Chester, 133, 183–184

Batson , 74

Bausch & Lomb, 280

Baxter Cereals , 248

Bay of Pigs fiasco, 104–105

Becker, Brian, 107–108

belief systems, 133

Benford's Law, 279–280

Benjamin, Walter, 82

Bennis, Warren, 115

Benson, Richard, 33

bias

performance evalutation and, 49

Biehn, David , 204–206

"big picture" argument, 279–280

Bixler, Susan, 189–190

Blake, Ginger , 200

blame

for organizational failures, 15–16, 29–34

power and, 148, 154–155

Blankenship, George, 266–267

blindsiding

and strategy, 159–160

body language, 219

Bolman, Lee, 35

bosses

fear of bending rules and, 233–235

Bremer, Frank, 38

The Bridge On The River Kwai (movie), 79–80

bridging technique, 51, 52

Broadcast News (movie), 238

Brown, Moore and Flint, 177–178

Brown, Roger, 199–200

built-in bias, 266–267

business literature, 212–213, 218, 219

cheap labor and, 129

cost-benefit analysis and, 276–277

myth of management science and, 22, 26–28

business success
new business failure rate
and, 17–19
organizational hypocrisy
and, 14
Business Week Online, 61
busy busy busy managers,
249–250

C

Cabell, James Branch, 191
The Caine Mutiny (movie),
229–230
Calvin, John, 71
Campbell, David, 178
Capital Holding Corporation
Direct Response Group
(DRG), 47–48
carefulness
memos and, 281
statisticulation and, 279–
281
tactics and, 229–231
whistle-blowing and, 281,
282–283
Carli, Linda, 33
Carpetpure Rug Cleaning
Company , 247
Case Method approach, 177
cause-and-effect, notion of,
214

CBS Television, 124
Challenger disaster (1986),
95, 146
chambers of commerce, 208
Chang, Lee Zhong, 193
"change," 30
Chapman, John Jay, 8
charisma
power and, 137
charts, 272
Chicago School Board, 13
Chrysler, 12, 122–123
Chu, Chin-Ning, 193
Cihon, Patrick, 210
Clavell, James, 117
Clay, Jason, 62
Cleveland Paint , 175–176
Clintion, Bill, 270
Clinton, Bill (U.S. president),
5, 85, 220–221
clothing, and strategy, 168–
169, 172. *See also* first
impressions
Clyde, Patsy, 109–110
coalitions. *See also* alliances
memos and, 281
power and, 120–121, 125–
126, 145–146
"cocooning trend," 31–32
Colamosca, Anne, 4
Collendale, Hendrick, 106

commitment
  attention-getting and, 272
  criticism and, 273, 278
  organizational power and,
    56–57
committees, avoidance of,
  237–238
communication skills
  getting attention and, 272
  manners and, 228–229
  ORGSPEAK and, 187–189
  rhetoric and, 180–181
  self-improvement strategy
    and, 164–167
compensation
  of executives, 35–39
  hidden agendas and, 39–41
  of workers, 29–30, 128–129
computer-skill training, 165
concern about employees, as
    pretense, 52–57, 128
Concerned Women for
    America, 54
confidence
  knowledge accuracy and,
    278–279
conflict
  sources of, 140–144
  as tool, 144–145
Confucius, 71
Connolly, Agnes, 282

consensus builders, 244–245
consistency, 195–196
control freaks, 245–249
control myths, 133–134
cooperation
  interdepartmental, 261–
    262
  resistence to, 196–197
  social realities and, 183
  spirit of, 161–163
  strategic use of, 197–199
corners
  and power, 138
corruption
  visionary leaders and, 151–
    152
Cortland, Henry, 121–122
cost-benefit analysis, 276–277
cost overruns, 283
coworkers
  bluffing and, 85
  pretense of trust with, 227
  Seldom-Seen Susans as,
    252–253
  victims of humor and, 99–
    100
  virtuousness and, 85–86
CPR Institute for Dispute
    Resolution, 210
creative bookkeeping, 268
Crisp, Quentin, 68

cruelty, as human, 92–93, 94

cultural audit, 48

Cuneo, Nicholas, 145–146

D

Dabney, Marjorie, 77

Dallas Semiconductor, 112

Daly, John, 29

dangerous people, 110

Danter, Gladys, 65–67

Darley , 74

Data General, 81

Dawn, Sheila, 269

deception as tactic, 162–163

decision processes

  agenda stage, 180

  cost-benefit analysis and, 276–277

  criteria in, 180

  group behavior and, 103–105

  naming of alternatives and, 180

  strategy and, 179–180

decorum, 172–178

Defining Moments: When Managers Must Choose Between Right and Right (Adario), 170–172

De Herder, Rick, 217–218

Demara, Ferdinand Waldo, 84

Demary, Jim, 218

democratization, 126–128

denial, 70–72

DePaulo, Bella, 69–70

Dick, Philip, 220

Dickens, Charles, 214

Digital Equipment, 11–12

dignity, 195

Direct Response Group (DRG) of Capital Holding Corporation, 47–48

discretionary funds, control over, 221

Disraeli, Benjamin, 8

Dole, Bob, 85

doubt, as tactic, 245

Downs, Marsha, 39–41

downsizing

  concern about employees and, 54–55

  job insecurity and, 3–8

  trend in, 3–7

DRG. *See* Direct Response Group (DRG) of Capital Holding Corporation

Drucker, Peter, 17

Drummer, Cynthia , 177

Dunn, Sandra , 200

E

Eagly, Alice, 33

EarthRite household
  cleaners, 62
The Economist, 20–21
education. *See also* training
  importance of, 165
  organization of, 13–14
effectiveness, and resistance,
  197
efficiency myth, 5–7, 8
Eisenhower, Dwight D., 131
Emerson, Ralph Waldo, 191
employee rights
  power and, 59–60
  protection of, 11, 54–56,
    209–211
  "validation" and, 211–212
empowerment, 58–59
  organizational power and,
    119
  phony empowerers and,
    248–249, 262
  as pretense, 130–131
endings, 178–179
entrapments
  adjustability and, 193–194
  consistency and, 195–196
  cooperation and, 196–199
  dignity and, 195
  negative thinking and,
    191–193

norms of exchange and,
  199–200
Equal Employment
  Opportunity
  Commission, 209
Esar, Evan, 264
Esposito, William, 279
ethics
  altruism and, 73–74
  authority and, 94–95
  the easy way and, 90–92
  individual, 67–70
  organizational hypocrisy
    and, 60–62
  strategy and, 170–172
"Ethics, Inc.", 61
Ethics Officer Association, 69
Ethics Resource Center,
  Washington, D.C., 69
ethos, 180–181
etiquette, rules of
  different viewpoints and,
    167–168
  group behavior and, 113–
    114
exchanges
  norms and, 199–200
  power and, 201–203
  psychological, 198–199
  tit for tat and, 200–201
exercise routine, 169, 204, 205

experimentation
  power and, 150–151
  risk-taking and, 236–237
  tactics and, 231–235
expertise, 136
eye contact, 181

F
Faiola, Anthony, 62
fairness, 110–112
falsification, 84–85. *See also*
  statistics, use of
family-friendliness, 53–54,
  171
Farnsworth, Rick, 121–122
favors. *See* exchanges;
  unofficial power
FBI laboratory scandal
  (1997), 279–280
Federal Reserve, 21
feuding, 105, 106
Fidelity Investments, 13
first impressions, 172–173,
  242–243
Fisher, George , 186–187
Fitzgerald, Ernest, 282–283
Ford, Henry, 11, 43, 154
forecasting, 20–21
Fortune magazine, 4
Foster, Mary, 115–116
Fountain, Sally, 266–267

Frankfurt, Harry G., 1, 68
Fremson, Bill, 9–10
Freud, Sigmund, 86
Fuller, Craig, 124

G
Gandhi, Mahatma, 195
Garrison, Tom, 177–178
Gates, Bill, 165
Georgetown University
  Hospital, 117
getting along, 182–190. *See
  also* communication
  skills; coworkers;
  etiquette, rules of; social
  reality
Gill, Daniel E., 280
Giraudoux, Jean, 215, 244
GM, 24–25, 31, 196
goals, personal, 178–179
Godfather movies, 174
Goldfinch, Shaun, 3
Goldman Sachs, 21
Goldstein, Walter, 155–156
Gomez, Francis, 266
Gore, Al, 5, 29, 91
Government Retirement
  Benefits, Inc., 7
Grant Study, 89–90
Gray, Heidi , 175–176

The Great Imposter (movie), 84

green marketing movement, 62

Greenspan, Alan, 21, 274–275

greenwashing, 62

Greyhound Lines, 26

grievance procedures, 209

Grote, Nick, 96

group behavior
fairness and, 110–112
feuding and, 106
in-group humor and, 101–102
job protection and, 106–108
Lazy-Susans and, 109–110
molehill men and, 108–109
rivalry and, 105–106
self-interest and, 102–105
sincerity and, 112

Groupthink, 104–105, 236

Guantanamo Bay Naval Base, Cuba, 65–67

Guccione, Robert, 72

guilt trippers, tactics with, 255, 256–258

H

Haas, Robert, 54–55

half-truths, 271–272, 278

"halo effect," 49, 166, 242

Hamlet (Shakespearian play), 160

Harriman, Pamela, 163

Harvard Business Review, 27–28, 33, 56

Harvard Business School, 18, 19, 177, 182, 201

Hawthorne studies, 102–103

Hayakawa, S. I., 219–220

Hayes, Randall, 62

Hazard, Howard , 247

Hazlitt, William, 166

Heffner, Hugh, 72

Hellman, F. Warren, 54–55

Henry, James, 210

hidden agendas, 39–41

"higher ups." *See also* managers
access to, 154
confrontation and, 232–233
diffusing control by, 221–222
manipulation of, 212–214
tactics for dealing with, 225–227

hiring practices. *See* job interviews; recruitment

Hoff, Ann, 242

Hollander, Sharon Flynn, 117

honesty, personal, 67–70, 227

Honeywell, 12, 120, 121

hooks, and impromptu
    meetings, 219
Howard, Kelley, 43–44
Human Relations industry,
    52–57
humility, 160–161, 241
humor
    in-group, and strategy,
        101–102
    organizational hypocrisies
        and, 98–100

I

Iacocca, Lee, 12, 122–123
IBM Credit Corporation, 75–
    76
idealism, 2, 193–194
ideas. *See also* presentations
    absurdity and, 31–32
    implementation of, 263
illegal aliens, 129
Illich, Ivan, 155
impromptu meetings, 217–
    219
impudence, spirit of, 161
inconsistency, human, 67, 73
independent investigators, 61
individuality
    ethics and, 67–70
    teamwork and, 88
information systems, 7

in-group humor, 101–102
Ink magazine, 177–178
insecurity
    group behavior and, 113
    martyr managers and, 253–
        255
    use of space and, 138
integrity. *See also* ethics
    personal strategy and, 160–
        164
    vs. virtuousness, 163
    whistle-blowing and, 283
interdepartmental
    cooperation efforts, 261–
        262
interdependencies, 134–136,
    141–144
interdependencies, and
    power, 224
International Institute for
    Management
    Development, 148–150
IRS, whistle-blowing at, 282

J

James, Audrey , 212–213
Janis, Irving, 104–105
job description, ambiguity in,
    219–221
job enrichment, 57–58

job interviews
   first impressions and, 172–
      173, 242–243
   legal knowledge and, 211–
      212
   lying on resumes and, 84–
      85
   preparation for, 166
   tactics and, 232, 239–243
job protection
   being careful and, 230–231
   group behavior and, 106–
      108
job selection, and power-
      building, 215–217
Johnson, Samuel, 21
Jones, Dave, 282
The Judas Economy (Wolman
      & Colamosca), 5
Jung, Carl, 97, 215

K
Kanter, Rosabeth Moss, 124–
      125, 263
Karp, H. B., 196–197
Keillor, Garrison, 45
Kennedy, John F. (U.S.
      president), 14
Killingsworth, James R., 188
Kissinger, Henry, 118
Kiwanis Clubs, 208

Kotter, John, 182, 201, 204
Kropf, Daniel , 206

L
Langley, George , 205–205
language
   attention and, 272
   body language and, 219
   bromides and, 43–44
   ORGSPEAK and, 187–189,
      258–259
   prescriptive statements
      and, 28
   slogans and, 22
   strategic use of, 187–189,
      219–221
   tactics with managers and,
      254–255, 258–259
LaPiere, Richard, 73
Larson, Erik, 268
Lauder, William, 32
"laundry list" approach, 185
Lazy-Susans, 109–110
legal concerns
   rights in the workplace
      and, 59–60, 209–211
   statisticulation and, 280–
      281
Lenczowski, Fred, 198–199
leniency error, 49
Levi-Strauss, 54–55

Ligman, Bill, 235

Lipman-Blumen, Jean, 133–134

Lippencott, Seymour M., 156

Loeber, Judith, 155

logos, 180–181

loop, being in the, 137–138

losses, 214–215

loyalty, 38. *See also* commitment

Luce, Clare Booth, 223

Lund, Nancy Brennan, 71–72

M

Maccoby, Michael, 151

Machiavelli, 2, 117

McNeil, Kathryn , 170–172

Macy's, 238

magazines, 212–213. *See also* business literature

Management By Objectives (MBO), 130

management science, as myth, 17–32

  academic views on, 21–22

  bad luck and, 24–26

  blame for failure and, 29–34

  business books and, 26–28

  forecasting and, 20–21

management successes and, 17–19

meaningless use of words and, 19–20

productivity and, 32–34

slogans and, 17–19

managers, tactics with

  "busy" managers and, 249–250

  coaches and, 255–258

  consensus builders and, 244–245

  control freaks and, 245–249

  guilt trippers and, 255

  imprecise language and, 258–259

  interdepartmental cooperation and, 261–262

  martyrs and, 253–255

  Seldom-Seen Susans and, 250–253

  teamwork projects and, 259–261

  types of managers and, 244–263

Managment By Terror (MBT), 131

manners. *See* etiquette, rules of

Marcus Aurelius, 224

Margolis, Jan, 218, 219

Martens, Pamela, 145–146

Martin, John, 30

Martin Dressler (Millhauser), 31

Maslow, Abraham, 42–43

Massachusetts Mutual Life Insurance, 218

Mattel Inc., 217–218

MBO (Management By Objectives), 130

MBT (Managment By Terror), 131

means, medians, and modes, 269–270

mediocrity, and tactics, 229–231

Meese, Edwin, 124

Mellick, Bill, 23

memos, 281

Men and Women of the Corporation (Kanter), 124–125

Mencken, H. L., 225, 280

mentors, 189–190

meritocracy, as myth, 192

Merton, Robert, 75

Meyers, Gerald, 61

Mica, John L., 6

Midkiff, Susan, 109–110

Milgram Experiments (1961), 92–93, 94

military institutions

statisticulation and, 275–276

as theater, 176–177

U. S. Navy and, 60, 162

Mintzberg, Henry, 26

mission statements, 10, 43–44

Mitsubishi, 60

Mohajer, Mahmood, 58

molehill men, 108–109

money, tactics involving. *See also* statistics, use of

cost-benefit analysis and, 276–277

creative bookkeeping and, 268

discretionary funds and, 221

power and, 203, 221

use of averages and, 269–270

Monroney, Bea , 142–143

motivational techniques, 57–60

Motorola, 24

Musashi, Miyamoto, 117

"my hands are tied" reasoning, 95–96

N

NAM. *See* National
Association of
Manufacturers (NAM)
name recognition, 219
NASA, 95
Nast, CondŽ, 223
National Association of
Manufacturers (NAM),
128
National Cancer Institute,
277
National Transportation
Safety-Board (NTSB), 84
negative thinking, 191–193
networking, 206–208
Newsweek poll (1987), 188
New York Times, 14, 43, 274–
275
Nietzsche, Friedrich, 1, 117
norms of exchange, 199–200
Northridge, CA, earthquake,
23
not-for-profits, and
performance evaluation,
37
NTSB. *See* National
Transportation Safety-
Board (NTSB)

O

office furniture, and power,
138–140
office procedures, 231–233
Okun, Monty, 39–41
Olympic Games in Atlanta
(1996), 129
On Bullshit (Frankfurt), 68
Orange Utilities, 60
organizational genes, 128–
129
organizational hypocrisies,
155
adaptation tactics and,
193–194
avoidance tactics and, 237–
238
blindsiding and, 159–160
deception tactics and, 162–
163
ethics and, 60–62
hiring practices and, 49–52
human relations and, 52–
57
humor as tactic and, 98–
100
key examples of, 237–238
motivational techniques
and, 57–60
negative thinking tactics
and, 191–193

performance evaluation
and, 48–49

pretenses and, 45–48, 209–210

productivity myth and, 8, 32–34

response to failure and, 11–15

organizations. *See also*
organizational
hypocrisies

as American religion, 10–11

downsizing trend in, 3–8

nature of, 1–3

as organized hypocrisies, 8–15

resistence to
disenchantment with, 3

as theater, 172–178, 225–228

ORGSPEAK, 187–189, 258–259

Orwell, George, 132

The Outlaw (movie), 79

overstimulation, 197

P

Partee, Gloria, 105–106

Patagonia, 55

pathos, 180–181

Peale, Norman Vinbcent, 191–193

Pentagon, 282–283

people in organizations. *See
also* coworkers; group
behavior; "higher ups";
managers

adaptation and, 77–81, 97–98

aggressiveness and, 88–90, 194

altruism and, 73–74

cruelty and, 92–95

denial and, 70–72

different viewpoints and, 167–168

easy way and, 90–92

helplessness and, 95–96

honesty and, 67–70

humor and, 98–100

inconsistencies in, 67, 73

lying on resumes and, 84–85

memory and, 82–83

reasons for ineptness and, 63–65

role playing and, 65–67

self-perception theory and, 86–88

teamwork and, 88

values and, 90–92
virtuousness and, 85–86
work ethic and, 70–72
performance evaluation
executive compensation
and, 35–39
not-for-profits and, 37
organizational hypocrisies
and, 48–52
personal strategy
avoiding entrapments and,
191–199
being true your own self
and, 160–164
clothing and, 168–169, 172
decision-making as process
and, 179–180
decorum and, 172–178
different viewpoints and,
167–168
ethics and, 170–172
gains and losses in, 215
getting along and, 182–190
goals and, 178–179
language and, 187–189
legal rights and, 209–211
mentors and, 189–190
need for, 157–159
organizational blindsiding
and, 159–160
Plan B and, 167

rhetoric and, 180–181
self-improvement and,
164–167
subordinates and, 183–187
personnel manual
unstated policy and, 186–
187
persuasion, 180–181
Peters, Tom, 26
Philip Morris Company, 71–
72
Philips Petroleum Company,
56
phony empowerers, 248–249,
262
phrasing, 181, 188–189
Plan B
and strategy, 167
"pleasure revenge," 31–32
policy thinking, 12, 38–39,
122–123
Popcorn, Faith, 31–32
positive thinking, 22, 191
Potswana Power Company,
115–116
power, 115–132. *See also*
unofficial power
aspects of, 115–120
authority and, 115–116,
120

coalitions and, 120–121,
125–126, 145–146
delegation of, 123–124
democratization and, 126–
128
employee interests and, 56–
57, 59–60
gender and, 33
guidelines concerning, 132
job selection and, 216–217
military strategy and, 116–
117
official *vs.* unofficial, 133–
134
power bases, 121–123, 125,
148. *See also* unofficial
power
presentations
attention-grabbing and,
272
knowledge of numbers and,
264–266
politics and, 273
pretenses. *See also*
organizational
hypocrisies
of concern about employees,
52–57, 128
organizational hypocrisies
and, 45–48

ORGSPEAK and, 187–189
risk-taking and, 236–237
worker participation and,
130–131
private sector
access to the top in, 154
downsizing in, 3–5
efficiency and, 9
job protection in, 107–108
procedures and, 75–76
procedures
training for ineptness and,
74–77
trust in, 95–96
productivity myth, 8, 32–34
professional associations,
206–208
projective testing, 211–212
project premortem, 236
Prothro, C. Vin, 112
Proulx, E. Annie, 115
provisional appointment, 51
Prudential Insurance, 41
*Public Administration
Review,* 3
public sector
downsizing in, 5–7
irrational procedures in, 75
job protection in, 106–107

R

rain forest theme, 62

Raleigh-Durham airplane crash (1995), 84

Randall, Newton , 205

Rashomon (movie), 82–83

rationality

  group behavior and, 103–105

  procedures and, 74–77

recency, 48, 49

recruitment. *See also* job interviews

  interviewer techniques and, 239–241

  loyalty and, 38

  lying on resumes and, 84–85

  organizational hypocrisies and, 8, 49–52

  pay-performance link and, 36–37

  projective testing and, 211–212

  role playing and, 177–178

Reengineering the Corporation (Hammer & Champy), 27

"reinventing government," 5–7

resistance, value of, 196–197

responsibility

  in large organizations, 14–15

reward-for-performance systems, 35–44

  executive compensation and, 35–39

  hidden agendas and, 39–41

  policy thinking and, 38–39

rhetoric, 180–181

  personal strategy and, 180–181

Rice, Shirley, 230–231

Rider, Mark , 259–261

Riesman, David, 88

risk-taking

  challenging unofficial power and, 147

  experimentation and, 236–237

  organizational hypocrisy and, 46

rivalry, 105–106

Rivera , Geraldo, 85

RJR Nabisco, 78

role playing, 65–67

  costuming and, 172–173

  as management tactic, 175–178

  management tactics and, 175–178

pretense of trust, 227
researchers and, 277–278
scripts and, 173–174
tactics and, 239
tactics with "higher ups"
and, 225–228
understanding people
behind, 225–227, 229–
230
romanticism, 72
Rosenblatt, Roger, 153
routine work, avoidance of,
224
Rusek, Ray, 77
Russell, Bertrand, 82, 110
Rutherford Institute, 53–54

S
sabotage, 106, 136–137
sample bias, 266–267
satisficing, 179
"satisficing," 74–77
Satron, Bill , 247
Schechtman, Mark, 201
Scherrer, Lisa, 189–190
Schneider, Frank, 26
Schorr, Daniel, 112
Schrader, Janet, 110–112
Schrum, Barry, 6
screening devices, 49–50
scripts, 173–174

Seldom-Seen Susans, 250–
253
self-awareness
job selection and, 215–217
resistance and, 197
self-improvement, 164–167
self-interest, in groups, 102–
105
self-perception theory, 86–88
self-presentation. *See also*
personal strategy
clothing and, 168–169
first impressions and, 172–
173, 242–243
lying on resumes and, 84–
85
manners and, 228–229
seeing others' points and,
167–168
tactics of, 138–143, 228–
229
self-promotion, 241
set-up-to-fail syndrome, 148–
150
Shakespeare, William
on clothing, 168
Hamlet, 160
Shaw, George Bernard, 132
Shearson/American Express,
145–146
Sheeler, Charles, 153–154

Sheen, Charlie, 85
Shulman, Susan, 181
Simon, Herbert, 28, 179
Simpson, O. J., 90–91
sincerity, 112
singing, 181
"sink-or-swim" approach, 185
skewing, 271–272
Smith, Adam, 9
Smith, Roger, 24–25, 31
Smith Barney, 146
social reality
    cooperation and, 197–199
    getting along and, 182–183
    knowledge of, 182–183
    manners and, 229
    memos and, 281
    subordinates and, 183–184
space, use of
    insecurity and, 138
    and power, 138
spare time, use of, 166
speaking style, 181
spin-control techniques, 266–
    280
Stanford University cruelty
    study, 93–94
state labor protection law,
    210
statistics, use of
    averages and, 269–270, 271

biased samples and, 266–
    268
challenging others' use of,
    277–278
charts and graphs and, 272
combination of tactics in,
    280
confidence *vs.* accuracy
    and, 278–279
cost-benefit analysis and,
    276–277
creative bookkeeping and,
    268
invention of numbers and,
    279–280
selective subgroup
    comparisons and, 273–
    275
skewing and, 271–272
stupidity and, 280–281
testing processes and, 275–
    276
Stein, Gertrude, 178
Stetstrom, Michael , 162
Stevenson, Adlai, 169
strategic planning, 11–12
strategic relationships
    networking and, 206–208
    within the organization,
        189–190, 204–206,
        217–218

strengths and weaknesses
  as the same, 166–167, 243
  self-improvement and,
    164–167
strictness error, 49
subjectivity
  cost-benefit analysis and,
    276–277
  power relationships and,
    135–136
  recruitment and, 49–52,
    211, 241
subordinates. *See also*
    coworkers; managers;
    people in organizations
  errors in relating to, 184–
    186
  manipulation of superiors
    by, 122–123, 212–214
  social realities and, 183–
    184
  social reality and, 183–184
  strategy and, 183–187
success
  aggressiveness and, 88–90
  chameleons and, 243
  characteristics of climbers
    and, 223–224
  negative thinking and, 193
  prior failure and, 186
  subjectivity and, 211

Sulzberger, Punch, 14–15
Sun Tzu, 117, 153, 158, 225

T
Taco Bell, 30
tactics. *See also* managers,
    tactics with
  adaptation and, 193–194
  avoidance and, 237–238
  combination of, 280
  deception and, 162–163
  with different managerial
    types, 244–258
  experimentation and, 231–
    235
  humor and, 98–100
  for idea implementation,
    263
  interdepartmental
    cooperation and, 261–
    262
  negative thinking and,
    191–193, 192
  organizational roles and,
    225–227, 229–231
  phony empowerers and,
    262
  of self-presentation, 228–
    229, 238–243
  teamwork projects and,
    259–261

vague language and, 258–259

vs. strategy, 157–158

tailoring, 51

"take charge" attitude, 89

taking responsibility, 224, 260–261

Taylor, Elizabeth, 166–167

Taylor, Lynn , 233–235

Teal, Thomas, 27–28

teamwork

  individuality and, 88

  motivation and, 58

  tactics and, 259–261

testing processes

  manipulating results of, 275–276

  screening devices and, 49–50

theater, organizations as, 172–178, 225–228

Thick Black Theory (Chang), 193

Thiokol Corporation, 95

Tinker, Bob , 143

tipping, 199–200

tit for tat, 200–201

Tomlin, Lily, 1

Tooker, Gary L., 24

top management. *See* "higher ups"

Torres, Ralph, 206

Torret, Donna , 248

Total Quality Leadership (TQL), 162

Town Taxi Service, Phoenix, AZ , 142–143

toxic leaders, 134

TQL. *See* Total Quality Leadership (TQL)

training. *See also* education

  computer skills and, 165

  ethics and, 61

  for ineptness, 74–77

Trent, Bob, 108–109

Trilling, Lionel, 94

Trollope, Anthony, 169

Trump, Donald, 70, 72, 129

trust

  establishment of, 204

  organizational hypocrisy and, 46, 96–97

  pretense of, 227

  in procedure, 95–97

  "zone of indifference" and, 97

tube wars, 81

Tunney, Linda, 275

20th Century Insurance, 23

Tyson, Mike, 174

U

Uchitelle, Louis, 274–275

uncertainty

    forecasting and, 20–21

    taking control in, 222–223

understanding

    confidence in knowledge
        and, 278–279

    of people behind roles, 225–
        227, 229–230

    survival and, 15–16

unemployment figures, 271–
    272

uniqueness, and power, 217

U.S. Department of Defense,
    282–283

U. S. Department of Labor,
    87–88

U. S. economy, success of, 18

U. S. Immigration and
    Naturalization Service in
    Miami, 106–107

U. S. Naval Academy, 12–13

U. S. Navy, 60, 60, 162

U. S. Supreme Court, 50, 211

University of Colorado, 277

University of Michigan, 20,
    127

University of Pennsylvania,
    268

unofficial power

    being "in the flow" and,
        217–219

    being "in the loop" and,
        137–138

    blame and, 148, 154–155

    charisma and, 137

    coalitions and, 121–122,
        145–146

    control myths and, 133–134

    covert use of, 147

    ethical choices and, 94–95,
        172

    expertise and, 136

    hazards in, 147–152

    importance of, 131–132

    investment of, 201–203

    knowing your own, 202–
        203

    negative thinking and,
        191–193

    office factors in, 138–140,
        217

    origins of, 134–136

    ourselves and, 150–151

    personal qualities and,
        164–165

    position and, 124–125

    risks in challenging, 147

    sabotage and, 136–137

set-up-to-fail syndrome
and, 148–150
social knowledge and, 182–
183
sources of conflict and,
140–145
vagueness and, 147
ways to increase, 217–221
whistle-blowing and, 283
workplace bullying and,
150
Unruh, Jesse, 203

V
vagueness. *See also* language
myth of management
wisdom and, 19–20
unofficial power and, 147
"validation," as legal term,
211–212
values. *See* concern about
employees; ethics;
mission statements
verbal response methods,
273–275
virtuousness, 85–86, 163
visibility, 219, 223
visionary leaders, 151–152
vividness, 272
Vogue magazine, 223
voice quality, 181

W
Wall Street Journal, 282
Walters, Lisa , 171
The Washington Post, 71,
116–117
weaknesses. *See* strengths
and weaknesses
Weber, Max, 14
welfare reform, 110–112
Wheately, Bill, 96
whistle-blowing, 61–62, 281,
282–283
Whitman, Walt, 63
Whyte, William F., 105
Whyte, William H., 161
Wiegand, Dave, 240
Williams, Tennessee, 83
Willis, Maydeen, 105–106
Willoughby, George, 108–109
Willson, Howard, 113–114
Wilson, Sarah, 113–114
Wingate, Fred , 231–233
winning and losing, 214–215
The Witch Doctors
(Mickelthwait), 29
Wolman, William, 4
women
clothing and, 168
in leadership roles, 33
mentors and, 190

workaholics as managers,
    253–255
worker participation, 262
work ethic, 70–72
Working Girl (film), 158–159
workplace bullying, 150
Wouk, Herman, 229–230
Wyman, Thomas, 124

Y

Yale University
    obedience study at, 92–93,
        94
    School of Organization and
        Management at, 22

Z

"zone of indifference," 97